MARSHA'S SONG
A Celebration of Life

By

Ines Arnsberger Hatch

Stellar A Productions

First Published 2004
In cooperation with
Penman Publishing, Inc.
4159 Ringgold Road, Suite 104
Chattanooga, Tennessee 37412
www.penmanpublishing.com

Marsha's Song

A Celebration Of Life

By

Ines Arnsberger Hatch

ISBN 1-932496-19-X

Front and Back Cover Photography by:
Kristin L. Flanigan

Edited by:
Kristin L. Flanigan

Manufactured in the United States of America.
Printed by Penman Publishing, Inc.

Acknowledgments

After thirty-two years of counting my blessings since the accident, I have come to the realization that we control our destiny and the people in our world help mold us and our future. My gratefulness goes out to: Joseph and Elsbeth Meerfeld, Barbara Smikale, Anne Isenberg, Rudy Verrier & Hildegard Seifhart, Bill & Ingeborg Swayze, Eizenmenger, Hiener & Rothwieter Moers, Weiss, Marga & Dieter Bausch, Stephanie Bausch Kaufman, Amy & Lisa McCartney, Annie Jenkins, Linda Pompano, John Fitzpatrick, Salvatore J. Puleo, Tom Baxtor, Dr. Anthony Mussari, G.R. Armstrong, Mary Murrin Smith, Michael J. Holden, Richard L. Jenkins, Tim Knoll, Elizabeth Bradley Gouriche, Sergio Ubilla, Stroudsburg Community Hospital Emergency & ICU Staff (1970), Scranton ICU (1970), Mercy Hospital ICU & Pediatrics Unit (1970), St. Francis Hospital Pediatrics Unit (1970), and Allegheny Hospital Pediatrics Unit (1971), and Yvonne Johnson.

A special thank you to the specialists and nurses who made recovery and my chance to prosper possible. I extend special gratitude to Dr. Keonig, without whose expertise my ability to stand and walk would not have been possible.

My sincere appreciation to the musician, Yanni, who unknowingly provided soul searching and inspiring music. Throughout the creation of both *The Adoption Eclipse* and *Marsha's Song* I repeatedly listened to Keys To Imagination, Tribute, Reflections Of Passion, and

Ethnicity. Your music helped me go into the depths of my soul, bringing forth memories and inspiring truths. May these lessons learned inspire generations to come.

Gratitude goes out to Kristin Flanigan, my editor, for burning the candle at both ends with me, and to Linda Lee Ratto for her continued support and efforts in answering questions and helping to make my dreams become reality.

Dedicated with love
to
my mother and father.

Other books by Ines Arnsberger Hatch:

The Adoption Eclipse

Look For

More Than A Mother

Coming Soon

Foreword

Marsha's Song is an American story. It is a story about tragedy, perseverance, recovery, and resilience. Not unlike St. Paul, Marsha fell off a horse, and her life was changed forever.

Yes, Ines Arnsberger Hatch is Marsha, and her college professor is pleased to write this introduction, because Ines is the personification of what a college experience and a life well lived is all about. If *Marsha's Song* is anything like Ines's life, it will entertain, inspire, and free everyone who reads it.

I met Ines in 1985. She was a senior, majoring in Mass Communications at King's College in Wilkes-Barre, Pennsylvania. I liked her the moment I met her.
I remember to this day her beautiful smile and her engaging manner. Tall, striking, and very well mannered, at first glance she appeared to have it all.

After a few moments of conversation, one knew that Ines was a person who struggled mightily. It was all there in her eyes. Eyes yearning for friendship. Eyes yearning for support. Eyes that contained the roadmap of a lifetime of challenges encountered and challenges overcome.

Later, I learned this young lady had overcome the seemingly impossible. Deep in a coma, confined in a world of silence, she awoke after seven weeks. Ines experienced a kaleidoscope of life experiences that makes *Marsha's Song* a must read for anyone whose life is touched by apprehension, disappointment, pain, and torment.

We had a marvelous student-teacher relationship. She was determined to succeed. She was resourceful and very industrious. She met and surpassed her own expectations and mine as well, and she learned the important life lesson of freeing her spirit through hard work, intellectual and personal growth, and accomplishment.

Recently Ines told me the rigor of my senior seminar class caused her to believe that one day she would write a book. Quite a dream for someone who was told that she might not be able to have a normal life because of her accident. She also confided that it was the high expectations set for her as a student in my class, including the way in which it was taught, that helped her free her spirit and see herself in a different way.

As a college student, Ines was determined to meet every challenge she faced. Today, Ines is an impressive and inspirational writer. A woman of grace and courage, Ines is a model for all of us. Every day she overcomes obstacles that would thwart the faint of heart.

I hope you enjoy reading about her odyssey. I am sure that when you read *Marsha's Song* you will have a new outlook and understanding about a life well lived.

~ Anthony J. Mussari, Ph.D.
Professor and Chairman
Mass Communications/
Media Technologies Department
King's College
Wilkes-Barre, PA

MARSHA'S SONG
A Celebration of Life

Part 1: Changes

I. The Promise: Perseverance Is The Key

Marsha cradled her newborn in her arms as Grandma and Grandpa Walsch looked at their daughter and new grandson with sheer admiration. Both felt an immediate sense of attachment to this little boy, clad in blue. Their daughter accomplished her goal, adopting this child, their grandson. In the process, she reached her dreams of making a difference in other people's lives and blossomed into a woman. Even though there had been so many difficulties and worries, her husband Brad had only been able to assist over the telephone; Marsha handled the adoption process with minimal assistance. Marsha had acted with an iron will and utmost respect and dignity for herself and the birth mother. She had helped bring a doubtful, painful adoption situation to a positive outcome; so what father wouldn't have the utmost respect for his daughter?

"I can see the complete exhaustion in your face," Marsha's father said to her. "Your mother and I are so relieved that you and Justin are finally home safe."

"You are very strong my dear and we are so proud," her mother continued.

"In the face of adversity you became stronger and nothing stopped you," praised her father. "You were a mother willing to endure pain and anguish for the benefit of your child."

"I know, I've exerted myself beyond my normal capabilities," replied Marsha to her parents. "Months before Justin was born I had no choice but support and nourish a poor, uneducated child, in a woman's body. I encouraged and guided her through to our son's birth. It was an experience I'll never forget. These last eight months have really opened my eyes and educated me beyond what's conceivable."

Marsha sat quietly with tears in her eyes and a sob escaped her. In the back of her mind she knew her strength originated from her childhood and grew every day, every week and every year. These past eight weeks had been an ultimate challenge for her and again she succeeded.

Mr. and Mrs. Walsch sat in awe of their daughter's strength once again. Grandpa proudly exclaimed, "You were always steadfast in your pursuit of life and being the best you can be, Marsha. Life is a series of challenges. It is a copulation of problems and decisions. From your childhood onward it was undoubtedly difficult for you and you decided to persevere. Your struggle for recovery is responsible for your strength and persistence and you are a better-rounded individual as a result. Your experiences created your special personality and vision of life and I am convinced your difficult road is responsible for your strength these last eight months."

Marsha had surprised doctors, family, and friends with both her recovery and accomplishments through the years after she was given little hope for survival in the hospital's ICU. "You are a survivor of the odds," Marsha's father finished, as he gently placed his arm around his daughter's shoulders and gave a little hug of praise, love, and encouragement.

II. Recollections: Memories Are Golden

That night Marsha had a dream of life before the accident that had changed her life forever. A beautiful little girl with shoulder-length blonde hair was playing in her parent's garden. Marsha saw herself at five years old. "Oh Mama, look at these pretty flowers. Can I pick them for you? Will you come play with me when you're done?" called little Marsha.

"Give me a few minutes honey," answered her mother. "Why don't you go check the mail? And remember to be careful of any cars."

"OK, Mama," replied Marsha.

Like a fly on the wall Marsha saw images of her childhood flash by. She saw herself playing in the neighbor's pool. She was so happy and oblivious to danger and pain, she thought. Life was uncomplicated and Mama and Papa made sure she experienced comfort and happiness. While she was observing, Marsha now realized that material possessions were not abundant, but the love and devotion between herself and her parents was what made her happy.

Marsha dreamed of the first time her girlfriend was allowed to stay the night. Papa read us stories by the fire and Mama brought warm milk and cookies. Cari and I were so happy to sleep in our sleeping bags and so proud to stay up until almost midnight. We were both pretending we were big girls that evening. Mama brought a box of old clothes and we dressed up and pretended to be women we admired.

In yet another scene, it was cold and blustery and she had seen a cute but scruffy-looking dog, shivering and huddled against the neighbor's house. We coaxed the shivering animal inside and comforted her. After giving her warm milk and food, we gave the dog a bath. Since she didn't have a collar Mama said we could adopt her. We named her Brandy and it wasn't long before Brandy made herself at home and watched the ABC news with Papa. Anyone would have been comfortable and happy in our home, thought Marsha to herself.

The next morning, sitting in the midst of family photos, Marsha found herself recollecting about when she was a baby. We lived in a modest townhouse and my mother worked as a teacher and my father went to college, she remembered. Alice was there to take care of me until Mama came home from teaching in the afternoon. Marsha thought of her Mama's words of recounting, "Sometimes you went with me to the classroom and you quietly colored in the back of the room until class was over. Marsha, you were always such a cheerful and happy little girl."

Marsha looked at the pictures of the powerboat Papa bought when she was a child. We went boating on the Allegheny or Monongahela Rivers almost every weekend. Mama and Papa lived life to the fullest with me. I was the apple of my father's eye.

Besides embracing life, Marsha had a passion for anything that came her way and she welcomed every opportunity to learn, while her parents presented her with opportunities to blossom. Mama and Papa always put me first and spent as much time with their little angel as possible.

Marsha enjoyed kindergarten and was the brightest in her class. Marsha clasped a picture of herself at the petting zoo firmly between her two thumbs and index fingers as she stared at it for a long time. It was as if this photo had the power of a trance. The photo showed Marsha holding a lion cub in the petting zoo. It was the last field trip Marsha would take with her class. She realized this picture signified the end to her past. This was a photograph of the last outing before life for little Marsha hung by a thread and recovery was questionable.

Her parents reminisced with countless baby pictures, before stashing them away while Marsha's long and painful recovery process progressed. How Marsha knew this she didn't quite know. Only now, twenty six years later, after the adoption of her child, Marsha was sure this last image of her before the accident was forever embedded in her parents' minds. Little Marsha, shoulder-length, blonde hair with bangs, wearing a short, red dress, bobby socks, and white tennis shoes, looked so happy holding the little lion cub in her arms.

Marsha, a privileged little girl with many opportunities ahead, suddenly saw the pearly white gates of heaven before her. The dirt path that only hours before held promise for a family adventure now held devastation. Little Marsha lay motionless, lifeless, on the uneven dirt path with her parents by her side.

"We have little hope for her recovery. If and when she awakes from the coma there is no telling what, and how much, damage has occurred. There is little else we can do, Mr. and Mrs. Walsch," Marsha's doctor finished before leaving them standing helplessly and bewildered.

The reality of Marsha's life-altering experience subconsciously brought realization of the value of life itself. Marsha's appreciation of mere existence changed. Life took on new meaning, a new direction, without Marsha or anyone else realizing it. Twenty-some years later, what a miraculous recovery she had made from being the youngster in the intensive care unit. After a seven-week coma, Marsha came back to life; opening her eyes and uttering "Mama" as she saw her mother by her bedside. Looking back, Marsha was proud of what she had overcome and realized that she accepted problems and faced life's many challenges head on. Marsha's recovery would be fueled by intense love of family and friends and something more. She felt her extra strength, the power from within, inherent in us all, played a significant role. Marsha could not help but wonder whether God had given her a special blessing for her rebirth and recovery. Did God hold the trump card to her revival?

Marsha's initial recovery was truly a miracle and her forthcoming progress was years of hard work initiated by sheer strength and dedication from herself and her parents. Marsha recognized that the sometimes-unbelievable challenges helped to mold her into the woman she was today: strong, proud, and beautiful.

The few memories Marsha retained of her childhood and the ordeal she survived were quite vivid and she concentrated time and time again in hopes of more recollection. She was convinced, during her teen years, that her persistence to the lifelong struggles to become a success in her own eyes had a deeper meaning or significance. Her vitality and accomplishments were important. Marsha realized she had a purpose beyond personal accomplishment. She had no preconceived notion of what she would do to make a difference in the future. All she knew is that somehow, someday she would. One day an inner voice would tell her how to encourage those faced with extreme adversity. "I am providing help and making a difference for people who are faced with adversity like I was," Marsha says, "and my purpose is to bring light to a dismal situation. Life is a path of struggles and dreams, fulfilled by our strengths and faith. We can overcome and build ourselves a brighter future if we put our minds to it and persevere."

With pictures of lifelong memories strewn around her on the floor Marsha could not help but think back about the event that changed her life completely and forever.

III. Papa's Surprise: A Vacation Is To Create Memories

Little Marsha jumped up excitedly from the memory game she was playing with when she heard the garage door opening. "Papa is home! Papa is home!" she called to her mother upstairs. He had been away from home for two weeks this time. I miss my papa so much when he goes on those business trips, thought Marsha to herself, and his absence from home was becoming more frequent. "Why does Papa leave us?" Marsha asked her mama as she descended with a basket full of laundry and as Papa walked into the living room.

Papa, a young, tall, brunette man, dropped his bags and opened his arms wide to embrace the little girl who ran to him. As he hugged her lovingly, he answered her earlier question to Mama that he happened to overhear as he entered. "Papa needs to make money so you and Mama have a nice home to live in, food to eat, pretty clothes to wear, and so we can buy you games and toys you like. After I change, would you like me to play with you?"

"Oh yes, Papa! Yes!" responded little Marsha excitedly. "I have to show you my new baby. Mama bought Suzy at the toy store yesterday. She's my bestest baby and she's so cute."

"I can't wait to see her, sweetheart. Just give me five minutes and I'll admire your baby Suzy. I'm sure she's as beautiful as you," said Marsha's father taking off his tie haphazardly after a long two-day business trip. "I'm sure you and Suzy have lots to tell me."

Papa stepped towards his wife in the doorway of their living room. "I really like your miniskirt, sweetheart," and he admired her long, shapely legs before putting both arms around her waist and pressing her bosom to his chest. "Oh honey, I thought about you all day!" he whispered in her ear, and she let out a tiny giggle.

Sam and Helen were the typical young couple, still with fantasies and dreams of and for one another. "How was your day, honey? I hope you had time to get some work done," Helen said as she batted her eyelids at her husband.

"It was fine, but busy. So, how was your day, honey?"

"I've been watching Marsha play with that doll all day," Helen said with a smile. "It is such a pleasure to see her so happy."

"Marsha, do we have another baby in our house now?" Sam called to his daughter.

"Oh daddy you are teasing me and she's my baby and I'm already a big girl and can take care of her," responded Marsha as she saw her mother and father in an embrace.

"You know she misses you terribly when you're gone, as I do," said Helen. "Marsha asks about you all the time and counts the days till you come home. Every night we talk about you before she goes to sleep and sometimes I think I see the pain of missing you in our daughter's eyes."

Since the day little Marsha was born almost six years ago, she had been the pride and joy of her parents. Helen and Sam devoted themselves to their child. Marsha is such a loving and sensitive child and she really adores her papa. Helen decided to quit working to be a guiding light for their daughter and has enjoyed every minute. "Honey, I feel so lucky that I can be here with Marsha all day when you need to go away on business," continued Helen. "I think I provide an anchor for her because she sometimes thinks you're never coming back. I need to explain that you always come home and we'll always be a family. Usually, as Marsha clings to me for comfort, I tell her Mama will always be here with her each and every day. That seems to help."

"I wonder if all parents feel the way we do?" Sam asked out loud. "Whenever I hear her voice over the phone, my heart just melts and I can't put into words how I feel. Like you, I want to give her everything we possibly can and knowing you are here with her eases my heartache a bit. I am so glad you take such high regard in being by her side and take pride in teaching our angel. I'm sure it's not always easy."

Sam spent quality time whenever his work schedule and travels allowed. Most weekends, the Walsch family worked and/or played together. It was a habit the parents started early on. This way little Marsha could help, have fun, and feel important. "Would you like to help Papa wash the car tomorrow morning?" Sam asked his little girl.

"Oh yes, Papa! Can we use the new hose Mama bought and make the water bubbly?" screeched Papa's angel as she snuggled on the brown living room sofa between her parents. Marsha felt sad when she could not participate in convorsations with her friends about their daddies. "I wish you could give me a bath and tuck me in every day like Cari's daddy," said Marsha. She relished the hours together with her papa.

"I have a surprise for you," Mr. Walsch said to his ladies and watched how his daughter seemed to come alive and sit at attention, all sixty pounds of her. She sat there beaming, looking so beautiful in her red little shorts and dark blue t-shirt to match her big blue vibrant eyes, and now they were focused on him.

"Papa, what's the surprise? What is it? What is it?" she repeated excitedly. "Tell me! Tell me!" Little Marsha was bouncing up and down by now.

"OK, my little rabbit. Settle down," said Papa. "We are going on vacation to the mountains before school starts. The leaves will be starting to turn colors due to the cool nights of autumn and yet, it will still be warm during the day. Marsha, you will have fun exploring the woods and we can romp on the rolling hills. Maybe we'll even find some treasures you can bring back home to show your friends when school starts."

Papa sat smiling and observed his daughter's reaction.

"When are we going Papa?" asked Marsha. "Are there pretty flowers like in Mama's garden? Will we see a big brown bear like on Grizzly Adams? Can I take my baby Suzy with me?"

"Slow down sweetheart," said Papa. "We're not going

for a few days. Yes, you may take your baby Suzy. I don't think we'll see a grizzly bear, but there will be lots of other animals in the forest. I am looking forward to spending time with my family. I've been so wrapped up in work and I've missed my two favorite girls."

He gave his wife and daughter a loving hug.

"Oh Sam, it will be wonderful to get away. I hear the Pocono's are a wonderful place to vacation," said Helen beaming. "Where have you made reservations?"

"Erik and Carol have offered us their cabin for a week," responded her husband. "It's an old wooden cabin nestled in the Pocono Mountains. It has two bedrooms and a fireplace and Erik tells me that we'll see lots of nature because Stroudsburg, the town, is twenty minutes away. I'm sure this will be a wonderful vacation and we'll have lots of family memories for years to come," Papa smiled as he bounced little, squealing Marsha on his knee.

IV. The Pocono's: The Mountains Are Alive and Beautiful

Vast stretches of forest lined the cascading mountain ridges. They slowly appeared ahead of the Walsch family as they drove through the countryside. As they drove closer, the brilliance of the turning colors became more evident." Oh, look at the splendor of color before us," said Helen. "And it's just the beginning of fall. Just imagine this place in a few weeks time."

Settling into their mountain retreat the happy little family snuggled close in front of the roaring fireplace. It wasn't long before Marsha put her head in her papa's lap, closed her eyes, and fell fast asleep.

"Oh Sam, just look at her," sighed Helen. "She looks so peaceful in your arms. She is most happy when you tuck her in and I'm glad we have a week together in these beautiful mountains."

"I consider myself lucky to have you and Marsha in my life," said Sam. "Do you know how much you mean to me? I wish our family could spend more time together like this," he kissed his wife softly.

"I know how you feel about your job and the time it takes you away from home," Sam's wife responded. "But I'm sure it won't be like this forever. Let's make the most out of this week and make sure that Marsha has fun."

"I agree," said Marsha's papa. "We will give her experiences she will be proud to share with her friends. Now, I think we should take our angel to bed and enjoy the fire, just you and me," and he gave her a dashing smile.

"Why don't you tuck her in and I'll find a bottle of wine, honey?"

As Sam carried his little princess up the stairs, she stayed snuggled close. Her blonde, messed hair draped on his shoulder. Little Marsha seemed to be so comfortable and content. She kept her eyes closed and appeared asleep all the way to her bedroom. There, as Papa gently laid her in her bed and covered his daughter with her Cinderella comforter, Marsha said, "I love you, Papa. Will you sing me a song?"

"I love you too, sweetheart, and of course I'll sing you a song," Papa whispered. "Twinkle, twinkle little star. How I wonder what you are…" When he finished, he bent over Marsha and gently kissed her forehead.

This is what makes being a father so wonderful, he thought. She just takes my breath away and I will do anything for her. "Marsha was asleep before I finished Twinkle, Twinkle Little Star," Sam told his wife. "Come sit by me and tell me what you'd like to do tomorrow. I heard there's a riding stable nearby and we could see the area on horseback if we get in a few lessons with the horses first. What do you think?"

"It'll certainly be more of an adventure for Marsha than exploring the area on foot," commented Mama. "Do you think she's old enough, Sam?"

"I don't think it will be a problem. Marsha is both tall and responsible for her age and I've seen smaller children riding horses. Besides, we'll have a guide with us the whole time."

"You're right about Marsha, but we should make sure of the stable's rules before we tell her and get her hopes up."

"Certainly!"

"I'm sure Marsha will be excited once we know for sure. Oh, Sam, it will be lovely to see the countryside on horseback. Am I glad I brought a few pairs of jeans and hiking boots for everyone," Helen continued.

The sun shone brightly through the kitchen window as Helen fixed bacon, eggs, and biscuits for her family. We have a long busy day today and we need a hearty breakfast to get us off to a good start, she thought before a familiar voice interrupted her daydreaming.

"What are we doing today?" Marsha screeched as she came bouncing down the stairs. "What are we having for breakfast, Mama? I'm starving."

She climbed on the bench in the kitchen's nook.

"We have a special big breakfast of eggs, bacon, and biscuits to start our busy day off right. Papa has a big surprise for us today. It's supposed to be a lovely day today and we will be outside all day long," Mama said, beaming at her bright-eyed little girl.

"Where are my two favorite cowgirls this morning?" bellowed Papa as he entered the kitchen. "I see Mama has you dressed for our special day. Did you tell Marsha our surprise, Helen?"

"No, I wanted to give you the honors," said Mama, smiling at her husband.

"Papa, what's the surprise?" asked Marsha, bouncing up and down in her seat.

"Oh Marsha, we are going to have a week full of adventures. How does that sound?"

"Oh boy," squealed little Marsha excitedly. She looked like a little beaming angel to her parents.

"The three of us are going horseback riding. We need to get going right after breakfast so we can meet our horses and learn to ride them," instructed Papa. "Then, if everyone is comfortable, we'll ride some trails in a few days."

"You mean on a real horsy, Papa?" screeched Marsha.

"Yes, a real live horse just like in your story books," interjected Mama.

"I don't think any of my friends have ridden a horse before, Papa. I'll be the first to do that," she stated proudly.

"Now hurry up and let's eat breakfast so we can get going," said Papa.

On the way to the Stage Coach Stables, the road wound through rolling hills of green grass, wild flowers, and forest.

"Oh Sam, this is beautiful," said Helen. "This will be lovely to see on horseback."

"Mama, look at the pretty flowers and I see a bear," Marsha screeched in delight

"I think that's a cow sweetheart," Papa corrected with a grin.

"Oh Papa, I think it's a bear. Really! Will we see more bears this week?" she continued.

"I think we just might, little one," teased Marsha's father. Obviously Mr. Walsch's plan to give their daughter a memorable vacation was working and Helen squeezed her husband's hand in appreciation.

"Papa, are we there yet?" asked Marsha. "I want to see my horsy. I want to pet her. Do you think I will be allowed to give her a carrot, Mama?"

"I suppose we can ask whether or not you can."

"We'll be there shortly," sang Papa with a song on the radio. Moments later the forest opened to rolling hills of pasture as far as the eye could see. To the east, under a low-lying sun, stood a large, bright red barn with an adjacent well-kept home.

"Papa, look," screamed Marsha. "We're here! And it looks like Captain Kangaroo's house."

"Yes, it does," chuckled Helen and Sam in unison.

As Mr. Walsch was paying for their week-long excursion, Marsha was excitedly looking at all the pictures of horses on the office walls with her mother. Some had riders in various picturesque locations of the Pocono's. "Mama, will my picture get put up there, too?"

"You never know, sweetie. Which horsy do you think will be yours to ride?" she asked. "Which one do you think is the prettiest?"

"I like the one up there with the pretty lady," answered Marsha. "The one with the white bushy tail. It looks like Cinderella's horse."

"Do you think it could be Cinderella's horse?" asked Mama.

"No Mama, Cinderella's horse turned back into a mouse at midnight," said Marsha. Helen and Sam enjoyed playing with their little girl. They wanted to promote their daughter's originality and imagination.

"The lessons will be three hours the first two days and four on Wednesday, Thursday, and Friday," Mr. Walsch told his wife. "The last three days we'll have to be here at eight in the morning."

"That sounds OK. We'll just have to wear an extra layer for the morning chill."

"Let's go to the stables, cowgirls," called Papa to his wife and daughter. "Joe is the name of our trainer and he will meet us there."

"Yaaay," screamed Marsha with glee.

"Are you just a little excited?" Papa asked as he opened the door for his ladies.

"Papa, hurry! Hurry! I want to see my horsy."

"Good morning, Mr. Walsch, Mrs. Walsch," Joe nodded. He was a tall, blonde, handsomely rugged looking character, wearing blue jeans, a white t-shirt, and a denim jacket.

Little Marsha instinctively clutched her mama's hand at the sight of him. "He so big, Mama!" and she remained close, touching her mother for comfort.

"And who do we have here?" he questioned looking towards the little blonde child.

"My name is Marsha and I want the horse with the white tail just like the picture in the office," Marsha declared with sudden vigor, still standing beside her mother.

"I'm afraid we don't have Missy anymore, young lady. But, we'll make sure to get you one that's just as pretty,"

Joe finished before directing his attention to Sam and Helen. "We'll be ridin' inside the corral for two days and then head out on the trails the rest of the week. Would you like to get started right away? I'll get them saddled up."

"What do you think Helen?" asked her husband.

"I think that would be just fine. Marsha will be thrilled. You know how impatient she can be and it's a good thing we dressed the part this morning," Helen finished as Marsha rushed into her arms after hearing her mother give the OK.

Mr. Walsch drew Joe aside and said, "Our little girl is barely six years old and we want to make sure that nothing happens to her. Please make sure to keep the horses calm at all times. Given our daughter's age and experience I think it would be best not to gallop the horses."

"You needn't worry. The horse your daughter will be riding is our calmest and the one that the kids ride here all the time," indicated Joe with a good-natured smile.

"Let's go, Tonto," Papa called to his little girl who eagerly watched the horses grazing in the fenced green pasture.

As they watched Joe lead four horses into the corral, Marsha's eyes grew wider and wider with amazement. "Oh Mama, look! Papa, they're beautiful! Which one is mine? Can I ride him every day?" Marsha exclaimed in awe.

"Little lady," said Joe. "This is Glory and she's yours to ride, every day."

"She's beautiful, and look, Papa, she has a white tail," said Marsha excitedly.

"Now little lady we always have to be quiet and calm around horses and always stand in front of them so they can see you," instructed Joe. "When horses get frightened by a sudden sound, or can't see you, they kick with their hind legs and could hurt you. We certainly don't want that, do we?"

"Yes sir, I mean, no sir," answered Marsha looking at the horse trainer sheepishly, her head lowered as if she'd been scolded. Helen knelt beside her and put an arm around her small waist. Sam noticed how their matching blonde hair glistened in the morning sun and considered himself the luckiest guy in the world for having such a beautiful wife and daughter.

"These are big strong animals, honey," interjected Helen, in an effort to comfort her.

"Now let's see how you look in Glory's saddle," said Joe. Marsha quietly walked in front of Joe with a big smile on her face. She had anticipated being on a horse all morning and that was about to become reality.

Sam and Helen watched with pure love and pride as their little girl fearlessly climbed on the stirrups and swung her right leg over Glory's back. "I wonder how she knows to do that?" Helen said to her husband standing, watching proudly, next to her.

"From watching The Lone Ranger and from her books, I imagine."

Joe stood by little Marsha's side making sure Glory's junior rider was safe and secure. After her victorious mount onto her Cinderella horse, Marsha triumphantly beamed at her parents.

"Just look at her, honey. She's so happy and proud."

"Got it," said Papa Sam as he snapped a picture.

"This is definitely one of those images that will always remain in my memory."

"I agree," said Papa Sam. "This is definitely a Kodak moment and one I will also probably never forget. Now let's get on our horses and get this show on the road, shall we?" Sam marveled as Helen graciously mounted her horse, putting her left, booted foot into the stirrup and swinging her long right leg over her horse's back before sitting securely in the saddle and flashing him a broad, happy smile. "God, she looks good," whispered Sam under his breath before turning, holding, and mounting his own horse.

"Everyone good to go? Let's go then," agreed Joe and made sure all were secure on their horses before mounting his steed. "Let's start by just getting comfortable with sitting on your horse while I go over how to properly hold the reins, and a few other things, OK?"

Joe spent the next half hour demonstrating the proper use of the reins to guide the horse where it was to go. They all took turns practicing under the watchful eye of the instructor.

"Now follow me and get comfortable riding around the corral," he instructed.

Joe spent the next portion of their lesson demonstrating the proper methods of making the horse go the speed wanted. They each practiced walking, trotting, and cantering. Joe was careful not to have the girl on the horse gallop, as instructed by her father.

Sam and Helen kept close watch on their smiling daughter. Unknown to each other, they were both searching for the slightest hint that Marsha felt uncomfortable.

"How're you doing, Tonto?" Papa inquired.

"Oh Papa, this is great!" Marsha was obviously enjoying herself and Mama could not help but wonder if Marsha was pretending to be Cinderella or some other fair maiden. She thought about how their precious little girl looked so grown up riding the horse, and a tear escaped her eye before she was brought back to reality by Joe's authoritative voice.

"That's about it for today, Little Princess. Let's resume this in the morning. The horses need to get some rest now. Please follow me to the gate and I'll show you how to dismount," he said as he got off his horse and hurried to Glory's side to help Marsha.

"Tomorrow I'll see you at nine and we'll review and ride inside the corral for the remainder of the time," Joe relayed to Sam and Helen. "I hope you had fun today, Marsha."

He finished with the horses, said his good-byes, and took the horses into the barn.

"Papa, I want my own horse when I grow up," Marsha said dreamily as she fell asleep on the short drive home.

"We're making our daughter very happy, and it certainly tires her out. Maybe we can find some books about horses in Erik's library and learn a bit about the animals with Marsha. Do you think she'd enjoy that?" said Helen as she looked at her sleeping daughter in the back seat.

"I admire how you look out for our daughter's interests and how you pride yourself on furthering her education," Sam told his wife yet again. "Whenever an opportunity presents itself, you are there making the learning process fun. You really are a wonderful mother, and I love you," and he put his arms around her slender waist and kissed her lusciously, first on her neck and then her mouth.

Later that evening, Marsha spied some books on the coffee table, "What's this Mama?"

"I thought you would like to learn about horses. I found these books in Mr. Erik's library."

"You mean I can learn what Glory likes to eat, and where she sleeps, and stuff like that, Mama?"

"Yes, dear. There is so much to learn about horses that I thought we could read a bit after we eat. Why don't you look at the pictures while I fix dinner?"

After dinner, the happy little family snuggled together, and Mama started reading. Both she and Papa answered Marsha's questions until bedtime.

"OK, angel," Papa told his little girl as he carried her up to bed. "We've had a long day today, and you'll ride Glory again tomorrow, and he pulled the covers over his little girl's obviously spent little body. Now you need to get good night's sleep so you'll be bright eyed and bushy tailed in the morning."

Before Sam finished the sentence Marsha was fast asleep.

"Marsha is already asleep and it would probably be a good idea if we did the same," said Sam to his wife as he came down the stairs.

"I agree. Tomorrow will be an early and exciting day," she said, smiling at Sam and accepting his hand as he led her upstairs to bed.

V. A Road Of Paradise: Heaven Has Many Gates

The second morning of their vacation, Helen woke up early to the sounds of chirping birds. In her white terrycloth robe, she made her way to the overstuffed chair by the open window and indulged herself with the woodsy morning air. Everything was quiet except for nature's sounds. The beauty had her in a trance. Helen's eyes surveyed the backyard and spotted two squirrels chasing each other while not far from them a deer grazed lazily. This must be one view into paradise, she thought, and couldn't help imagining how much nature they would experience this week.

After another hearty breakfast, this time pancakes, eggs, and sausage, the three set out to the Stage Coach Stables. They practiced on the horses, fine tuning the skills they had learned the first day. Marsha progressed to the point that Joe felt comfortable enough to take them to a larger, outside corral to get the feel of riding the horses in the open. Marsha was ecstatic. The little family enjoyed the morning with the horses and spent the afternoon relaxing. After a lengthy afternoon nap, Marsha delighted in exploring around their cabin, even after dinner when the sounds of nocturnal animals filled the nighttime atmosphere.

"Papa, it's so noisy, much noisier than at home." Marsha peered over the ground and into the woods, diligently searching for the culprits with her big red flashlight.

"Well, Princess, there are lots of animals living in the woods, some so small you can't even see them. I think it's time to come in and get ready for bed. We have more riding to do tomorrow, remember?"

"Yah, Papa, OK."

"Ooh, you're here early this morning. The horses are still feeding. Would you like to come see and I'll show you the barn where they live?" asked Joe.

"Oh boy! Can we? Can we, Papa?" squealed Marsha jumping up and down.

"Yes dear, we'll go see where the horses are kept," and Papa grabbed his exuberant little girl's hand and she went pulling him towards the barn, following Joe.

Marsha enjoyed watching the horses eat their breakfast. It was over quickly and her daydream ended when she heard Joe's voice.

"OK, if you could all go back to the corral I'll have the horses brought out and we can get started," said Joe as he busied himself with gathering saddles and bridles, before joining them at the corral on his black stallion. "We are a group of eight this morning," reported trainer Joe to his group of riders. "Let's line the horses up with the little girl up front with her mother. Everyone else line up behind them."

Joe finished addressing the group and started his horse in a steady walk away from the stables, down the dirt path, into the woods. Sam let out a sigh of contentment as he sat tall on his chocolate mare observing his wife and little girl a few horses ahead of him. Sam knew his wife was entranced by the quiet solitude of the forest and he admired her as she inhaled the fragrant air and listened to the sounds surrounding them.

"We are in no hurry," exclaimed trainer Joe as he stopped at an opening in the forest and all the horses gathered in a circle. "This is nature at it's finest."

"You two are a vision of radiance," Papa said and positioned his horse beside them. Trainer Joe snapped a picture with Sam's camera, and stood by and observed their moment together.

"What a nice family. This is what makes my job special," he thought to himself with a smile of pleasure and contentment on his ruggedly, handsome, tanned face.

The bubbling stream next to the dirt path gave promise for a fruitful adventure that day, and Marsha gazed at the clear water gurgling across the pebbles and vegetation.

"Mama, look at that fish," she exclaimed in awe. "Do you think the frog prince lives here?"

An occasional rustle of leaves and snapping of twigs from squirrels and other creatures playing and frolicking in the underbrush let the visitors to the forest know that they were not alone. The gentle breeze rustling through the trees carried the sweet sent of russet leaves and the fast approach of fall.

As the group proceeded through this wooden wonderland, trainer Joe occasionally pointed out scenery and animals along the way from atop his horse. Squirrels, birds, and other critters were busy preparing for the winter ahead and the passers-by were obviously interrupting their ecosystem. As the horses progressed along the stream and through the woods, a mockingbird sang his song from a tree ahead. The clop, clop, clop of hooves became mesmerizing and in tune with the sounds of nature. Sam thought of his lovely wife and daughter and hoped they were enjoying their vacation as much as he was.

"Oh Mama, this is the best!" exclaimed Marsha. "I am having so much fun being Cinderella!" Helen smiled at her daughter's playful, joyous comment.

The forest opened suddenly and before the group lay mesmerizing rolling hills covered with wild flowers. Helen heard Marsha gasp in amazement as trainer Joe steadied his steed to prepare the others for a moment's rest to take in nature's newest breathtaking picture. The fluffy cumulous clouds spotted the sky and filtered the sun's rays as they slowly moved across the heavens before them. The soft breeze swept across the fields, slightly moving the heads of buttercups as far as the eye could see.

"This must be what heaven looks like," said Helen out loud and simultaneously everyone seemed to agree.

"We have a few miles of riding through these meadows before we return to the barn," said Joe. "Is everybody ready for our journey through the royal gardens?" He smiled and then cast his gaze on little Marsha, "Your Highness?"

"Yes, Sir!" Marsha replied.

Slowly the horses moved one behind the other and proceeded into the lush, colorful meadow.

Helen, Marsha, and Sam simultaneously inhaled the fragrant air and sighed in contentment. What could be more magical than this, mused Helen. She felt so happy to be able to share this beautiful experience with her family. "This experience is so special don't you agree?" she exclaimed and her husband nodded behind her.

The next two days followed suit, each more memorable than the next. The fall scenery, the colors, and smells of the Poconos were ever changing and felt like paradise to all the horseback riders.

VI. A Face of Hell: Devastation

The horses walked in tow, one after the other, like a chain gang through the lush paradise. They only had a mile or two before this week-long adventure came to an end and, with it, their vacation would soon draw to a close and reality would set in again. Joe held the reins of his steed firmly, yet all of a sudden and without warning, his horse, the lead horse, took off at a dead gallop. Helen's palomino, Marsha's Glory, and the rest of the horses followed suit. Almost immediately, Papa heard the high-pitched "Papa" and then nothing, silence. He sat straight up, strained on his saddle, extending, stretching as far as he possibly could and stretching his muscular shoulders and neck past the other riders to see what was wrong, what had happened. But he saw nothing except the fellow horses keeping time in front of him. His precious little girl would be changed forever. Her cry would be the last time he heard her voice for a very long time. He could not fathom what had just happened. Mama Helen heard the thump of something hitting the ground following that bloodcurdling scream. She looked in front of her, at her daughter's horse, expecting to see Marsha, a motherly reaction to the sound of her daughter's cry. Glory's back was bare, no Marsha. Helen strained to keep her balance as her horse kept in step with trainer Joe's horse.

What she saw made her heart stop and her blood curdle. Momentarily she was paralyzed as her images of paradise turned into sheer horror. Glory was dragging Marsha by her right leg, which was caught in the stirrup.

"Sam—!" Sam—!!!" Mama Helen screamed. "Oh my God! Sam!" She was in utter shock at the sight of her precious child dangling helplessly at the side of the horse. She was being dragged, like a rag doll, along the dirt and rock laden path.

At the sound of his wife's distraught voice, Sam sat erect and at attention in his saddle. He secured himself and strained to see his wife in front, second in from trainer Joe. Seconds passed and Papa realized the horror his wife was witnessing!

"Joe!" He was screaming even before grasping the full horror of the situation.

His usually composed face instantly went white as his gaze fell on his little Marsha. Sam kicked his horse's flanks, arrived at his daughter's side and yanked the two horses to a stop with more strength than he knew he possessed. "No! Marsha! Oh God, NO!!!"

As sheer terror erupted and panic ensued, Joe immediately kicked his steed in his sides and raced for help. Others on horseback formed a semicircle around the fallen child, speechless and some in tears at what they saw before them. This scene would haunt this group forever. A lustrous and exhilarating day turned into hell in mere seconds. What now? What can we do? Oh God! Please help us, came the cry inside Helen and Sam. Mechanically, Sam tended to their angel, avoiding movement and thereby possible further damage.

"Oh my God, Sam, what can we do?" Helen cried, as Marsha lay battered and lifeless on the dirt path that only moments before represented utter beauty and contentment. "Mama is here," Helen whispered to Marsha lovingly.

"Everything will be OK," whispered Sam as he ripped off his shirt to apply pressure to stop the bleeding. "I've got to stop the bleeding," he murmured, distraught, "where, though?" His words were to himself but spoken out loud, in despair because his baby's head was so badly injured and covered with blood and dirt. "There's blood everywhere!"

Gingerly he placed his shirt under Marsha's bleeding

chin and wrapped it around her little mutilated head. Then he proceeded trying to remove some of the dirt off of her face. "Oh my God! My baby's face," he said out loud. As if to shield Marsha from the air and any further pain, Sam took his denim jacket and covered his daughter's injured body. But he couldn't hide her mutilated face from view. Oh my God, he thought. What else can I do? What can I do to help my little princess? His mind raced with questions in utter pain and anguish.

"My baby! My baby! Oh please help my baby!" sobbed Helen as she held her child. My beautiful little girl is mangled beyond recognition. I don't even know if she's alive. Mama held Marsha's limp little hand and felt a tiny pulse. She sobbed, "You are our everything and we will take care of you. Oh Sam, what can we do?" She was gasping uncontrollably. "We need help. We need an ambulance!"

"Joe already went for help," Sam said flatly.

"You'll be OK, sweetheart. You need to hang on, sweetie. Stay with Mama!" Helen continued crying. She sat weeping beside her motionless child. Mama reached for her other small, motionless hand and felt a slow pulse. She was greatly relieved. "Oh baby, hang on. Please hang on. Help is on the way," she could barely whisper as tears ran down her face uncontrollably.

"Marsha must have lost consciousness with the shock of the fall," Sam said to his wife. At least each secretly hoped so. They could not imagine the horror and pain their daughter endured in those horrific seconds after she lost her balance.

Looking to her husband for comfort and strength, Sam's eyes met hers and the two shared a moment of connection and strength. "We'll get through this! We'll do whatever's necessary. We'll do whatever it takes!" Sam said defiantly.

"The ambulance is on its way," called Joe as his horse galloped towards them, slowed, and came to a halt. "Is Marsha conscious yet? What else can I do to help?"

"I think you have done enough, thank you!" spat Sam

bluntly and he heard the ambulance siren in the distance, coming ever closer at what seemed like an agonizingly slow pace.

"Give us room to take care of our daughter," Mr. Walsch grumbled at the spectators as he and Helen kept watch over their mangled child.

Both parents were numb, with no idea what was next, what to do, or even if their precious child would survive.

Mama sat with Marsha's hands cupped around her head and prayed silently. Marsha's blood oozed from her beautiful, innocent, now badly damaged face. "Please God, help my little girl," she begged yet again. "I love you so much, baby!" She cried because she was feeling totally powerless. The life had drained out of her. She functioned by mere necessity, determination, and resolution. It was mere strength of character that kept her going in the face of the unimaginable. But she had to survive, do what needed to be done, for her little girl.

As the paramedics quickly tended to the limp and deformed little body, Sam gave them a rundown of what happened and how he and Helen had handled the situation so far.

"Our daughter's horse took off. Marsha lost her balance. My wife heard the thump as she fell to the ground. We hope she lost consciousness immediately. Her leg was caught in the stirrup and she was dragged. My wife screamed, as she was able to get our attention. It seemed a lifetime until I could get the horse to stop. Is there anything else I can do to help?" Sam's voice quivered and tears were in his eyes.

"You did the right thing to move her as little as possible," said the first paramedic.

"Her right leg is obviously broken and we can't tell the extent of other injuries," continued his partner. "Mr. Walsch, we will do everything we can for your daughter while we get her to the hospital."

The pair worked on Marsha almost mechanically as Sam and Helen watched in horror, and she was whisked into the waiting ambulance in minutes, which seemed too long.

"The drive will take about half an hour," said the first paramedic as he quickly directed Sam and Helen to follow the stretcher into the ambulance. Utter silence gave way to sounds of sirens screaming as the ambulance navigated through the serene field onto the vacant road. Helen and Sam sat huddled side by side, staring blindly at their limp, mangled daughter as the ambulance sped to the hospital.

In mere seconds, Helen and Sam's world turned from happiness and tranquility to sheer horror. Their world was torn apart instantaneously, their heart and souls torn apart. They clung to each other mentally and physically to get through each and every moment of the torture, the not knowing what to expect and how this nightmare would end.

"This is Hell!" Helen sobbed. "What's next? Where to from here? Oh Sam, what are we going to do?"

"I have no idea," responded Sam, clenching his blood-covered fists for control.

Both parents felt the grip of death close by, as a presence seemed to engulf the rear of the ambulance. The paramedic worked on Marsha in front of them, yet seemed not to notice the ever-increasing feeling of doom the Walsch's were feeling.

"Sam, do you feel it?" Helen stammered as panic set in.

"Hang on Marsha, baby, we're here," Sam whispered, feeling Marsha's life fading before their eyes.

The doom loomed over them and seemed to engulf the small space they occupied inside the speeding ambulance.

"Oh my God! Sam!!!"

"Baby, don't give up. Stay with Papa. Honey, Papa's here," begged Sam as he and Helen prayed their precious child would not die in front of them.

As Marsha's parents clung to faith and hope, the attending paramedic looked up and nodded approvingly and Marsha's vitals appeared weak but steady on the monitor.

"Marsha, my name is Arella," said a meek voice in Marsha's head. "Hang on. Hang on. I will help you."

"I'm still Marsha, right? I feel so different. I feel like I'm floating. What's that light in the distance? Who's there? I feel you near me, calling me, although I can't see you, I hear you calling me. Who are you? Tell me, please," Marsha was hearing not only her own voice, but another voice as well.

"*Come with me, Marsha. I am Arella, your messenger and guide to your new world. You'll feel continuous love and no sadness where we'll go. You will always be happy. If you come with me, towards the light, you will come to know more and more love and joy as you move closer to God. You'll be free forever—.*"

Marsha turned her attention to her crying mama and papa. She felt their pain and heard their voices pleading for her not to go away.

"Baby, you are our everything. You are our angel. You can't leave us. Oh, honey, your mama and papa will do anything for you. Stay with us!" Mama cried.

"Arella, I feel so strange. I can feel what's going on around me, and around my body too, and I can understand you. I still feel so small and helpless," Marsha answered the voice.

"You are still a child, Marsha. Come with me, you will understand more and more as time passes. You will be able to understand your loved ones feelings. You will be able to get inside and help make a difference in their lives."

"My sweetheart! You know how much we love you, baby. How very much you mean to us. How very much we want to do everything for you. How we want to make you well and happy," stammered Papa with great emotion.

"I wish I could make Mama and Papa feel better. They are so sad. They feel so bad about what happened and I want to let them know it wasn't their fault," Marsha said to the voice.

"Sam, I wish I could talk to her—, hold her—," Mama sobbed as she held Marsha's limp, bloody little hand. "Remember how we used to sit together and read stories? I want to do that again, Sam. I can't bear the thought of losing her, Sam!"

"I wish I had spent more time with her, Helen. I wish I

had told her how much I wanted to, and now I might never get the chance. —Did the accident happen as punishment for never being home or for putting her on the horse in the first place, Helen?"

"Sam, don't blame yourself!" responded Helen quietly. "You're a great father and you do what's necessary for our family. I think things happen to us for a reason and our actions are responsible for the final outcome. We have to fight for Marsha until the very end."

"My parents feel guilty and scared. I can see how strong they are despite how scared they are, Arella. It's incredible how much they love me and I never knew," Marsha said to the voice.

Marsha felt her father's pain as he spoke, "I'll never understand why this happened to us."

"How will we be able to deal with the pain—if…" sobbed Helen uncontrollably.

Now Marsha heard Arella's answer or was she feeling it?

"*Your parents are trying to make sense of it all. They need to understand and come to terms with what happened in their own way before they can go on and be free of this pain. Marsha, you will never be forgotten, though your loved ones will move on with their lives, as it should be. Come with me. You will be free to travel and help those you love without them even knowing. It is so gratifying. Remember, the closer you get to the light, the closer you will be to God.*"

"I'm so confused," thought Marsha. "I feel like I'm in the middle of a tug-of-war. I don't know what to do, Arella. How can I leave this world I barely know? I am so curious about life and I love my mama and papa so much. I don't think I am ready to leave. I have too many things I want to do and Papa always told me I am strong. But how do I tell them I'll be OK, Arella? Please tell me."

"*You are already connecting with your father, Marsha. He just doesn't know it yet. You are your daddy's girl and he will feel your words soon, just like you feel him. You two will give each other strength to go on, Marsha.*"

"How's that possible?"

"Just think of how your father used to encourage you, even over the phone, when he traveled. Remember how he always had the power to make you try a little harder?"

"Yes."

"Well now, he'll give you the strength you need to go on, to fight your road of recovery, and you'll give him the knowledge that you're going to survive and the strength to keep encouraging and fighting for you."

"But how am I going to tell him?"

"That's the special power you have with your parents and I can help it become stronger."

"Why are you helping me?"

VII. Reality: Life is fragile.

The emergency team at Stroudsburg Medical Center is ready. They have been alerted of a little girl with extensive injuries. Although Stroudsburg Medical Center is a limited care facility (Appendix 1), it is the closest hospital. The magnitude of injuries treated here are less life threatening than what is required now," one of the paramedics told Sam. "We needed to get her to the nearest hospital regardless. She will be moved if need be."

ER nurses and doctors surrounded Marsha as she was wheeled in. Sam watched as their angel was whisked down the hall and the doors closed. Helen, white as a ghost, shook in her husband's arms as she sobbed, "My baby! Oh God! My baby!"

Papa squeezed his wife in his arms to comfort her, "She'll be OK, with God's help," was all he could muster in his cracking voice. Mr. Walsch was doing everything to stay strong for his family and his strength was fading. He was so tired and shaken and worried.

"The doctor's will do what can be done. We'll do everything we can to make that happen," Sam whispered to the woman by his side, the woman he loved.

"I feel we haven't slept in days and I will never sleep

again until Marsha is out of danger. What do you think is happening with her Sam? What are they doing to her?" Helen cried and hung on to him for strength.

"Arella, do you see how much my parents love me? My mama will be lost forever if I leave," Marsha told the voice.

"They will be lost only for a short time and then go on with their lives. They'll never forget you. Remember, here you can live for eternity and see them forever."

"Sweetheart, we will stick this out together and do whatever we need to for our angel," said Papa with new determination in his voice. He never imagined the strain and stress he now faced and he swore to himself he would hold his family together.

"I can't bare to see Papa like this, Arella. He's not himself. He's making me nervous. He's scaring me. I feel his pain, too."

"Of course you do."

"How come?"

"Up here you feel your loved ones emotions."

"Oh, I don't like this. I want to be with Mama and Papa. I want to hug my mama and papa again. I want to plant flowers with Mama and go to school with my friends."

"OK, Marsha. You can. But, you'll have a long and hard road to recovery. Make no mistake. It'll be a long hard battle and it is going to hurt, a lot! But, if that's your choice, so be it. You'll be like a baby when you wake up. You will have to learn everything all over again. It's going to be hard."

"What do you mean?"

"You'll not only have to learn everything you knew before the accident, but you'll need to work harder than anyone else, harder than your friends, for the same outcome. Nothing will come easy."

"I'm confused. Could you please explain?"

"You won't be able to balance, or walk and you won't be able to feed yourself. You won't know how to go to the bathroom, or get dressed. You won't be able do much of

anything. You won't even know how to talk. You will be a big girl, but helpless like a baby."

"I have Mama and Papa to help me. They said they'd do whatever it takes. You heard them. I don't want to go with you, Arella."

"That is your choice, Marsha."

Arella wanted to guide Marsha through the pearly white Gates of Heaven. She knew that a child is special, without the knowledge and experience a lifetime provides. Arella was a special messenger angel, sent by God, to bring Marsha to the upper echelons of Heaven with the other children. With Marsha's decision for life, Arella's mission was completed.

"There is coffee and juice for you. It may be awhile," a nurse explained before disappearing.

The minutes ticked by while Mama and Papa sat pensively for news on Marsha's condition, even though they knew deep down that the news could not be good. Finally, after what seemed like eternity, a doctor walked out of the heavy, blue doors into the waiting area where Sam and Helen sat quietly and alone.

"Mr. and Mrs. Walsch? Your daughter is lucky to be alive. She is listed in critical condition, with a head injury. We don't know the extent at this point. She is in a coma and her right femur is broken," he said. "She is on her way to ICU. Dr. Alvarez will be her attending physician and will see you upstairs."

Helen and Sam sat frozen in their seats as the doctor gave them the devastating news. He had their full attention. Slowly tears flowed from Helen's eyes again as she digested every word and, her husband's grasp tightened around her quivering hand. Both sat like statues and did not say a word until the doctor left. Sam took his wife in his arms and they both sobbed.

"Marsha will be all right," Sam said, meeker than in his normal positive tone. "We have a strong little girl and we've got to be strong for her, too."

"Yes we do," Helen cried in despair. "We will stand by her and Marsha will get everything she needs, and more."

"Mr. and Mrs. Walsch?" said a cheerful voice.

"Yes," Helen said looking up, hopeful.

"Your daughter is being moved to ICU," said the nurse. "She will be in 13A."

"Marsha. Marsha. I am Brisa, your guardian angel. Arella told me you would need my help. You have made the decision to live and it is my duty to help you with that decision. You just had to let me know for sure which direction you wanted, heaven or earth. I am your friend, God's angel, remember?"

"Are you really *MY* angel? Wow, am I that special that I have my own angel? Was Arella an angel too? She didn't tell me."

"Yes. Everyone is special and everyone has his or her own guardian angel. Some people let us help, while others don't. Mostly, we angels are called upon in emergencies, when life is threatened, especially when they have chosen to fight, like you."

"Will you be my friend?"

"I will watch over you. For as long as it takes to make you well, although no one will ever see me. I am the force within—your will to survive, Marsha."

"Oh—and can I talk to you?"

"Yes, when you're thinking and battling with your inconceivable problems, troubles, and pains, you'll be talking to me and hopefully I'll be able to help you."

"How?"

"I'll try to make you understand what you can and cannot do."

"OK."

After a long pause, and more silence, Sam quietly suggested, "Let's go upstairs and give our daughter some support."

He helped his Helen up and slowly, painstakingly, they walked hand in hand to the elevator.

In ICU, Marsha's room was across form the nurses'

station. Sam and Helen gazed at their little Marsha, lying in a bed with bars on either side. She looks like a wounded cub in her cage, thought Sam. It's so unfair. Marsha was covered with a white sheet from her chest down and her head was bandaged so only the lids of her eyes showed. A pillow was placed on either side of her head to restrict any motion, involuntary or otherwise. A respirator was connected to help Marsha breathe and the IV was pumping fluids and medicine into the little girl.

"Sam, she looks so helpless," breathed Helen.

"Yes she does. What have we done to deserve this? We've always looked out for her, made her happy and now this," he said in a trance.

"Sam, please don't blame yourself," said Helen. "You told the trainer to be careful. They told us kids always rode their horses. We did everything we could."

She stood sobbing beside her husband at Marsha's bedside. Although she tried to make her husband feel better, she still also felt the same inside. Sometimes her pain became so bad she experienced total and complete exhaustion and would break down in uncontrollable tears.

"I know it was a freak accident," responded Sam. "But why us? Why Marsha?" He wiped the tears from his eyes.

"How long will I have to see my parents so sad, Brisa? How can I make them understand I'm going to be OK? It really hurts me to see them in so much pain."

"*Sweetheart, you may have to wait a few more weeks before your body is strong enough to show them you are going to recover. Be patient. We will work on it together, you and I.*"

"I am Dr. Alvarez. I am your daughter's physician while she is here," the doctor said as he looked down at the chart in hand. "Marsha suffered a major concussion. She has damage to her cerebrum, that's the forebrain. We just don't know to what extent. She is in a deep coma and has a badly broken right femur. There are further tests needed, but her condition is too serious at the moment. We will get her stabilized and she'll be moved to Scranton Hospital for further treatment."

"Can you tell us what our daughter's chances are?" Sam questioned.

"What I am telling you is all we know so far. She is holding on. The cerebellum, which is necessary for life, and the brain stem do not appear affected," responded Dr. Alvarez.

"Thank God!! Why the pillows on either side of her head. She doesn't have a spinal injury does she?"

"We are restricting any movement until we know for certain the extent of injuries."

"How long will she be in a coma?" asked Sam. "What does our daughter need to be stabilized?"

The desperate look intensified as he realized the doctor could not answer his request for answers. His devastated psyche was on overdrive. Sam was on the brink of insanity with the dire prospects for his little princess.

"Your daughter's head trauma is severe, due to her fall, that is all we know for certain at this time," Dr. Alvarez repeated. "Further complications could surface. As soon as she stabilizes we will do some x-rays to determine the extent of her head injuries. We're monitoring her very closely and making her as comfortable as possible. We just can't do any further tests until she's stabilized because they could be detrimental.

"How long will it be before she wakes up from the coma?" questioned Helen, visibly shaken at the news herself. She appeared exceedingly pale, quiet, and battered.

"There is no way of telling, ma'am," responded Dr. Alvarez. "In the OR your daughter's vital signs plummeted and we revived her. Right now she is being kept alive by machines and the next few days will be critical. Your daughter has been very lucky."

"You mean she died?" Sam whispered.

"It was a close call, Mr. Walsch."

As Helen and Sam listened to Dr. Alvarez, Helen's eyes filled with tears and Sam's posture stiffened. Helen was holding on to her husband's arm, also at attention. They were both numb, realizing and foreseeing their grim situation and the prospects for Marsha.

Holding Helen in his arms and mustering all the energy he had left, Sam told Dr. Alvarez, "Do whatever you need to for her..."

"Oh my God, Sam, Marsha d-died. She came back to us, Sam. But she may still d-die!!!" Mama sobbed uncontrollably beside her husband, realizing the magnitude of their daughter's circumstances.

"No—, don't think that," stammered Sam. "Marsha is strong. She is a fighter and will continue to fight."

They both sobbed as they stood hand in hand at their daughter's bedside.

"You are welcome to stay through the night," said the nurse attending to Marsha's ventilator. "We give the parents of critically injured patients that option."

"What are you doing to that?" questioned Sam.

"The ventilator is set to deliver certain breaths per minute. At the moment it is keeping her breathing. We need to monitor all her machines closely, twenty-four hours a day. The negative factors of her condition have to be controlled so her battered little body can begin to heal and recover." The nurse finished her duties quietly and calmly.

"I can't leave Marsha when she is fighting for her life," cried Helen.

"I am sure we can arrange to stay close by her," answered Sam.

"Extra beds can be brought in," commented nurse Bridgett, a petite, pretty, black-haired lady.

"We'll both stay by our daughter's side," said Mr. Walsch emphatically to nurse Bridgett and his wife tearfully nodded in agreement.

"Your parent's presence and attention is helping in your recovery Marsha. They are giving you strength. You do realize that, right?"

"I feel their love, yes."

"Your parents talking to each other, and to you, their

words are registering in your brain. Your vocabulary is being formed again. The accident wiped out your memories and speech. Remember, Arella told you that?"

"Yah, I guess so. I really can't remember anything. I mean it's like I don't know where I've been. I can talk to you, but not to them. This is so confusing. Can you understand that?"

"Yes, and that's OK, Marsha. I'm here and we'll work on everything together, for the most part, and remembering too. But, first things first."

"I know, you said we have a long hard road."

"Yes, and you need to be patient with yourself and with me."

"Good morning, Mr. and Mrs. Walsch," said Nurse Molly. "I have Reverend Mike from Hope Christian Church here."

Reverend Mike was a small, rather plump fellow and he looked a little comical in his black suit, holding his Bible in his hands. "With your permission he would like to bless your child in light of her condition."

Helen looked at her husband with watery eyes for approval and said, "I would feel comfortable if we share God's blessings with her before she..."

"She won't," Sam persisted. "OK, it will help us to pray together."

He nodded approval to nurse Molly.

"May God bless this child," began Reverend Mike, "Forgive her all her sins and give her peace. Give her everlasting light. Shall she remember the good and the love we share upon this earth and may she continue to shine in the heavens. In the name of The Father, The Son, and The Holy Spirit," Reverend Mike finished and sprinkled holy water on the child's little bandaged forehead and closed his own eyes to pray with Marsha's parents.

"I am so thankful that everyone is trying to help us," Helen sobbed through her tears after Reverend Mike took his leave. She moved over to her daughter's bedside and stroked her bandaged forehead lovingly once again. It was an unconscious ritual and she hoped Marsha could feel her touch.

"I feel your love Mama and I wish I could let you know I am here," Marsha thought to herself as she tried to force her body to move in the slightest way, but nothing happened. There was no movement anywhere.

"Marsha, you're putting the cart before the horse. Your body can't function without its essential building blocks in place. You must rest and let all energies focus on rebuilding."

"Mama is hurting so bad and I want her so much, Brisa."

"I know, you will be with her in time. For now you must sleep and rebuild your strength. Let your body take over to the point where death can not take you anymore."

As each day passed there was little observable change in little Marsha's condition.

"My wife and I will alternate staying with our daughter," Sam informed Bridgett.

"We can alternate the day and night shift," Helen said somberly. "I can't bare the thought of one of us not being here if her condition changes."

"I understand you making sure your precious little girl is not left alone at this critical stage," reassured Bridgett soothingly. "This is perfectly understandable and that is no problem."

She finished and left them alone.

"Any little step is progress," Papa informed his devastated wife trying to comfort her. "We'll go day by day and write the rules as we go, honey. We've got each other to lean on and we'll cope as we go."

VIII. Scranton Hospital, PA, Will She Survive? Life Is Precious, And So Delicate

Mama Helen and Papa Sam were at their daughter's bedside two hours away from where their life had been shattered only days before.

"Marsha is in the ICU unit at Scranton Hospital and is

still unconscious," said Sam into the phone. "She was moved here this morning from Stroudsburg. Her condition is still so critical, doctors felt a full fledged trauma center was necessary for her injuries."

"Is the condition still life threatening?" asked the voice on the phone.

"At the moment Marsha is being carefully monitored. There's no telling what will happen next in her condition," Sam finished, trying to keep his composure.

"You need to be with your family a few days. We'll be thinking of your little girl," the voice finished.

Sam directed his gaze at his bruised and battered little girl. She was lying so still. The only sign of life was the image of weak beats of her heart on the heart monitor next to her bed.

Sam resumed his seat beside his wife and put his hands over his face in desperation. There was dead silence in the room and Sam suddenly said, "I have never been in a life and death situation like this. Oh Helen, what are we going to do?"

"I don't know," responded his wife, sliding closer to comfort her husband. "I would give anything to see those pretty blue eyes smiling at us. I wish we knew more. I wish we knew when Marsha will wake up."

Regaining his composure and trying to sound positive for his wife's benefit Sam explained, "My boss gave me an extra couple days off. I'm sure we'll have better news by then. Marsha will wake up soon. She's getting the care she needs and she'll pull through. Remember, this is *our* daughter and she's strong."

A yawn escaped him. Sleep had not been a priority for either of them since the tragedy. Emotions ran high, making sleep next to impossible. Misery was evident in their physical appearance and mental composure. Both parents seemed to have aged ten years in the last few days. Their faces looked tired and worn and Helen's vibrancy, which made Sam fall in love with her, was only a memory now. Likewise, Sam's 'on top of the world' feeling and intense vigor to experience life and his enthusiasm were gone. In its place, shared by his wife, was a burning need to help and provide for their child. Nothing else seemed important anymore, except Marsha's welfare. It consumed every aspect of their lives. Days became unimportant, routines were mere struggles, and yet it didn't matter somehow. Nothing mattered anymore. The couple didn't think of themselves, and somehow knew the only way to get through was to keep going blindly, oblivious to their own needs. Both counted the hours before seeing Marsha again. Each proceeding day brought further gloom and less anticipation for normal or even partial recovery as Marsha's condition didn't change. Yet, something brought Sam and Helen hope.

"I know our baby will come back even if her doctors say she's not. I just know she will, Helen."

"Mr. and Mrs. Walsch, my name is Dr. Franks. I am a trauma surgeon and will be on Marsha's case," he said. "It seems that her initial crisis is over. Marsha has stabilized and is responding to medication. However, until she comes out of the coma, things could still turn for the worse. We just have no way of knowing. The ventilator and IV are sustaining her now, and until she wakes up we cannot remove them. The longer your daughter stays in a coma the likelihood of brain damage escalates and there's a good chance she won't ever wake up."

When he finished he observed his patient's parents visibly wither further in their chairs.

Helen, in tears, exclaimed, "Oh, how can this be?"

"Give it to us straight, what are her chances Dr. Franks?"

"Marsha is lucky to be alive. Due to your daughter's age she is more likely to recover than an older patient. Unfortunately, in cases like this, patients often recover with severe trauma and inoperable conditions. It is apparent that the most important parts of the brain are intact, making recovery a possibility for the future. Unfortunately, there's nothing we can do right now except wait for consciousness to return, and make her as comfortable as possible."

"How long?" asked Mama Helen, distraught.

"It could be days, weeks, or even months, ma'am," responded Dr. Franks. "There is no way to tell."

"Now, now, let's not give up, Helen. We're strong for Marsha. We decided to be positive for her, remember?"

"Yes, and we're talking to her like she can hear us, and she'll understand our messages and come back," Helen stammered, placing her quivering hand in Sam's to draw strength.

"Good morning, Mr. and Mrs. Walsch," said Sandy, Marsha's new nurse. Sandy seemed pleasant, and the more Helen looked at her the more she thought, this could be Marsha in twenty years. Long, wavy blond hair was tied back into a ponytail that fell down a shapely fit body. I wonder what Sandy's like, Helen thought and abruptly shook her head to return to reality and listen to what Sandy said, "We have good news: Marsha's heart is beating stronger and her vital signs are slightly better."

During the following three weeks Marsha stabilized to where her vital signs became normal. It was long awaited good news. Nightmares of losing their only child, their precious little girl, became commonplace for Sam and Helen.

"I had a dream last night that Marsha woke up today," said Helen out loud.

"The odds for her coming out of the coma are increasing," said Dr. Franks, who had entered the room. "We are still monitoring her very closely though."

Although reserved, he was smiling.

"What about her leg," Sam asked.

"We can't fix the leg until she regains consciousness and right now we don't know when that will be," answered Dr. Franks solemnly. "Your daughter's progress has been remarkable so far and we'll promote her further recovery as best we can. You need to be patient."

"When will we be able to move Marsha to Pittsburgh's Mercy Hospital?" Sam persisted.

"If Marsha stays stabilized, she'll be ready to leave here by end of the week," answered Dr. Franks.

"Oh thank God!" cried Helen. "Our baby is getting better Sam."

Helen was both smiling and sobbing at the possibility.

"It looks that way," said Sam, smiling at his tired, teary eyed wife. He was having problems keeping dry eyes himself. "Let's hope that Marsha keeps improving. Attitude and commitment are worth so much. The highly recommended neurologist from Philadelphia will be here tomorrow. Dr. Bence is supposed to be here in the morning. He has dealt with many trauma patients and will be able to shed more light on Marsha's condition.

"I need some good news, Sam. I think we both do."

"Dr. Bence is supposed to be one of the best in his field, according to Uncle Bob."

"How did Bob know of him?"

Bence is a friend of an associate of Bob's. You can imagine how many different people Bob comes in contact with through his worldwide travels. Oh, I almost forgot, Bob talked to a Dr. Hanks about Marsha's leg. This doctor is confident about an operation on her leg that would restore her ability to walk again."

"Oh, that is wonderful! My baby...w-walking. Oh Sam!"

"Bob tells me that Dr. Hanks was a doctor in World War II and was very successful with unconventional bone surgeries for the times. According to a book he published, his methods were remarkable."

"OK, yes, maybe he can help us," Helen said with a spark of hope.

"Yes, maybe he's the answer to our prayers," said Sam.

"I brought Marsha some music by Simon and Garfunkel," said Helen. "When Marsha was sick, the soft music would comfort her. Do you suppose Marsha hears and enjoys these songs like she used to? Maybe it'll help her."

She sat back and listened herself.

... When times get rough
And friends just can't be found,
Like a bridge of troubled water
I will lay me down...

"Marsha, are you listening?"

"Why's Mama crying?"

"Remember when you listened to this song with your parents? Your parents are thinking about you now, about your time together. Music was always a part of your lives. This song reminds them of the good times with you. They want to be your bridge for recovery. Just listen and learn—"

... Like a bridge over troubled water
I will lay me down...

"Yah, remember when she was born, how we talked to her continuously and played soft music for her," interjected Papa, also in a world of his own. "Remember how she amazed us with her wit. She was always so bright for her age."

Papa sat with a dazed look on his face as he thought of those fond memories.

"You're right," said Mama defiantly, returning their world back to reality. "We'll do this...we have to Sam. I guess she'll be like a baby again and we'll have to teach her like we did when she was first born six years ago. We will dedicate ourselves to Marsha's rebirth."

"I'm so proud of you, my dear. You're making positive decisions to bring Marsha back. This'll work, Helen, you'll see."

"I know Sam. It's just got to."

"Sweetheart, I can see the toll it's taking on you already though," Sam continued, looking lovingly at his wife and taking her hand and then embracing her in support.

"Oh Sam, what else can we do?" she sobbed in her husband's arms. "I remember how Marsha and I spent hours together in the garden and how much she loved flowers and she'd ask if she could pick her dolls some. I want my little g-g-girl back... I-I-I need her Sam."

"Marsha won't leave us," whispered Sam in Helen's ear. "Marsha has beaten the odds so far and she knows how much we love her. We just have a long road ahead of us—a long road to recovery... You need some rest, Helen."

He gave her a kiss and pulled her to her feet, steadying her. "Marsha is stable now, and we both need to stay strong for her for a long time."

"I know, honey... I'll be back in the morning to relieve you. At least a comfortable bed will add to the possibility of a little rest," Helen said before bending over Marsha's bed and gently kissing her bandaged forehead. She then quietly and laboriously left the hospital.

I have never been so devastated and tired in my life, she thought to herself.

IX. Hope And A Prayer: Faith Gives Us Strength

It had been three weeks since the accident, the horrible event that forever changed the Walsch's lives. For over a week now Sam had been back at work. He managed to fly to Scranton Hospital weekends and return on a red eye flight in time for work Monday morning.

The question lingered: how will Marsha recover, if she does? Sam could not bear the thought.

Dr. Bence had no guarantees either, "Everything is up to your daughter's body's willingness to recover. There are no more medications we can give her to improve her chances. It is up to her now," and the doctor exited after acknowledging Sam and Helen were doing right by their child.

Marsha's parents persistently encouraged their daughter and themselves by being by her side.

Sam and Helen needed to be by their daughter's side whenever possible. Mama and Papa gave all they could give.

"Marsha is being moved to Mercy Hospital today," Helen announced to her husband. "Marsha has stayed stable long enough and hasn't wavered for three weeks and there's nothing else they can do for her here."

"Yay, that's good news, honey. We'll be in driving distance of the hospital."

"No more commuter flights to see you," and he smiled openly with newfound vigor and relief in his voice. "Our little angel is getting better."

"Dr. Franks says Mercy Hospital has a specialty care unit. He praises our presence twenty-four hours a day and said communication to Marsha has likely made a difference in her recovery. He gave a thumbs up and told me Marsha will be taken to Mercy Hospital via private plane this afternoon around one o'clock."

"You'll accompany Marsha, honey, in the plane. I'll drive the car back home and be at Mercy Hospital as soon as possible," said Sam.

"Are you sure you want to drive all the way to Pittsburgh?"

"I'll be OK, and you heard what Dr. Franks said, the constant attention helps Marsha's recovery and I would feel better if you stayed with her," he finished with finality.

"Of course I'll stay by Marsha's side. But I'm worried about you d-driving the long distance alone..."

"I'll be fine," said Sam, giving his wife a hug and kiss. "Besides, how else would we get the car home?"

He was obviously oblivious to comfort for himself. The blue Chevy, their only vehicle, was valuable for Sam to travel between airport and hospital every day the preceding week. A rental car would have been one more bill for the newly financially stressed family. They were now living paycheck to paycheck and there was no end in sight for their financial problems. Fortunately, his boss had lent Sam a second car on the other end.

The half-hour plane trip seamed like forever to Marsha's distraught mother. Helen sat before her comatose child. Three seats preceding hers, in the medical helicopter, were folded flat and her child lay motionless, strapped to a stretcher. Marsha's IV was strapped to the floor and again to the overhead luggage compartment to prevent the instrument from falling. Helen sat motionless, observing her only child.

"Oh God, please help us," she murmured as tears trickled down her pale face once again.

It was the first time she was by herself, outside the hospital environment, dealing with horror, with the tragedy staring her right in the face. Her head felt like it was on fire. She didn't know what to think. She didn't know what to do. She still didn't know how long this would go on. Helen still didn't know if her daughter would finally make it. If she did survive, how extensive would her handicaps be? Would she be forever dependant? What would be the quality of Marsha's life?

At the airport, Helen watched carefully as her daughter was lifted into the waiting helicopter that would transport them to Mercy Hospital. The admitting team was waiting as the helicopter landed on the Mercy Hospital roof. Nurses and doctors surrounded the little patient and rushed her inside with IV, blanket, and all. They didn't know how much time there was before life slipped away.

Helen climbed out of the helicopter and hurried after the stretcher, doctors, and nurses.

Inside, procedural vital signs, fluids, IV, and monitoring lines as well as wounds were checked and recorded.

"Didn't they say Marsha's vitals were stable? Why does my little girl have to go through tests and procedures again?" asked Helen.

"This is procedure, ma'am," answered the nurse.

"It's just that Marsha is still in such bad shape, and I'm worried it may be too much for her!" Helen felt like a mother lion protecting her cub, yet she had no idea how. I've never been in such utter pain, she thought.

"This is standard procedure for our new patients, ma'am, and we have state-of-the-art equipment," answered the nurse. "We need to monitor her very closely. Please step over to the side so we can get to her."

"Yes ma'am. Please, do what you need to for her..." Helen answered as she moved to the side of the room.

When the checking was done, they prepared Marsha to move to her room. "Your daughter will be in the Pediatric Ward on the third floor. You can go upstairs with her. She will be in room three," said the nurse as she motioned towards the way upstairs. Helen walked to the elevator and rode up to the third floor. She followed the signs to the ICU area and checked in with a nurse at the nurses' station.

"Thank you... Oh! My baby, what's all this?" she blurted as she walked into the room.

"What's wrong?" asked the nurse as she adjusted wires and settings.

"Marsha has twice as many machines connected to her. Has her condition worsened? And doesn't she get a private room, in her condition?"

"We're running a few more tests," proclaimed the nurse. "I'm Susan and I'll be Marsha's day nurse."

Helen immediately perceived Susan as cold and regimented. Susan stood erect and domineering.

"She really is OK, ma'am. If there's anything you need, let me know. The call button is next to the bed."

"OK, if you say so. I'll be back in a moment, my dear. Mama's going to get a cup of coffee downstairs," Helen leaned over and kissed her angel before leaving the room.

"I'd really be more comfortable if Marsha had her own room. I'll have to talk to Sam about that," Helen thought as she walked to the elevator.

"Hey baby, you have a new roommate. Look I brought your brother and your little friend Bobby today," said a heavyset lady to Marsha's roommate as she entered the room with two young boys in tow.

"Yaa, Mom, sanks," a little meek voice answered. The little boy in the neighboring bed lay motionless. Almost his entire body was in a cast and his head bandaged severely, secured by a neck brace. He had been in a serious car accident and thrown from the car. Just that once, he hadn't worn his seat belt.

"You kids have a good time together and I'll be right back, OK?"

"OK!"

"Lets play hide and seek. You're it, Bobby."

"OOOO!"

"Come on, count from one to ten and I'll hide."

"I'll get you, Yaaaaaa."

"Ay Tommy, are you having fun watching us?"

"Ya, ya."

"I hope Sam's OK. He must be getting close to Pittsburgh by now," thought Helen. "I can't wait to see him. It's really hard being by yourself when your baby's in danger."

Helen quietly turned the corner and entered Marsha's room, dropping her coffee at the shock of seeing tubes hanging disjointed from Marsha's medical equipment.

"What on heaven's earth. What are you kids doing? What have you done? Marsha's tubes, Susan!!!" Helen screamed at the top of her lungs, as she ran to her daughter's side.

"Yes ma'am!" Susan answered as she came running in.

"Marsha's tubes are disconnected! These kids—I knew something would happen! Oh Marsha—! Baby—!" Helen held her daughter's hand and quietly sobbed at the sudden rush of adrenaline from the scare.

"I'll get them right away, ma'am," said Susan as calmly as she could muster.

"She needs her own room. Marsha could die! She's on the brink anyway! Oh my God, Susan..."

"Yes, I'll put it on her chart and you can talk to the doctor."

"Oh, we will talk to more than just the doctor! Wait till my husband hears about this!" Helen was beyond protective at this point. Nothing on this earth was going to stop her from getting the best for her wounded cub. "I will not put our child in danger any more, ever," she thought.

Within the hour, Dr. Sears came in to check on his new patient.

"Marsha is holding steady this morning," said Dr. Sears as he walked next to the hospital bed that engulfed the small motionless child. "Marsha's vital signs are OK and she's being moved to a private room shortly."

"You heard about what happened then?"

"Yes, I got a phone call from the nurses' station. Although she was in no immediate danger, she will be better off in a private room. I have ordered a series of tests and your daughter will have a CAT Scan to determine the extent of brain damage; and I have ordered a physical therapist to work with her extremities, starting tomorrow."

"Oh thank God nothing happened!"

"You caught it in time, ma'am."

"Oh, thank God I was here! Thank God I walked in when I did!" and Helen lovingly and possessively placed her hand on Marsha's bed and peered at the doctor with relief in her eyes. "Will Marsha be able to m-move again?" Helen asked in response to the information about the physical therapist.

"Marsha is lucky to be young," answered Dr. Sears looking up from the chart now. "The younger the patient the greater chance for recovery. Mrs. Walsch, we have a close eye on her and if anything changes we will attend to your daughter immediately."

He was trying to waylay her fears of the worst happening. He finished his checkup and left.

"Can I leave the cassette player in the room to help stimulate Marsha's brain?" Helen inquired of nurse Susan.

"Yes, by all means. You might want to put pictures on the cork boards in her room and bring colorful artificial flowers. We have observed that bright colors help patients' focusing ability when they awaken from their comatose state without the worry of keeping the flowers alive. We also highly encourage interaction between patients and family members," Susan said with a smile. Helen had to admit she was good, but her bedside manner needed improvement.

Outside the room Helen heard Susan directing to Sam, "Marsha and your wife are in here, Mr. Walsch."

"Oh Sam, I'm glad you're here—Now there's one less worry for me," she sobbed, holding on to her husband.

"Are you OK?" Sam asked his crying wife.

"Better now."

"How is our angel," Sam questioned, leaning over Marsha. "Papa prayed for you the entire trip, my sweet. I love you, baby and I would move heaven and earth for you." His eyes misted as he looked on his little girl, his precious little angel, and remembered how everyone always said she's Papa's little princess.

"Marsha had a close call today."

"Oh?" Sam turned to face his wife, with sudden concern, as he directed his full attention to his wife. This must be the reason she is so upset, he thought.

"Visiting kids, who were left unattended, pulled her tubes out. Thankfully I came in almost immediately."

"Where were the parents?"

"Stepped out, I guess. Oh my God, Sam—I was so scared."

"Yes, I can imagine," and he reached for her quivering body. "So that's how she got the private room."

"Yes, I insisted!!" Helen said with a defiant nod of her head.

"Good for you. Your mama takes such good care of you," Sam said to his resting daughter.

"Oh Sam, I need a hug," Helen said as she wilted into her husband's arms. She sobbed from fright and exasperation, "I am so glad I was here and Susan was here immediately when I called, too. You know—the staff here doesn't sugar coat anything and Marsha's nurse is optimistic—and I think I like that."

"Of course. Marsha will get through this and persevere," he said again, quietly but confidently.

"The staff here agrees that music helps the brain of comatose patients and Susan advised to decorate the room with bright colors for when Marsha wakes up, Sam. They agree patients learn to focus quicker just like infants do. It's so nice to hear the medical team believe in more than medicine alone," she whispered to her husband.

"Marsha is a lucky little girl to have you as her mama, you know that, honey?"

With a weak smile, Helen sighed, "Thanks—I just wish I could do more."

"Your brilliance in early childhood development will help her tremendously, honey. Our family will get through this," Sam assured as he and Helen embraced and comforted each other. After what seemed a long time, Sam straightened and said, "Go home while it's still daylight and get some rest. I'll stay through the night tonight."

The next morning Sam awoke with a start. He had fallen asleep in the big chair next to Marsha. Quickly his gaze fell on his child, still motionless.

"My name is Carmen," said a nurse entering the room. "I kept watch last night and left you sleeping since Marsha had a restful, uneventful night, Mr. Walsch."

"I guess I really was tired... So she's OK?"

"Yes sir. No change. Would you like breakfast ordered before the therapist comes at ten?"

"Oh yes," said Sam as a yawn escaped him and he stood up to stretch his legs. "That would be great."

"I'll bring Marsha a full intravenous bag in a bit too," she said checking the IV lines and the bags that fed the little girl.

"She gets all her nutrition from that right?" Sam asked.

"Yes sir. Until Marsha wakes up we can't give her anything else. It's sugar water for now, sir."

"Of course!" He said, smiling at the nurse as she left the room. He turned to the bandaged little figure in the bed. "I feel so sorry for you, angel. I wish there were something, anything Papa could do for you."

"Oh Brisa, Papa is so sad. Isn't there any way to let him know I'm getting better, that I'll be OK?"

"Not yet Marsha. He'll see little hints of improvement and that will help him. It is going to take time—lots of time, perseverance and patience for everyone."

"I can't tell I'm getting any better though, Brisa. I still can't even move a muscle."

"I know. Be patient with your body and with me, OK?"

Later that morning, a lean, yet powerfully built young man entered the room.

"Good morning, Mr. Walsch. I am Bill, Marsha's physical therapist. I will manipulate Marsha's limbs every morning and afternoon to improve her circulation."

He proceeded to move Marsha's left leg and her arms gingerly.

"I will be moving her limbs through the appropriate range of motion for her condition. Most patients react favorably to physical therapy at this stage and it helps in recovery," he spoke to Sam as he gently moved the wounded little girl's limbs.

"OK, if you say so!" Sam said skeptically.

"When the time comes we'll get Marsha out of bed and onto her feet," he continued with optimism.

"Oh, she's a long way from getting out of bed," gasped Papa. "She's still in a coma. Won't all this movement hurt her?"

"No, I'm being very gentle and we must get the muscles working again. Walking and even sitting requires more ability than one imagines," counseled Bill. "Maybe through physical stimulation we'll get response from her."

He continued moving the limp little girl as Sam looked painstakingly on. Her limp, thin arms were extended, moved up and down and side to side. There was no reaction as the little extremities obeyed their guide. Then, Bill let his firm but gentle grasp slide down the little girl's forearm and gently bent her elbow. First the right side then the left. No response.

As Papa watched, breathless, tears formed in his eyes as he realized this was the first time he saw Marsha moving with only gentle guidance and assistance. He watched carefully for any sign of movement, any voluntary, or involuntary, sign. There was none. Marsha still lay comatose. However, Sam thought he saw a hint of improvement. Something moved, a twitch of Marsha's wrist maybe? He wasn't sure what just happened, or was it a figment of his strained, exhausted imagination.

"Oh baby, that's it, that's it, you're my strong l-little g-g-girl!" Sam stammered as the sight of his little motionless girl tore at his heart yet again.

"I did it. I did it Brisa. I showed Papa."

"Yes you did and I'm so proud of you."

"Oh Brisa, you're right. I ***can*** do this. Oh boy!"

"Calm down little one. The steps will be slow. Progress will take effort and time."

"Now I know it works though, and my papa knows, Brisa. He knows!!"

"I'll be in the office this afternoon and will be back to relieve you afterwards," Sam told Helen before he left later that morning. "Call me if there's any change, if you notice the slightest movement. Be prepared for Bill. It really hurts to see him move Marsha's limbs. Although, I suppose, he knows what he's doing—because our baby moved better. He spent about forty-five minutes with her this morning and you'll see him back this afternoon. He did warn me that PT is a long process, that it'll take a long time to get her moving and walking. Remember, call me if anything happens, honey."

"OK, Sam. I'm so happy she's making progress. You have no idea!" Helen smiled with hope.

"Oh yah, I know! I love you!" he said as he kissed his Helen good-bye and almost skipped to the elevators with the glimpse of improvement he had seen in his daughter's condition. It really was improvement, wasn't it? Or, was it really only imagination, he wondered again. "It's been so long since I've seen my angel move at all."

"Good morning, I'm Alex, your daughter's occupational therapist."

"Why does Marsha need an occupational therapist?" Helen asked, confused. "She's not conscious yet."

"I will massage Marsha's facial muscles so her speech will come easier when it's time. Just as the physical therapist have to get her arms and legs back into working order, I have to get her facial muscles in shape so that they work when she is ready," Alex said before turning his attention to the little girl.

"Oh," Helen said, not quite understanding yet.

"We find that this really benefits the speech process, and sometimes the increased blood flow to the head helps with recovery," he continued as he touched the little girl's bandaged face.

"Hello, Sam," Helen said into the phone.

"Hello honey," responded Sam hopefully. "Has our baby woken up?"

"No, not exactly. The occupational therapists explained that manipulations to her face would expedite her recovery. Isn't that amazing?"

"I guess that makes sense," said Sam. "How are you holding up?"

"I'm fine. The nurses seem more attentive now. The attention we are getting really surprises me," she finished as she yawned into the telephone.

"I'm glad you two are having a good day," Sam told his tired wife. "I'm leaving here shortly and am going home to sleep an hour before relieving you for the night. I'll see you around seven. I love you!"

Helen continued holding the receiver close and cried form exhaustion and desperation, and newfound hope. It's been weeks since I've spoken with Marsha, remembered Mama. We've only been able to talk *to* her and I can't erase the thought that we may never talk *with* her again. Mama felt her cheeks becoming damp at the awful thought.

Two weeks specialty care at Mercy Hospital and Marsha's responses were improving to the point doctors decided it was time to move her to a rehabilitation center. The movements of her extremities increased little by little each day and at times, Bill reported Marsha's body resisting pressure during physical therapy.

"Sometimes patients do respond even in the comatose state. It's definitely a sign of recovery," Bill continued.

Marsha had overcome her critical days, where it was never clear whether she would survive to see the next morning, Dr. Sears recorded in his notes. *Our patient clung to life and her body began to heal until she was upgraded to stable. The patient is ready to be moved to St. Francis hospital for further treatment and therapy.*

"Your daughter will be transported to St. Francis, a rehab hospital. They have the specialized equipment for her further recovery."

The possibility of losing their daughter and the intense steps to preserve her life strained Sam and Helen immensely and with that calamity erased, Helen and Sam focused on their daughter's recovery and rehabilitation.

"Stability brings new hope and steps for success at the next level," counseled one of Helen's friends. "All your love and care has made the difference for her, I'm sure."

Individually and as a couple, Helen and Sam struggled with feelings of guilt, helplessness, and ineptitude. Yet, something intense, inside, continued to make them fight for their child. The love for her and each other kept them going. Dedication and positive attitude for her recovery paralleled and overshadowed their numbness.

"Our psyche is forever changed," observed Sam. "We must go day by day, write the rules, and cope as we go. We have no choice but to go forward, to strive for what seems impossible now. Faith will guide us and give us strength for the future. Our balancing act will continue as we help our daughter build her new life."

"Yes, we're dedicated to her and we'll get through this together," Helen sobbed in her husbands arms. "Do you realize what we do for Marsha now, how we get her to recover, will determine the rest of her life, Sam?"

"That's why we must do whatever we can for rehabilitation. That includes physical therapy, occupational therapy, speech therapy—anything the doctors suggest."

"A tutor would be helpful down the road because her brain needs to be stimulated more, if our budget can manage it," Helen added without thought.

"You're right, Helen. Marsha's missing first grade right now, and she was always so bright, remember?"

"Yes, I do. She can always take first grade when she gets better. But for now it's best to get her brain stimulated as much as possible."

"We'll do what we can, honey."

"After seven weeks of amazing progression, Marsha has turned the corner from barely alive to stabilized," said Dr. Sears. "She will be moved to St. Francis this afternoon."

"Why is our daughter being moved again? Why's she being moved to another hospital Dr. Sears?" Helen asked, beginning to panic.

"St. Francis is a Rehabilitation Center. It is a state-of-the-art facility and Marsha will get the specialized care and attention she needs and can't get here. We just don't have the resources," Dr. Sears explained.

"Marsha—? Marsha—? It's time. You have a long…road ahead of you, but I'll be with you every step of the way," said Brisa as she drifted into Marsha's conscience.

"It's really nice to know I won't be doing this by myself."

"Ah, sweetheart, I have to warn you, you and your body will be doing most of the work. You're the one who will feel the pain."

"That's OK, as long as I have someone on my side who really understands."

"I'll be your best friend for years to come because you are going to struggle and have hard times for years to come. You'll likely have affects from the accident forever…"

"I understand."

The morning was spent in preparation for Marsha's transfer. Her belongings were gathered and the entire plethora of bags, tubes, and monitors were checked and prepared. Finally, it was time for the transfer. Two paramedics came to get Marsha and Helen for the trip. Helen bid farewell to the nurses as she followed her daughter to the waiting ambulance.

"OK darlin', in you go," said the paramedic as he lifted Marsha's stretcher into the ambulance and motioned for Helen to climb in and sit beside her.

"We are taking a ride to St. Francis Hospital, sweetheart," said Helen to Marsha, lying calmly and motionless on the stretcher before her. "I hear it's a nicer place and you will have more fun things to do there."

She sat by her daughter, in a daze, imagining Marsha consciously taking part in physical therapy. Oh how she wished her little girl was sitting beside her now.

"Mama," said a childlike, almost inaudible voice.

"Sweetheart?" Helen exclaimed as her eyes flashed to Marsha's bandaged face. Her heart seemed to suddenly beat out of her chest. "Did you just call me, baby?" Helen was surprised, alarmed, concerned, she didn't know exactly which.

Marsha's blue eyes blinked a few times as she tried to focus on something, anything. Knowing that she couldn't move her head, Helen moved her face into Marsha's line of vision. The little girl searched as if she saw only blurs and shadows.

"Mama?" Marsha said again in her weak voice.

Helen tearfully smiled and gazed into Marsha's eyes, searching for any clue of recognition.

"Oh baby! I've waited so long," Helen whispered and gently clutched her daughter's small, limp hand as tears of joy now streamed down her young but haggard face. She couldn't find the words to express her now frazzled emotions.

Was their little girl, their angel, really coming back to life? Was she really returning from her comatose state?

"Oh baby, we'll see Papa soon and he'll be so very proud of you. You know we love you so very much and we'll get through this, I promise!!" Helen said as the tears of joy rolled down her face. She did her best to keep Marsha's attention, for as long as possible, although she knew her length of alertness would be very short at first. No matter, when Marsha closed her eyes, only moments later, Mama Helen continued holding her little hand and hummed to her softly until they reached their destination, St. Francis Hospital.

This is a much more comfortable atmosphere than at Mercy Hospital, Sam thought as he walked down the hall to find his ladies. The colors around here are friendlier and it's less sterile, he observed. Entering room 24, Sam rushed to his daughter's bedside as he saw Helen next to her, crying.

"What's the matter? What happened?" Sam asked sternly and concerned.

"Marsha said Mama. Twice!!" whimpered Helen. "She said her first words, Sam."

"Oh my God!" breathed Sam as he dropped to his

knees beside his little girl's bed and took her other hand in his. "Mama and Papa are here and you'll be OK. I knew it. You're our strong little one. You're our angel. You're coming back to your Mama and Papa. We're so proud of you."

He reached for his wife's hand in celebration. They sat side by side in silence, marveling at their still-bandaged little girl.

"You're in a friendlier surroundings, honey. Can you hear the music playing?" asked Mama, without expecting a response. "You always liked music, sweetheart."

"Good afternoon," said an older man as he walked into the room. He had gray hair and a moustache. He was wearing a blue suit rather than a lab coat. "I am Dr. Franks, a Neurosurgeon and your daughter's doctor."

Checking his chart he continued, "This little one has been through a lot. I see that she has been improving continuously. And I hear that you spoke your first words today, my dear. It's time for you to wake up now and get moving. The physical therapists and speech therapists will help you out there. They'll get you going."

"Is there anything we can do?" asked Sam.

"I'd continue whatever it is that you have been doing. Obviously it has helped so far," Dr. Franks said as he took a seat in the big chair across from Marsha's bed and her alert and attuned parents.

"I'll do whatever I need to do when I know exactly what that is," continued Sam. "Other than talking to her, I'm lost."

"Talking to her is the best thing you can do," remarked Dr. Davis. "Hearing your voice will comfort and teach her. She needs your communication as much as she needs her body to heal itself and the help she'll get from the occupational and physical therapist."

"Marsha's still in such bad shape and I'm afraid for her, Dr. Davis," interjected Helen, concerned.

"I know, and most parents are. Marsha is out of danger now and is recovering at a remarkable pace. I know it doesn't seem like it to you, you'll have to trust me on that. Marsha's complete recovery will take a very long time and everyone needs to be patient. She's come a long way already but she has a long way to go. One day at a time, may I remind you."

"What else can we do though, doctor, to help her, I mean?"

"Spend as much time with her as possible and mirror what her physical and occupational therapist does with her. They'll talk to you and if not, ask."

"I think we can do that, Sam."

"Yes, I definitely think so."

"Oh Sam, what will they do with her leg? Can it be fixed Sam?" asked Helen desperately. "I've never seen such a thing. Look at the bone sticking out—and the swelling!" Helen was working herself up and she began to sob again.

"Now, now, Helen," said Sam. "One thing at a time, like the man said. Whatever is wrong will be fixed in due time," he soothed, looking concerned himself. He had problems keeping his own composure too after Marsha's lower torso was exposed from under the clean white sheet while Dr. Davis examined the little patient.

"This certainly is unlike anything I've seen in a patient so young and I'm not sure anything can be done. But I'll see what I can do," commented doctor Franks.

Sam and Helen hadn't seen the damaged limb in weeks and although not forgotten, had not been their immediate concern. Seeing it now brought the concern to the forefront of their minds.

"We need Dr. Hanks," said Sam as he wiped his brow. He had a terrible headache. This was too much. How much more could he handle? How much more could they handle?

"Honey, go home and get some rest. I'll call you if there's any change," he finished as he kissed her good-bye. "I'm gonna call Dr. Hanks."

"Mr. Walsch, you look like you could use a rest yourself. Marsha's bandages need to be changed and I'll be with her about half an hour. Why don't you get some coffee in the lounge and relax a bit? We'll be OK, won't we, sweetheart?" Cara, Marsha's nurse, said softly before directing her full attention to Marsha.

Sam watched nurse Cara talking soothingly to his little girl. She was so gentle with her and talked so kindly and soothingly. Sam heard her asking, "Are you comfortable little one?" There was absolutely no response from her, and it broke his heart.

Why did this happen? The question churned over and over in his mind. What could he have done differently? Why did he have to take his family riding? What could he do for his daughter now? How could he comfort his wife? Why did God let this happen to his family? Sam wondered yet again.

"I trusted you wouldn't give me anything I couldn't handle," he said to God silently. "Please give me strength and direction and help my baby girl now. Help her with her struggle and the burdens she'll bare, the struggles we will incur!"

He sat on the dark blue overstuffed love seat in the corner of the lounge, hunched over, with his hands over his eyes. How much more can I cope with? How much more can my dear Helen handle? How and when would this nightmare end? He contemplated, in sheer misery.

Cara met Sam at the door with a smile and reported; "Marsha's eyes fluttered open for a moment then closed again. They're closed now. She's sleeping peacefully again."

There was a slight chirp in her voice. She too was excited at the prospect of her new patient's recovery.

"The one time I leave and I miss seeing my baby open her eyes," said Sam, rushing to Marsha's side as he heard Roberta Flack's, *The First Time I Ever Saw Your Face* playing softly on the bedside radio. Sam sat in the big chair beside his princess, his elbows on his knees and just broke down from frazzled emotions and fatigue. Though he found himself drifting in and out of sleep, Sam thought he heard Marsha's voice time and time again, only to see her peacefully sleeping. But he kept hoping he would see those beautiful eyes reopen.

"Oh sweetheart, please let me see your pretty blue

eyes again. Please come back, come back to us," he whispered with tears in his eyes.

Sam sat, dazed, remembering how sometimes his daughter's eyes had reminded him of the endless sea. Their blue was bluer than blue and when the sun hit a certain way they'd sparkle on her beautiful doll-like face. He had seen endless passion and zest in those eyes. Now, as he sat patiently by his little girl's bedside he came to terms with the situation. Marsha's battered body is the only thing that is here now, he thought in anguish. Her injuries have sent her on a long journey and she may never return to the way we knew her. He cried in the privacy of the hospital room, and looking at his motionless little girl he said, "I know you're strong and you have done great so far. Come back to us, Princess. Papa loves you so much. Come back, baby, please—!" He then settled back in the chair and eventually nodded off.

Marsha's eyes suddenly became alive as if something in her brain activated. She was dreaming. Her eyes moved almost rhythmically as she drifted through her dreams. Claire noticed the activated heart rate on the monitor at the nurses' station and hurried into the room to check her patient. Claire's observation of Marsha's REM flutter brought a smile to her face and she turned to Mr. Walsch. Noticing him sleeping she quietly turned back to Marsha and said, "Your daddy will be so happy."

She checked the monitors again and left with a slight spring of satisfaction in her step.

"I must have nodded off early, Claire," said Sam as he saw her entering the room with a big smile the next morning.

"I know you have been through a lot, Mr. Walsch," she said. "This morning I have some good news for you."

"Oh?" Sam said dazed and confused.

"Around 2 A.M. your daughter's heart rate became elevated and her eyes were in REM flutter. Marsha was dreaming."

"Marsha's eyes have not done that before. Nothing has moved voluntarily since the accident," he expressed, holding back tears. "First, she called for her mama, now this? Our baby is really starting to wake up!!!"

He picked up the phone to call his wife.

"Hello," Helen yawned into the telephone.

"Good morning, sweetheart. I'm sorry for waking you so early, great news though! Marsha was dreaming last night. Her eyes were moving in her sleep. Claire says its REM flutter. She was dreaming, Helen. That means her brain is working," he continued exuberantly. "Oh honey, Marsha really is coming back to us!" He was unable to hold back tears from her any longer, as Sam jubilantly cried to his wife on the phone.

"Oh Sam!!! I can't believe it! Our baby is…"

"Claire said her heart started beating faster all of a sudden and her eyes fluttered like ours do when we sleep," Sam explained happily. She saw the increased brain activity on the monitor.

"That's great news!" Helen replied also in tears. "Does that mean our baby girl will wake up today? I can be there in an hour."

"Claire said it's a good sign. The doctor hasn't been in yet. Marsha is resting now and I'm not moving from her side again until you get here," Sam finished.

"Hold Marsha's hand in yours, Sam, and talk to her," instructed Helen. "Tell her how much we love her and that Mama will be there very soon."

"I will, honey," assured Sam. "Now I'm convinced she hears me, Helen. Her brain is working! Oh, and Sweetheart, please be careful getting here."

Helen sprang around the house like a jackrabbit. "My baby love, my baby love," she sang out loud. She hurried through her usual necessary tasks before jumping in her car and driving to St. Francis Hospital. She was perspiring and gently quivering with anticipation.

Soon I will have my little girl again, she thought to herself. I wonder if Marsha will have any recollection of what happened to her? Will she have any memory of her past? Will she be able to recognize us? Will she be able to communicate? A string of questions ran through Helen's mind as she paid special attention not to exceed the speed limit.

"Oh—where is she?" Helen whispered hurriedly to Claire in the hall.

"I suppose you heard the good news, Mrs. Walsch," exclaimed Nurse Claire. "Marsha is still resting quietly this morning. Dr. Davis just left."

"Thank you, Claire," Helen responded as she walked into Marsha's room. "How's my baby?" she questioned, gazing at the still lifeless bandaged little girl. "Oh, I expected too much I guess. My expectations are always too high."

"I know what you mean. I expect her to wake up all at once too. But Dr. Franks told me it just doesn't happen that way. He did confirm that dreams are a good sign though. That means her brain is functioning and Marsha's vital signs and heart are fine."

"Is she going to wake up, Sam?" Helen asked, her hopes rising after being dashed just moments ago.

"The odds are she will, although Dr. Franks wasn't specific. He couldn't say when. Nobody can, really."

"Oh Sam, I'll do my best with her today. Marsha, I brought some of your favorite books from home. Look, we have *Go Dog Go*, *The Cat In The Hat*, and *Pooh's ABC*."

"I'll be back tonight to relieve you, Helen. I'm heading straight for the office and in case anything happens, I'll tell Grace where to find me. There's meetings all day," he finished and kissed his wife.

"I love you and I'll call with any change, I promise," she whispered to him and looked up for another kiss for energy and encouragement. Helen lightly touched and caressed her daughter's limp right hand and arm again and again. It became a routine of comfort, touch between them and this time Helen started humming, "Hush little baby don't say a word, Mama's going to buy you a mockingbird..."

Helen saw the slightest twitch of Marsha's fingers. "Did you just try to touch me, sweetheart?" she questioned, startled and in disbelief. "Oh my God," Helen cried and pushed the call button.

"My baby moved her fingers!" she said to Claire when she hurried into the room.

"She is having more reflexes. Good!" exclaimed Claire. "This is common with comatose patients and is part of further recovery."

She walked beside Marsha's bed to check the monitors. "You're doing very well, little missy. You're a trouper and we're so proud of you!"

Helen was looking on the scene with an expression of hopefulness.

"Hello, Ruby. Is Sam there please?"

"Oh, hello, Mrs. Walsch, he's in a meeting. Just one moment and I'll get him."

"How's Marsha?"

"Marsha m-moved her hand in mine. Claire said it's a natural reflex of recovering patients. Oh Sam!"

"Yes, honey, yes, that's wonderful news. Has the doctor been in to see her yet? Will her reflexes continue?"

"Dr. Davis has been notified. This is further s-sign of r-recovery Sam, and I needed to share it with you," she cried, sorry that she had interrupted his meeting.

"Hang in there, sweetheart, and I'll be there as soon as I can."

"OK."

"I was singing a lullaby to her, Sam, and she squeezed my hand in recognition, Marsha's c-coming back, Sam!! She really is!"

"That's terrific. I love you, and keep up the good work, baby. I need to get back to my meeting, and I'll see you soon, OK?"

"I love you too!"

I need to find some aspirin, Helen thought as she felt her head throbbing again. These days she really should carry a bottle of aspirin in her purse, she thought, because headaches came on so frequently. "Where can I find some medicine for a headache," she asked Claire as she kept an eye on her sleeping daughter.

"The gift shop downstairs should have something."

"I'll be back in five minutes then."

"I need to change her dressings. It will take five to ten minutes," she continued, already uncovering her little patient.

"OK, I'll only be a few minutes," Helen said over her shoulder as she left to find some headache relief.

"Your mom tells me you moved your fingers. Are you going to make your parents proud and move a little more?" Claire questioned the motionless little body. "You can do it. I know you can," she persuaded.

Methodically Claire changed each bandage being extremely careful not to upset little Marsha, who still appeared to be sleeping. All of a sudden Claire noticed motion in Marsha's left hand. Her fingers were curling in slightly.

"That's it, Marsha. You can do it," she continued, and hoped that Mrs. Walsch returned quickly.

Helen watched as Claire covered Marsha with a clean white sheet and couldn't help imagining Marsha as an angel.

"My baby, oh my baby," she whispered before Claire noticed her in the doorway.

"Mrs. Walsch, Marsha moved again, and this time, her left fingers, all five at once," she finished with a demonstration and a big satisfied smile. "She's advancing, getting stronger, Mrs. Walsch!"

She glided out of the room leaving Helen amazed and looking at her watch to see when Sam would arrive. "Papa is coming soon and you can move your beautiful little fingers for both of us again, darling."

"How are my two favorite ladies tonight?" Sam questioned as he came into the room. Immediately he felt the sense of resilience from his wife. "I have the feeling something positive happened here this afternoon," he guessed and embraced Helen warmly.

Helen let herself wilt in Sam's arms saying, "Marsha's left fingers moved. All of them at once, Sam," she blurted as she sobbed into his chest.

"That's wonderful! Did you see her?" Sam questioned with a wide smile of joy.

"No, I wasn't here. Just like you, I missed witnessing Marsha's progress too!" said Helen, still sobbing. "I went out for aspirin, just for a few minutes. Claire saw it. Oh Sam!"

"It's OK, honey!" he felt her frustration.

"But I'm with her all the time and…"

"I know, baby. It's frustrating."

"I just want to see her move, Sam!" Helen continued crying.

"I know Helen, I know."

"Claire told me the reflexes are common and will continue. Maybe I'll see it tomorrow or maybe you'll see it to…" she couldn't continue, she was sobbing so hard.

"Come here, my sweet. You look so tired and worn out," and he pulled her close and hugged her gently.

"Oh Sam, it's so hard and hurts so bad to see Marsha like this. I wish I had the power to make her all better, make everything go away, all the pain..."

"I know how you feel. But we can do this, baby! Remember? The two of us, together, with a positive attitude," Sam said in the best confident tone he could muster.

"Yes, honey…"

"Look how far we've come, how far Marsha's come," Sam counseled his wife, as optimistically as possible. "And she'll continue recovering the more we focus and believe, the more faith we have."

Helen released herself from her husband's arms and sat in the chair opposite their daughter's bed. She thought about how she and Sam were bonding as a result of this tragedy. They were depending on each other more than she imagined possible. They were fighting for a common interest and it brought both vigor and vitality to continue their quest. It gave both the inner strength to keep going. Helen leaned forward and took her daughter's hand in hers once more and again began to hum Hush Little Baby as she had done earlier. She was hoping for another reaction. But there was none. After Helen fell silent, both parents sat quietly, watching their little girl's chest rise and fall, rhythmically.

"We love you!" both parents whispered, almost in unison.

"And we won't let you down," Helen finished with certainty.

"Good evening, Mr. Walsch," said Dr. Davis. "I heard your daughter is having more reflexes."

"Yes," said Sam. "Two that we know of."

"There have probably been more. You just didn't recognize they happened and it's certainly a positive sign. PT five times a day is helping Marsha's muscles regain strength, and their healing is likely causing further stimulation. Now we have to wait to let her body do its thing. The body is truly amazing. Do you have any questions?"

"How long will movements be mere reflexes? When will my daughter move consciously again?" Sam questioned.

"When will Marsha wake up, doctor?" Helen whispered, knowing the doctor could not answer, but hoping for an answer all the same.

"Movement in the comatose stage is always good," responded Dr. Davis. "The body is beginning to function again, and we're helping it along through physical and occupational therapy. Recovery depends on Marsha's body's ability to mend. Everyone heals differently and at his or her own pace, unfortunately. I'm sorry there's nothing else we can do and there's no timetable. Marsha has her very own schedule, and we need to heed her rate of recovery. We can only reinforce her progress."

Sam and Helen had their routine. Helen continued staying with Marsha all day, during the week, so Sam could go to work. Evenings, Sam arrived and stayed until visiting hours were over or sometimes all night. The Walsch's life revolved around their daughter. Nothing else seemed important. The stress of the situation quickly took its toll as both parents continued seeing their little girl fighting for life the way they knew it. Nonetheless, day after day, Mama and Papa read to Marsha. They talked to her. They played music for her, even while she was sleeping, in hopes that she could hear them. Helen and Sam were in agreement that this was the only way to reach their daughter. Her brain must be stimulated, the little patient's parents agreed with the rehab doctors and nurses.

"Your daughter's brain must be handled like a newborn's. The information you feed her will register for life. You are teaching her like an infant. You are building a new person."

The morning after Marsha moved her fingers, Helen and Sam were meeting with Dr. Davis to go over all progress so far.

"I wonder if Marsha will remember anything when she awakens?" Helen wondered out-loud again.

"She's unlikely to because of her head injuries, and there's really no way of knowing how her memory was affected until she wakes up completely and we can converse with her," responded Dr. Davis. "The best you can do is what you've been doing and wait."

"You mean talk to her? Will she be able to speak when she wakes up?"

"Unlikely," responded the doctor. "But we'll be able to determine comprehension and vocabulary much better than now."

"I need to get going, Helen," said Sam. "I'm running a few errands before heading to the office this morning and I'll see you tonight. I'm sure our angel will do well today."

Then he gently kissed his two ladies and left.

Again, Helen missed her daughter's movement as she excused herself for lunch and then again for a cup of coffee. Each time in her conversation to Marsha afterwards, Mama told her she knew she was playing a game.

"I know you are getting better, my darling. You just go right ahead and keep moving and one of these times I'll catch you. Your progress is making Mama and Papa so happy and very proud of you."

Helen looked at her bandaged daughter while straightening the sheet that covered her.

"You are welcome to bring in family pictures and teddy bears for Marsha to see and focus on when she wakes up," nurse Abby told Helen. "We encourage a warm environment for our patients. It promotes a sense of security, especially for the little ones."

"Do you think Marsha will wake up soon?" asked Mama excitedly.

"She's certainly becoming more alert," replied Abby.

"Marsha has always moved when I am not here," said Mama with exasperation.

"Sometimes that happens," responded nurse Abby. "Be patient with her. Marsha is bound to surprise us. She's an extremely strong young lady."

"Are you going to surprise Mama, young lady?" questioned Helen without expecting a response. Out of the corner of her eye Helen thought she saw her daughter's right foot move or was it her imagination?

"Baby, do that again," she said. There was no movement and Helen felt her headache returning. She went to take some aspirin and called Sam with the progress she thought she just witnessed.

"Hello, honey," she said excitedly. "I think Marsha moved her left foot. But it could have been my imagination too."

"She probably did, honey. Did you see anything else?"

"No, she hasn't moved since. But Abby said she'll probably surprise us."

"I'm sure she will, our little fighter. I can't wait to see you both."

"Can you bring some of Marsha's teddy bears tonight? I'll look for some family pictures to bring tomorrow I want to make her as comfortable as possible when she wakes up."

"Are we to the point where Marsha could wake up?" gasped Sam in pleasant surprise.

"According to Abby, Marsha could surprise us, yes, anytime! And friendly surroundings are likely to help her."

"I'll bring the teddy bears. I love you and I'll see you soon," Sam assured, not believing his ears. Can it be possible my angel is returning? Maybe tonight will be the night I'll see Marsha move or open her eyes again, Sam thought as he hung up the receiver. He couldn't help fantasizing about life with his precious little girl. "I'll do anything I can for you, baby," he whispered to himself. I'll build you a nice little play area in our yard with a special little seat so you can see the flowers and birds you used to enjoy so much.

"Papa is bringing your teddy bear friends, Marsha," Mama said to her little girl. "They will be here, waiting for you to wake up, just like Mama and Papa. We love you so much and are looking forward to saying hello.

That afternoon Marsha moved her fingers three times. Each was a special, momentous event. Each time Helen pushed the call button for the nurse, and every time brought increasing hope.

"You are our strong little princess and you can overcome this. You've battled this far and you're moving ahead honey, in the right direction. Keep going. Promise me you won't give up and I'll promise never to give up either," Mama whispered close to her daughter's ear.

As the minutes and hours passed without more signs, no visible improvement, Helen felt more and more fatigued and disappointment set in again. "Sam, please get here soon," she whispered under her breath. "I am so tired and need emotional support."

"Mr. Walsch?" said Abby. "Can I help you with those?

"No, it's OK," said Sam as he juggled five teddy bears in his arms.

"What a lucky and loved little girl," commented another nurse as Sam disappeared into room 24.

He stopped short as he saw his wife crouched forward on the chair with her head on Marsha's bed. "Sweetheart, are you OK," rushing to her. "Is Marsha OK?"

"I'm exhausted Sam. Marsha moved her fingers three times and I've been talking all day, encouraging her. I just want her to open her eyes, Sam! I want my baby back!!"

"Now, now, it's OK. You're trying so hard and giving all you've got, honey. Let's set these bears around Marsha's bed. We'll let Abby know where we are and we can have some coffee together before you go home."

They went to the nurses' station and then hand in hand to the elevators.

"Tell me again what happened this afternoon and what did you talk to Marsha about?"

Rather than answering the question, Helen told her husband what had been on her mind for quite a while now. "Do you know how much I appreciate you, standing by us?"

"You don't have to, honey," Sam said, embarrassed by his wife's statement.

"You work all day and come to the hospital every night to see us, so I can go home and rest. Your dedication means so much to me, to Marsha too."

"I wish I could spend more time, give you more help."

When they returned to Marsha's room, the sight of the motionless little girl surrounded by the teddy bears made the entire situation all too real for the exhausted parents.

"Oh Sam!!"

"Now, now, you're tired. Go home and get sleep and I'll see you in the morning, Helen, I love you," Sam said, leading his tired wife by the hand to the elevator.

A little while later, the phone rang in Marsha's room. "I arrived home safely, Sam," Helen said in a tired voice. "How is Marsha? Has she moved again?"

"Yes," Sam replied proudly. "Marsha's whole hand actually moved this time. I'm keeping close watch. Now please get some sleep, sweetheart. We'll be fine here, I promise."

"I love you, Sam," said Helen.

"I love you too, baby."

The next morning brought ice and snow and the weather report predicted snowstorms all day long. Sam called his wife early in the morning.

"Sweetheart, I think you should stay home today," he

told her. "I spoke with Dr. Davis and he said Marsha is fine. Get some rest today. I'm sure you can keep busy and I'll be home after I stop by the office. We need to wait out this storm together and regroup," Sam continued. "We need to take care of ourselves too, now that Marsha is not critical anymore."

"Do you really think she's out of danger, Sam?"

"Yes, she's stable and improving every day Dr. Davis told me this morning."

"If you insist, I'll see you when you get home," Helen was both skeptical and relieved at the same time. She hadn't had a day to herself since before the accident.

This is the first time in almost six weeks I will concentrate on our lives, she thought. It will be the first time I'll think about anything besides Marsha. There's so much to do, so much that's been neglected. Where do I start? The laundry first. A short time later Helen heard the familiar sound of the garage door opening and closing and she quickly finished putting away the sheets.

"I'm in here, Sam," she said, feeling herself being scooped up from behind.

"How's my beautiful wife this morning?" Sam was practically beaming.

"Why are you in such a good mood?"

"Marsha's eyes fluttered open. Abby was giving her a bath when it happened. Isn't it wonderful?" he stated. "Our baby is close to waking up and now we have the rest of the day alone together."

Helen dropped the socks she was folding and threw her arms around his neck. "Yes we do!"

"While we're stuck here today let's get as much done as possible so we can devote our full attention and time to Marsha again."

"Yes. I miss her terribly. Other than at night, we haven't been apart in—how many days? Or has it been weeks?"

"Weeks, Helen, weeks."

"Yes, weeks."

"Abby said the nurses expect phone calls from parents

when bad weather keeps them from the hospital," Sam finished, still holding and rocking his wife for comfort.

"I've been cleaning and doing laundry all morning and need to keep busy to keep from going insane. When will this pain end, Sam?"

"We have to look at the bright side, darling. Marsha is over the worst, continuing to improve. We're very lucky and we have to keep taking it day by day, honey."

"Oh Sam, I know. You're my anchor. What would I do without you?"

"We're helping each other. This is hard for me too, Helen. Like you, I'm just going through the motions each and every day and the pain sometimes gets unbearable. We need to be optimistic though, just to go on, baby. That's all we can do now. There's no other choice. There's no other option. And I have no idea how we're going to handle this."

Sam showed her the first of Marsha's medical bills. Helen realized another realm of the utter devastation of her husband, one she and he had undoubtedly put out of their minds, until now.

"I'm at a loss myself," Helen admitted. "We're doing all we can and still feel it's not enough. Oh Sam, what are we going to do? What will be our baby's future, our future? We're living paycheck to paycheck. How're we going to pay all the bills? There will be more and more expenses, and we have to continue helping our child!"

Sam didn't know how to respond. He answered as honestly as he could. "I don't think there's anything else we can do and somehow we'll make it, honey. You're right; we just need to plow forward. Thank goodness we have medical insurance. Even with our medical coverage we have to make sure we choose the best services they cover and be patient."

"Patience is the hardest aspect to deal with. How can one be patient when your child has a brush with death and you still don't know if she'll ever be healthy again? If she'll walk again? Oh, Sam!!"

"We'll do what needs to be done," Sam said quietly. "I'm sure the storm will subside and roads will be clear tomorrow so we'll go to the hospital to see Marsha. Maybe she'll finally wake up."

"Yes," agreed Helen. "That will be a happy day."

"Try to get some rest today my darling," Sam whispered.

"Please hold me and tell me she'll be OK, Sam."

"We will overcome!" whispered Sam in her ear. "Ssshhhhhhh...relax..."

The evening was as relaxing as possible. After calling the hospital to check on Marsha, Sam and Helen had a nice dinner together, and watched the television for an escape. They went to bed early and had the first restful night in a long time.

"It's currently a balmy 22 degrees outside. The high will reach nearly 29 today," said the cheerful radio announcer. "Salt trucks have been on all major arteries all night. But be careful. Side streets may still be slippery. Please take caution today."

"The sun is beautiful on the snow," said Helen as she gazed out their bedroom window. "I hope it's safe enough to drive to the hospital this morning."

"Oh, I think so. The car can handle it anyway. I was just going to call to check on Marsha," Sam said as he picked up the phone and dialed the number for the nurses' station.

"Good morning, Abby. How's Marsha doing this morning?" inquired Sam.

"REM Flutter continued throughout the night," reported Abby. "Marsha's sleeping comfortably now and Dr. Franks is scheduled to come in a little later this morning."

"My wife and I will be there in a while, and thank you, Abby, for looking in on her."

He hung up the phone turning immediately to his wife's inquiring eyes. As he scooped up his wife in his arms, Sam relayed, "Marsha's been dreaming all night. She's resting peacefully right now."

"I can't wait to see her blue eyes again," said Helen with a dreamy look.

"Remember, it's only REM flutter."

"Yes, but she's opened her eyes before. I wonder what she's thinking, what's she dreaming about?"

"Sweetheart, don't get ahead of yourself," said Sam. "I don't want you to build your hopes up too much and be disappointed when we get there. Remember, there's a long road ahead, even after she wakes up."

"I know. I'm just so happy Marsha's making progress. I just need to hold my baby girl again," she said. Sam opened his arms comforting arms to her yet again.

"Cry as much as you need," Sam soothed his wife. "We'll draw strength from each other, OK? We'll make it, baby. You'll see!"

Marsha was sleeping soundly as both parents entered the room and instantly started fretting over her. They independently were thinking about the road they had traveled to get to this point and how lucky they were Marsha was still alive.

"Good morning," whispered Abby. "The doctor was in shortly after we spoke this morning. He was pleased with Marsha's increased stimulation and said he is very optimistic. It is wonderful how she's progressing and I can only imagine how thrilled you must be."

"I'm having trouble seeing it," cried Helen, both a little depressed and anxious at the same time.

"You will, honey, and possibly today. Remember, Marsha is getting stronger every day."

The morning progressed and little Marsha slept peacefully.

"I suppose Marsha's wild dreams got her very tired last night," Sam joked with nurse Abby after she confirmed her vital signs were steady and there was nothing to worry about.

"Oh, I am sure the recovery process is very hard on Marsha and takes all her energy. That's why I want to do what we can to make her comfortable. Marsha is so lucky to have a mom and dad like you," exclaimed Abby. "You are willing to give more and more of yourselves, even though you're worn out. But I guess that's what being a parent is all about. Is there anything you need before I end my shift?"

"I don't think so," responded Sam and looked adoringly at his wife. He really was so proud of her for how she stood up for their daughter and he remembered the vow they had made eight years before. For better or for worse, and he was determined to stand by those words too.

"These past weeks have been a strain on our relationship," he said, looking at Helen.

"Honey, we are in a crisis and we're holding together the best we can," she exclaimed, surprised at the concern.

"I mean we should spend family time together. For now I guess it'll be in this hospital room," he continued. "And as much as possible when Marsha wakes up. She should see both her parents beside her."

Sam touched his daughter's bandaged brow lovingly, and said, "I need to run out and take care of a few things and will be back around lunch time. I'll bring us something yummy for lunch. No hospital food today. Then we can spend all afternoon together."

He kissed his wife gently before leaving. Helen waved as he left the room. She turned to her bandaged daughter and said a silent prayer, imagining the angels looking over her little girl were listening closely and answering in the affirmative.

"I'll let you rest for awhile now, sweetie," Mama Helen declared after a few minutes, which seemed longer, of course. I'll be right here reading *Gone With The Wind* and maybe later, after you've rested some, I'll read you a bit," Mama finished before falling silent.

Moments passed and Helen became entranced in her novel and faintly heard Dionne Warwick's *I Say A Little Prayer*. Helen felt a tear fall as she was drawn away from her book to listen, and prayed for a miracle. Wiping her eyes, Helen looked up at her sleeping child next to her, only she wasn't sleeping anymore.

"Mama," a faint confused voice questioned and then

nothing more. Marsha lay there with her eyes open, blinking from time to time and looking around at nothing in particular. Was she trying to focus?

It was only the second time Helen heard her daughter speak in seven weeks. Marsha's wide blue eyes looked over to the faint sound of her mother breathing, or did she actually hear her heart pounding with excitement and anticipation?

She again questioned; "Mama?" Searching for her mother's face.

Mama Helen felt her heart beating even faster instantly, as her now-sweaty hands quickly laid her book aside and gently grasped her daughter's hand.

"Hello, sweetheart," Mama said, now weeping openly with happiness. It was all she managed to say. Helen was speechless. The flood of emotions made words impossible. Instead she kept looking into her daughter's beautiful sapphire blue eyes, and gently massaged her little arms while tears continued rolling down her weary, fatigued face, dropping onto the clean, white sheet covering Marsha's frail little body. My prayer's been answered! A miracle just happened! thought Helen as she reached for the call button.

X. Holidays To Remember: A Cherished Time For Our Family

Marsha was progressing visibly every day now. With her eyes open and focusing and noticing her surroundings, Helen and Sam noticed increased movement, both reflexive and voluntary.

"Therapy will increase your daughter's ability over time," reported Dr. Davis, "And we have removed the feeding tube since Marsha is alert now. It says here that she's eating with an appetite."

Dr. Davis had been correct in Marsha's recovery to this point, and Helen and Sam counted their blessings every day. Both parents marveled at Marsha's obvious zest to go forward, to persevere, from moving her little blonde head in recognition when they arrived to visit with her, to learning to control her food intake, to doing her very best at both physical and occupational therapy sessions.

"Patient is doing extraordinary with recognition and initial motor skills," Dr. Davis read aloud from Marsha's chart.

"How can you say she's doing extraordinary, when she's still in a virtually immobile state?" questioned Helen anxiously.

"Honey, you are tired. Marsha is not a vegetable, like the doctors had first thought, remember? She's responding and shows signs of further recovery. That's what the doctor is referring to."

Dr. Davis was no stranger to exasperated, fatigued parents. He continued to explain, "We will not give up on your daughter; she's responding well to all treatments and keeps making progress."

"Like I told you, honey, Marsha's a Walsch and she won't give up!" Sam tried consoling his wife. "Let's keep that positive attitude for her.

"Therapists work with Marsha every day and her reflexes and motor functions are improving slowly," Helen spoke into the telephone. "She's been responding with a smile when we talk to her and she's eating well. I think the doctors and nurses consider her a miracle, we do anyway! Oh, and there's even a chance she'll be able to come home for Thanksgiving."

"Oh my gosh! That's terrific! When will you know?" asked Uncle Bob.

"Dr. Davis said by end of the week."

"We'll make plane reservations, so we can spend Christmas together." said Uncle Bob to no one, as Helen quickly gave the phone to Sam as she saw one of Marsha's support pillows fall to the floor.

"Say that again, Bob."

"We'll come see you for Christmas. I'm sure Marsha would enjoy seeing her Aunt and Uncle," Bob repeated.

"Yes, I'm sure she'd enjoy that. Marsha's face lights

up when anyone walks into the room. She loves attention, although visits tire her immensely. By then I'm sure her condition will have improved even more, and Dr. Davis tells us she needs more and more stimulation and interaction for the best recovery."

"Of course, and we'll do whatever the doctor advises, Sam," assured Uncle Bob.

"I'll ask him what he thinks about her prognosis for Christmas time tomorrow."

"Did you speak to that Dr. Hanks yet?" Uncle Bob inquired.

"Yes," Sam replied.

"What did you think? Will he be able to help Marsha?"

"Dr. Hanks said he couldn't do anything until Marsha is totally stabilized," Sam said while in his mind he already visualized Marsha back on her feet.

"She is, isn't she, stabilized, I mean?"

"Yes, now she is, and we have an appointment with him the day before Thanksgiving," answered Sam with hope and anticipation in his voice. "He seemed positive and very knowledgeable about fractures. I've done some research on him myself and we're hopeful, Bob. Hanks has done some amazing work with bone fractures and reconstruction, some of which is still controversial to this day."

"I heard about injured soldiers he treated during World War II and even with limited resources, Hanks's unconventional methods saved limbs, even lives."

"Yah, I suspect so," responded Sam. "He used elongated nail-like metal pieces to mend badly broken limbs by inserting them through the center of realigned bone parts. It worked then, so why not now? Why not on our child?"

"You're absolutely right, that *was* years ago. So, why not now, Sam?"

Sam thought to himself again how lucky that Uncle Bob had known of this man, this obviously brilliant doctor, and how research and persistence brings forth answers and solutions to an incident, in this case a life altering situation and decision.

"I'm looking forward to talking to Hanks about Marsha's condition. Every other surgeon has refused to operate on Marsha. Controversial or not, Hanks's track record is good and he, at least, wants to see us."

"It's a great start and I have a feeling this'll be a good thing. Marsha will get the help she needs, Sam. I have a good feeling about this!"

"I do too, and I promised myself I'd do whatever I can for her, Bob. The operation sounds nasty, but not when you compare it to a life with a deformed leg. I just can't stand the thought. I will do whatever it takes for her," Sam said with a heavy sigh of burden.

"Of course you will. She's your daughter."

"Talk to you soon and thank you, Bob. I'll call you after we see Dr. Hanks."

Sam turned from the window and hung up the telephone. He saw his wife sitting next to his sleeping little princess and thought, how could their baby not get better with all this positive energy, love, and guidance? He shuddered at what cost that recovery might be to Marsha. What price will Marsha pay? What physical and mental impairments will she have? How will my baby deal with life? Life and its fruits will never be the same for her or the Walsch family.

"We will do what needs to be done," murmured Sam in response to his mind-boggling thoughts.

Dr. Davis spoke to the Walsch's outside Marsha's room so as not to be overheard by the recovering little girl. "You can take Marsha home for the Thanksgiving weekend, but she will need twenty-four hour care, and you must report to us morning, noon, and evening. I'll inform her nurse you'll call in, so she can make notes on Marsha's chart. You have my permission if you're comfortable with that."

"Oh Sam, we can have her all to ourselves for the entire weekend!" Helen said, beaming with excitement.

The following few days were filled with preparations at home for Marsha's stay as well as the daily routine of visits in the hospital. This was going to be both an exciting time and a stressful one too—for all involved.

"Remember, she gets tired very easily," finished Claire as she helped Sam position the little girl into the back seat of the family's Chevy.

"I'll sit next to Marsha to make sure she's OK on the drive home, Sam," Helen said, climbing in the back of the car.

"I think that's a good idea. A curve or a bump could throw her off balance or upset her," cautioned Sam.

"Oh honey, I have a feeling this weekend will be harder than we expect," whispered Helen quietly to her husband as he drove carefully through the streets to their home.

"Sweetheart, we'll be fine. I promise. We'll make our little angel feel as comfortable as possible. Just think, we'll be together just like before, only this time my little sweetheart is an invalid," and he pushed the thought quickly from his thoughts. Positive thinking, remember, he reminded himself. He glanced at his ladies in the rearview mirror.

"Yes, it'll be so good to have our angel home again!" Helen smiled.

"It sure will. I just wish—she felt better."

"Yes, Sam, I know. I do too. I wish we could run and play with her. But we'll do whatever to make that happen, in time, remember? It'll just take time, right?" Helen was reminding her husband, and herself at the same time.

"Yes, dear, and lots of work. But that's OK. We can handle it."

Soon Sam was pulling into their driveway. It was a wonderful feeling to have Marsha coming home, all the same, even with all the worries and trials ahead.

"Helen, make sure that wheelchair is sturdy and in the locked position so I can lift Marsha right into it," Sam said as he opened the back door of the car.

"Got it, Sam. There's a small pillow in it so her bump is padded. Remember, Claire warned about more bruising," reminded Helen.

"Let's get her upstairs and after her tour of the house, maybe we'll put her in the living room love seat."

"Good idea, she can watch us in the kitchen, living, and dining room from there. We need to make sure Marsha sees us as much as possible," Helen nodded.

"Agreed—It'll give her a sense of security!"

"Absolutely!" Helen noticed how she and her husband worked together to make Marsha's brief homecoming as stress free and comfortable for her, although she had the feeling that she and Sam would fall into bed at the end of every day.

After a quick tour of the house to remind Marsha of her home and family, the protective parents placed Marsha on the love seat and surrounded her with pillows for both support and comfort.

"Here you go, sweetie. This is for you," Helen said as she put a teddy bear next to the frail child.

"S-an-k oo-u, Ma-ma," Marsha whispered as she settled onto the family's love seat.

"Is there anything else I can get for you?"

"N-o-o, Ma-ma."

"Papa's right, you look like you could use a little nap and, maybe we'll go for a walk in the sunshine afterwards. Would you like to go for a walk in a little while, sweetheart?"

"Ya, Ma-ma," Marsha whimpered with a yawn.

"She is getting soars on her buttocks and shoulders. Is there more you can do? Can she be moved more often?"

"You can massage her when you come in. Maybe apply some lotion. There really isn't anything else we can do except move her from time to time, which is already being done," Claire answered over the phone.

"You poor thing. I know you must be uncomfortable. Maybe she's even in pain, Claire."

"Mr. Walsch, we're doing the best we can for her."

"I know you are," and Sam was thinking ahead to ask their pharmacist about wound cream.

"The soars are a result of your daughter being immobile for so long. As Marsha becomes mobile and we can move her more, the soars will get better and eventually go away, sir."

Sam thanked her and hung up to go see what his family was doing.

"Let's take a little nap first," Helen said covering her child with a blanket.

"Ya, Ma-ma," Marsha said again, as she laid her head on the pillow against the back of the love seat. Her eyes closed almost instantly, and soon came the rhythmic sounds of her breathing.

"Oh Sam, are you as tired as I am?" Helen said, sitting down in one of the kitchen chairs where she could see her sleeping little girl.

"Probably!" Sam sighed.

The only time Sam or Helen were alone that day was when Marsha was asleep and then there were endless chores to be done. The couple discovered that having their precious little angel at home required more work than they had ever imagined. But neither complained. Rather, at the end of the day, before nodding off to sleep, one or the other might suggest a better, easier, or quicker way of doing something. Sam and Helen were consumed in making Marsha's world, their lives, the best it could possibly be, with the finances they had available.

"We'll see what Dr. Hanks has to say tomorrow," said Sam, before closing his eyes and falling asleep with Helen in his arms.

"I'm hopeful too, honey," she whispered to her already sleeping husband. "He's our last hope, really."

Again, the sleeping pill she took half an hour ago finally allowed for sleep.

Sam, Helen, and little Marsha, in her wheelchair, waited for Dr. Hanks in his small office waiting room. They were his first appointment of the day. The television stood mute in the corner and the receptionist was still turning on lights and machines.

"Coffee will be ready in just a few minutes. Have you signed in? Can I get your daughter something to drink, maybe some milk?" the lovely young receptionist asked.

"Oh, no, we brought hers. But thank you."

"The doctor shouldn't be long," the receptionist said as she returned to her station.

"Thank you," answered Helen. Silently, to herself, she prayed today's appointment would bring good news.

"Dr. Hanks's surgery ran late. He just called and is on his way," said the receptionist, apologetically. They had been waiting almost half an hour at that point.

"These appointments are never on time," Sam grumbled.

"You're right, but a surgery, I guess he really couldn't do anything about, Sam. I imagine he must have had his first surgery start at five or six o'clock this morning to still be there at eight. I'm just hoping he'll have answers for us, some good news. I just can't imagine what we're going to do if Marsha's leg can't be fixed. I mean, our baby'll n-never walk again…Oh, and we can't forget to point out the bed soars, Sam."

"I think she'll get help. I've got a good feeling, honey. I have a good feeling about today, Helen," Sam said, and he continued reading his Time Magazine with his wife sitting pensively between him and Marsha.

From time to time Helen touched their little girl who sat motionless, passively in her wheelchair. She looked so pale and weak. What will it take to bring the life back into her, thought Helen. What else can I possibly do to help her? What can we do? Where do we start?

"I am so sorry I'm late, Mr. and Mrs. Walsch," said Dr. Hanks as he walked into the waiting room to greet them. "And who is this?"

Marsha looked up at the doctor's inquiring eyes from her wheelchair, a sheet covering her legs. She said nothing, but looked at him with vacant, yet sad, eyes.

"Marsha, this is Dr. Hanks. He is going to take a look at your leg and see when you can walk again, honey," explained Papa as the group moved down the hall and into an office.

As the group settled into the exam room, the doctor set aside the chart he had been reading. He looked at the feeble little form in the wheelchair.

"Can you move the sheet so I can take a look?" questioned the doctor quietly of the little girl. There was still no answer or movement. "OK, may I remove the sheet?"

Sam and Helen sat side by side, touching, watching as Dr. Hanks introduced himself to their daughter. Helen whispered, "I like the way he's handling her, Sam."

"He's letting her trust him so he can look at her legs, I suppose," commented Sam.

"OK, Marsha, I'm going to see if you have reflex in your legs. I'll just use this little hammer here, OK? It is just going to tickle a little bit."

Marsha nodded, and her guard seemed to relax a bit.

There was absolutely no reflex in the shorter deformed right leg. The doctor did a series of manipulations and touched many sections of Marsha's lower extremity. He reviewed the x-rays and examined her a little more. Finally, after he was completely satisfied that he had gathered enough information to make a decision; he directed his attention to Marsha's parents.

"Your daughter is a prime candidate for this operation, and is likely to reap all its benefits because she is so young. Her right femur would be extended to within two inches of its standard length, and exercise and massage will promote further growth to coincide with her growth. She's a lucky young lady. Her body is growing rapidly and is still manipulative because of her age. I think we can do something to get you walking again, young lady, and it won't take long before you're up and around," and he smiled at the still expressionless child.

"Will this really work, Dr. Hanks?" inquired Helen. "Will Marsha really walk again?" she expressed in utter relief, excitement, and anticipation.

"There's never a guarantee, but in this case, I think chances are very good, yes. If everything goes as planned I'll have your daughter walking a month after the operation."

"A month? You're kidding, right?" gasped Sam, his eyes wide.

"Not at all. The nail that will be holding Marsha's femur together will allow her to stand up in a few days and the intense therapy program will strengthen her, teach her balance, and ultimately how to walk again."

"In four weeks?" questioned Sam, doubtfully.

"Yes, with hard work and positive reinforcement from you," Dr. Hanks then proceeded to explain the entire procedure in great detail. Portions of the process were quite vivid and made the parents squirm at the thought of what their baby will go through. He then excused himself from the exam room to let the parents talk about the information he just presented to them.

"Oh Sam, it will be hard on her. It sounds so harsh," Helen sighed, a little nauseous from all of the details just presented to her.

"You heard the doctor. We have to push her a little to get her well again."

"Yes, dear. We just need to keep convincing ourselves it's for her own good," Helen nodded reluctantly.

"Maybe she'll surprise us," Sam shrugged.

"Ya, maybe. Oh Sam, this is so amazing!"

"Yes, it's amazing and…" Sam stopped talking as Dr. Hanks entered the room.

"My next available appointment is January 15th. Let me know what you decide," said Dr. Hanks as he regarded Marsha. "Here you go, you may cover yourself back up, young lady. Maybe your Mom can help you," and he gave Marsha a reassuring smile for encouragement.

"Oh, I think we'll go for it. No one else will even talk to us. No other doctor wants to touch Marsha. Of course, until now, her condition was too critical. Now, since her bones are grown together improperly, they tell us it's impossible to break them. It's too risky!" Sam stated. "Every doctor is of the same opinion."

"Not at all. It's not impossible, the way I see it. Set it up with my secretary and I'll see you January 15th," and he looked at Marsha and winked. "You continue to be a good girl, OK? I'll see you in about two months."

"Dr. Hanks, maybe you can shed some light on Marsha's bed soars," Helen interjected. "I mean, they look painful and we don't know what to do."

"The soars are a result of your daughter being immobile for so long. As Marsha becomes mobile and we can move her more, the soars will get better and eventually go away, Ma'am. In the mean time, get some wound cream at the pharmacy and see about getting pressure off those areas."

"We're doing the best we can for her."

"I'm sure you are," Dr. Hanks shook hands with Sam and Helen and exited the room.

"I like him. He's confident and makes sense. What do you think, Helen?"

"I'm with you, and he's our last hope."

"That too, but he's good, I think!" Sam had a renewed sound of confidence in his voice that had been missing for quite some time.

"How's all this going to work, Sam. I mean she can't walk, can't even stand. Marsha has absolutely no fine motor skills or balance. How's she going learn that? How do we teach that?" Helen was sounding hopeless again.

"She's improved a lot already, right?" Sam said, trying to convince his wife there was great reason for hope.

"Well, yah."

"We need to take it day by day and little by little, honey, remember?" Sam coaxed his tired despaired wife.

"I've noticed that Marsha can't hold anything in her little hands, she's so shaky. Oh Sam—what're we gonna do? Oh dear God, help us!"

"I know honey—it hurts. But we'll just have to work with her. We'll ask her therapists what exercises we can do at home to help her. We don't have to do this alone."

"We need to encourage Marsha as much as we can, Sam. Do you think we can make a difference, I mean, help her?" Helen almost had a sound of hope in her voice. It was almost there, Sam thought.

"Of course—we just have to put our minds to it and gather as much information as we can to help us help her."

The day was busy but wonderful. The little family took the long way home from Dr. Hanks's office to enjoy the late autumn sunshine. They returned home for a nice lunch and Marsha took a long nap on the family room love seat. The evening was restful, and the first night at home was without incident. The following morning, Thanksgiving, was cool, but sunny.

"Is Marsha's wheelchair still downstairs, Sam? A walk by the lake may do all of us good. Would you like that, honey? You can see the ducks, smell the forest, and hear all the birds singing. Wouldn't that be nice?" Helen asked.

"Brisa—Brisa, are you with me—? I can't seem to be able to let Mama and Papa know how much I'm enjoying being home and how much I appreciate all the things they're doing for me. All I can do is smile. I can't explain it to them, and I can't move much, either. How do I tell them Brisa? How?"

"Just keep smiling, Marsha. They'll know. Your face speaks a thousand words. Your parents know you're doing your very best. I know everything you took for granted before the accident seems impossible right now. Give it time and we'll work through it together, you, me, and your mom and dad. You will prevail through both strength and help from others around you."

"I feel safe with Mama and Papa, Brisa. Why is that?"

"Your parents have been by your side since the accident. They are dedicating themselves to your recovery."

"But why do I hear their voice of encouragement when I know they're not with me. Like when I'm sleeping?"

"Marsha, your mother and father have been giving you inspiration and encouragement since your accident. One, or both, has been by your side continuously. They love you so much they will not give up on you, nor will I—nor will you."

"Sam, I think I see a little glimmer in Marsha's eyes. Look, do you see it? I'm so glad we have her with us this weekend! I think time away from the hospital is actually helping her."

"You may be right, Helen," Sam shrugged and gave his wife a knowing smile.

"I think we are helping her. I mean, can you imagine being in the hospital for as long as she has? Under those artificial lights? Sam—I bet this is like a vacation to her. Look at her—, look how she's looking at the ducks on the lake. Nature seems to be therapeutic for her. Just look at her taking it all in, Sam. She's really enjoying it," Helen said with a smile that Sam hadn't seen for a long time. It was therapeutic for Helen as well.

"Yah, I think you're right. She's perking up a bit in the sunshine. It must be nice to be in the openness again, in the brilliance of sunshine, instead of those florescent hospital lights," he reiterated.

"I'm thinking of Marsha as a flower. She's budding—, like flowers in the spring. Just think of what we feel like after being cooped inside the house or office for days on end!" Helen cringed.

"Look—, she's smiling. Isn't it beautiful—? Funny you should refer to her as a flower, because that is how I've always pictured her," Sam smiled to himself.

"I wonder if she'd tell us she likes this, if she could, Sam," Helen whispered.

"I'm sure Marsha would, honey. Remember how she always had the brightest smile...and gave those great big hugs when she was happy?"

"Being home is good for Marsha, you're right. She seems happier and more content, and I'm really enjoying seeing her happy, Sam!"

"We're helping her unconsciously, too—giving her hope, for further recovery," Sam suggested.

"Oh I hope she knows how much we're trying, Sam.— Oh, I guess that's silly, huh?"

"I'm sure we're making a difference for her Helen, whether she knows now or not. And I think she's making a difference for us, too. Let's go home and have some dinner, just our little family," Sam said as he started heading for the car, and home.

A little while later that afternoon, the Thanksgiving feast was about ready.

"All I need is for the turkey to finish and we're all set. Can you get Marsha's wheelchair to the table?" Helen called from the kitchen.

"Yup, it's here and we're getting the little princess situated, isn't that right, honey?" Sam said as he locked the wheels in place.

"Here we go. Here's the turkey. Doesn't this look yummy?" Helen observed Marsha as she saw her eyes widen. "Honey, these are mashed potatoes. Here are cranberries and these are candied apples. This, of course, is the turkey."

Helen and Sam knew the importance of labeling everything by its name for Marsha's sake. This way she was learning.

"Can you pass me a small piece of turkey for Marsha?" Helen said, settling down in her chair. "OK sweetheart, here's a bite of sweet potato. Isn't it yummy?

"Aha..." Marsha said with enthusiasm.

"Be careful to cut the turkey in tiny pieces Helen. I'm not sure how well she'll be able to chew solid meat. Here, I'll finish feeding Marsha so you can eat, my dear, OK?" Sam got up and changed places with Helen.

"Thanks, honey. You know, our angel has really made strides, Sam," Helen said with pride in her voice. Saying this was partially for Marsha's benefit, and partially for her own.

"She certainly has, baby. I'm going to miss her when we have to take her back to—," and Sam swallowed the rest of his sentence, realizing he might upset Marsha with mention of the hospital and her return there on Sunday.

"Me too—. Let's not think about that right now," Helen said as she tried to enjoy the delicious Thanksgiving meal with her family.

Friday and Saturday were filled with time for and with Marsha. Sam and Helen had to do everything for their little girl, and managed to squeeze in some short walks and lots of playtime. They tried to include Marsha in everything, from fixing dinner to folding laundry. The entire time, they talked and explained, teaching her as they worked. It made the work harder, but they were imagining that the rewards would be worth it.

Sunday morning Helen found her husband in the kitchen. It was six in the morning. "Sam—what's wrong? What on earth?"

"I wanted to fix my ladies a special breakfast."

"Oh, honey…" Helen was filled with love and admiration for her husband.

"I wanted us to have a meal together, a special occasion, before we take our angel back to the hospital this morning. You've outdone yourself this weekend. We're both in lots of pain right now and I wanted to show you how much I love you."

"I love you, Sam!" She hugged and kissed him, and her eyes momentarily filled with tears of gratitude, yet pain for what had to transpire later that day. She pulled him upstairs to Marsha's room and they knelt by her bedside and said a prayer before their angel opened her eyes.

"We'll get through this and Marsha will shine, my sweet," Sam whispered with his right hand resting on his daughter's outstretched hand and his left squeezing his wife's right hand as she stood beside him, her left arm holding him lovingly.

"You will come visit home again soon," whispered Mama softly as she took her daughter in her arms and dressed her with Sam's help. Sam and Helen did their best to keep their spirits up during breakfast, but this morning was just not the same.

"Oh Sam, it feels like a piece of my heart will be pulled away," Helen said, fighting tears welling in her eyes.

"I know what you mean, honey. Try to look forward to the next time. It won't be long, I'm sure. Christmas isn't too far away and with Uncle Bob and Aunt Liz coming it'll be really busy preparing for the holidays. Time will fly, you'll see!" Sam felt it his job to encourage his wife when she became discouraged.

"I know it's a lot of work, but I want our baby home, Sam..." Helen let the tears fall this time without holding back, as she reached her hand out to Marsha's, who gazed at her mother, questioning and a little confused.

"Just think Helen, next time Marsha comes home she'll be healthier and we'll be even better prepared. I'm sure we'll have her home for Christmas and that's only about a month away, just around the corner."

Helen thought of that as they ate their special breakfast, and gathered up Marsha's things afterwards. They were returning to the hospital and they were all saddened that they wouldn't be together. Marsha was in good spirits most of the morning, until later in the afternoon when they entered the hospital.

"Oh, sweetie, don't cry. Please don't cry. You're breaking Mama's heart. You heard Papa; you'll be home again soon. Baby, don't cry baby, shhhhh. Oh Sam, she's so unhappy. Marsha doesn't want to return to the hospital. This is killing me. Help me, Sam. Please help me with her!" Helen was desperate. She was trying to be strong for Marsha, but the little girl's tears were more than she could handle as she prepared to transfer Marsha from the car into the wheelchair.

"Honey, oh my little angel, Papa's here. Now we have to take you back to your hospital bed cause the doctor's gonna make you better, sweetie. I promise he will and then when you come home for Christmas we can have more fun. OK? Sshhhh, baby, it'll be OK. You can come home again very, very soon, I promise, honey!" Sam was doing his best but his daughter's tears were getting to him also.

"Here, here, let me help," said Claire as she saw Helen and Sam coming down the hospital corridor with Marsha, crying.

"She's so upset at coming back here after being at home," Helen explained.

"I understand, Mrs. Walsch. I'm sure she'll calm once she's comfortable in bed and we'll see about giving her something to help her sleep if she doesn't calm down by herself. We'll give her a little time though. I'm sure she'll be fine," Claire assured.

"My wife and I will stay with her for awhile, if that's OK?" Sam said.

"Oh, certainly, Mr. Walsch. I'll just get Marsha into bed comfortably and leave you alone with her. The doctor should be in to check on her soon," indicated Claire, and Sam walked out into the hallway with her to discuss Marsha's bed soars.

"Mr. Walsch, we're doing the best we can for her. I'll see to it that her pillows are checked and repositioned more often, though."

"And some wound cream too?"

"We'll need doctor's orders for that. But you can certainly apply some on your own too."

"Yes, thanks, Claire."

"You are so welcome," and Claire disappeared into another patient's room.

"Marsha, honey, you just relax, listen to the pretty music and Mama and Papa will be right here. Maybe later I'll read you a story like *Little Red Riding Hood*, how does that sound?" Helen looked worn out as she settled back in the chair. She closed her eyes and Sam stood behind her and massaged her shoulders gently.

Marsha soon fell fast asleep and the Walsch's had a moment to relax. It seemed as hard on them as it was on Marsha. Just about the time Helen was nodding off, the doctor arrived.

"How did our patient do at home this weekend?" inquired Dr. Davis walking into Marsha's hospital room.

"It was good having her home. But we really did have to do everything for her," Sam whispered, since Helen was apparently asleep. "Everything seemed OK. We tried to stimulate her as much as possible for short periods of time and she seemed to enjoy herself."

"That's good—. That's very good," as he wrote the information in Marsha's chart. "Marsha cried this morning as we brought her back," said Helen abruptly, with a tear in her eye at the recollection. "It was hard to see her so unhappy, crying like that..."

"This weekend meant so much to her and we had no idea before then, this morning!" Sam added.

"Good news. Marsha's showing emotion. If all goes well, you can have her home for Christmas. With this news, she'll have something to look forward to," urged Dr. Davis. "I was hoping she'd enjoy being home. That was part of the reason I ordered it."

"If she remembers. I mean, if she can remember," Helen interjected.

"Talk to her about the weekend at home to stimulate her memory—her mind. Be positive and encourage her for her next visit home. This is all good for her. It will stimulate thought and reasoning. It might even help with the concept of time," Dr. Davis stated, confidently.

"Of course—oh yes, if you think it'll help!" Sam responded.

"Oh Sam, all this must be so painful for her. Do you think she remembers life before the accident? Or the accident itself?" Helen panicked at the new thought.

"I don't know," Sam shrugged with a slight tingle at the possibility.

"There's no telling what Marsha remembers, ma'am, but I doubt it," responded Dr. Davis. "Memories of incidents after the trauma might appear in time."

"Like all the time we've spent with her, by her bedside I mean," questioned Helen.

"For example, yes," responded Dr. Davis.

"For now we have to forget the past and move to the future, Helen. We need to help make good things happen for Marsha. We need to strive to help her succeed," Sam exclaimed with his positive tone returning, and attempting to move his wife ever forward to positive thinking.

"You're absolutely correct, Mr. and Mrs. Walsch, and I am prescribing physical exercises as well as mental ones for the speech therapist to stimulate Marsha's entire structure, including her mind. We've already seen signs of improvement in her reactions, and speech therapy reports that she's repeating sounds and words. Her language skills are improving. The nurses report that they see you reading and otherwise communicating with Marsha constantly, and that's to be commended!"

"Yah, I guess we do," Helen nodded.

"That's paying off, you know? Marsha's like a newborn baby. She's absorbing everything—everything she hears, and now everything she sees," encouraged Dr. Davis.

"It makes sense, really. I guess," Sam agreed and Helen nodded.

"Yah, it's how we learn—how children learn," Helen remembered from her education classes in college.

"Marsha's been learning since she woke up from her coma. She's been registering every word that's been said, the music she's heard, stories she's been told, and your words of love and encouragement. But I'm sure other doctors have shared this information with you," Dr. Davis said.

"Yes, it's been mentioned, but the impact and positive implications of our devotion haven't been evident until recently."

"Marsha's making phenomenal progress," Sam breathed to no one in particular as in his mind he replayed his daughter's progress these past weeks.

"Yes, Marsha's progress has been outstanding, and you can hold yourselves largely responsible," responded Dr. Davis, looking at two very emotionally drained parents.

Helen was openly, yet quietly, sobbing as tears rolled down her face. Her whole body seemed to respond to the confirmation of their daughters' recovery, and she let herself slump in the oversized chair from total exhaustion. Sam stood erect, taking in all the information Dr. Davis provided.

"What more can my wife and I do for Marsha. She's still so helpless. How else can we help her? How can we further her recovery?"

"Keep doing what you're doing. Work with her hands.

Take a doll and let her hold it, explore it with her hands, play with it. Let her handle play dough. Her motor skills need to be exercised, brought back to full efficacy. It can be done, in time, with lots of work and patience on everybody's part."

"OK, that's fine. But how long?" asked Helen.

"I can't answer that. Even though it will take a very long time, for her to be considered normal, you'll see improvement quickly. It will come in stages. But, it will be there. You'll see!" Dr. Davis encouraged, but not to the point of false hope.

"Seems to me it's gonna be a long—d-difficult time," Helen said at the thought of the monumental task ahead.

"Yes. Years, I'm afraid," said the doctor softly but firmly.

"It's what we have to do!" stated Sam sternly, grasping the importance of their work ahead of them for Marsha's rehabilitation.

"We'll get you well, baby," Helen said as she bent down and gave her little girl a hug and a kiss. To her surprise, Marsha moved her head and her lips kissed in response. Helen froze and was sorry she didn't have her face positioned to receive the kiss, the first kiss from her daughter in almost four months. "Dr. Davis, Marsha just responded to my kiss. She actually tried to kiss me back. Did you see it? Oh my God!"

"The more you reinforce her, the better she'll develop psychologically and the harder she's likely to fight her injuries. Like I said, work with her."

"Oh yes sir, we certainly will!"

The weeks seemed a lifetime for Helen, as she was busier than ever preparing for their daughter's homecoming and for Christmas. Sam and Helen wanted to make their home as safe and comfortable as possible for Marsha. Furniture was reorganized and strategically set for easier accessibility, and Helen took special care in preparing her little girl's room. She found favorite toys and placed them down low. With the shortage of funds, Helen used the plastic milk crates the milkman left as little tables and cubbyholes for dolls and stuffed animals. "I don't want my baby to be lonely," she thought.

"You really have outdone yourself, Helen. Did you do all this yourself? I mean look at the little pillows and blankets and the teddy bears over there. Marsha will love this. She always loved playing dolls with all the frilly, girl stuff," Sam said, amazed at the things Helen had accomplished in such a short time.

"I guess the sewing Mom taught me is paying off," Helen shrugged.

"It's really nice," and he kissed her affectionately. "When did you find the time?"

"Oh, while I was sitting with Marsha, when I wasn't reading or singing to her, I was sewing. It was another way to keep my sanity."

"I know, and I've immersed myself at work when I wasn't with one of you. But that's behind us now and we'll have her home tomorrow night."

"Yah, I still can't believe it!" Helen sighed at the thought.

"And Bob and Liz are arriving Christmas Eve," Sam reminded.

"Are you getting the tree tomorrow, Sam?"

"Oh yes, and we'll set it up with Marsha watching. What do you think?"

"She can help with the ornaments, get them out, I mean—oh, with my help. It's so hard for me to remember she won't be able to do things, even the simplest things," Helen sighed.

"Just imagine her face the first time she achieves what seems impossible. No matter how hard or cruel it seems, we've got to push and encourage for that to happen as soon as possible, even the smallest accomplishment!"

"Yah, that'll give her the will to go on. Then we can keep reminding her that her struggles will lead to success, with an example she'll remember, Sam."

"Yup, that's very important. I agree!"

"Oh honey, this is gonna be so hard!" Helen was starting to feel overwhelmed again.

"I know, baby. We've got to do it though," Sam soothed his tired wife.

"I know and we should be as positive as possible around her, always!"

"You're absolutely right, my dear. We're going be drained, but we've got to do it for our little girl, so she'll have a chance at a normal life."

"I wonder if every parent in a situation like we're in feels as powerless, yet determined, as we do?" Helen wondered aloud to herself rather than to her husband directly.

"Don't forget tired and drained, honey. I need to get sleep, baby, I'm sorry. I know you're worried beyond comprehension. But can we continue this in the morning?" Sam said through a yawn.

"Yah, sure. I'm beat too. I love you!" Helen turned toward the window. "I love you, Marsha—sweetheart."

"Come here—babe—so I can hold you and you'll fall asleep!" Sam held his arms open to his wife.

"Thanks, honey—I love you—good night."

"Good night, honey."

Sam and Helen fell asleep cradled like spoons. It was no wonder they fell asleep almost immediately, considering their anxieties about their only child. Would they have the strength and energy to care for Marsha at home? How would their lives change? What changes were awaiting the Walsch's? Both parents needed each other for strength and comfort.

XI. Challenges: For One And All

Marsha continued making progress and the day of her release from St. Francis Hospital was here.

"Sam, did you grab the pillows in the laundry? They'll act as bolsters in the back seat for support, remember?"

"Got 'em, Helen," Sam called from the open front door as he tried to go out to start the car so that it would be nice and warm for his wife. Sam quickly started the car and dashed back in through the nippy December air.

"And the little bag with her pretty clothes to wear home?"

"Yup."

"Great, I'll be there in a minute. Let me just grab the welcome home teddy bear," called Helen, with her anticipation rising.

"OK, I've got the car running."

"I'm coming. I'm coming... Here I am," Helen almost sang.

"Let's go get her, honey! Let's get our angel, our little girl, our beautiful Christmas angel," Papa sang. He was looking forward to having Marsha home again and he couldn't wait to see her reaction to Santa, the Christmas tree, the Christmas lights, and her presents.

"Sam, do you think she knows? I mean, that she's coming home today?" Helen asked as she settled into her seat and fastened her seat belt.

"She must, we've been talking about it for days," Sam said as he put the car in reverse and started to back out of the driveway.

"You think she's excited?"

"I would think so. Remember how she wanted to stay with us at Thanksgiving and how she cried, all the way back to the hospital?" Sam reminded his wife.

"Only this time she'll stay. I'm not sure she can possibly have the concept of forever. I don't think she knows she's staying here this time," Helen's smile stretched from ear to ear.

"Yah, I guess that would be pretty hard to imagine. Just think, Marsha will be in her own bed again tonight and we'll be able to see her every morning for breakfast and can read her bedtime stories again. This house will have life to it again, after months of quiet."

"I know, baby. It's wonderful," said Sam with a sigh of relief.

"Uh—huh," agreed Mama, with tears escaping.

"Don't cry, honey! It'll all be OK! Everything will be fine, in time. Remember, with Marsha's strength and ours we'll make it happen, together," Sam soothed as the car rolled slowly into the hospital parking lot.

"Sorry. These are really happy tears. Oh Sam, I am finally happy again!" Helen smiled and cried at the same time.

"Why does it have to be so crowded here this morning?" he questioned as he drove around and around for a parking space.

"There's one, and you'll bring the car round to the entrance to get us anyway," Helen reminded absentmindedly.

"Yah, OK!" Sam said as he pulled into a spot near the back of the parking lot.

"Bag, Teddy, purse. OK, let's go," Helen joked to lighten the mood as she got out of the car.

Sam joked back as he joined his wife in the lobby, "Our sanity? Check! OK, let's get our angel, honey."

Walking through the hospital lobby felt different this morning. Maybe the realization this would be the last time, except for the occasional appointment, brought feelings of relief and exhilaration. The knowledge of their coming hardships in caring for their daughter did not come to mind as Helen and Sam eagerly made their way to room 24 in the pediatric ward.

"How's our angel this morning?" asked Papa as he spied his little angel in the hospital bed.

"Pa-pa! Hi," Marsha smiled brightly.

"Do you know what today is?" Mama asked as she gave Marsha a gentle hug.

"Ma-ma," Marsha smiled at her mama and the cute teddy bear she was carrying.

"Today you get to come home, little lady, sweetheart. Isn't that wonderful? Are you excited?" Sam said as he pulled a chair next to Marsha's bed.

"W-is Ma-ma n Pa-pa?" Marsha struggled with the words, but managed.

"Yes, baby," responded Helen, trying to keep her composure. She just wanted to grab her little Marsha, hug her, and never let her go. Helen was so filled with emotion at the realization that this marked the end of a continual hospital stay for Marsha.

"I'll go see when she'll be discharged," said Sam, as he had the same thought run through his mind.

"OK. Look, sweetie, Mama brought you a special bear to take you home," and Helen placed it snugly next to Marsha.

"S-an-ks, Ma—," and Helen sat beside her and marveled at how far she had come. After not knowing if Marsha would ever wake up, after overcoming the odds of speech, movement, and so much more, Marsha was really coming home. How incredible. It is truly a miracle, Helen thought again, and knew that these thoughts would be with her forever.

"Marsha will be discharged later this morning. They've started the paperwork already and I've made sure that we get all the records, or at least a copy of them," exclaimed Sam excitedly as he walked over to Helen's side to help gather Marsha's things.

"They'll just give them to us?" Helen questioned.

"We'll have to go to the records department to get them and that should be it," Sam replied.

"Oh, Sam, I can't believe we've come so far!" Helen was smiling from ear to ear.

"I know what you mean," Sam smiled back at his wife.

"P.T. has left instructions for Marsha's continued therapy and they want her to get outside P.T. a minimum of three times a week. You have an appointment with Dr. Hanks, at his office, in three weeks and Dr. Davis would like to see her back for a check up in a month," instructed Abby enthusiastically, yet inside she knew she would miss Marsha. She wrote all of the information on the discharge papers, as was standard procedure, and to assist the Walsch's remember all of the things that needed to be done.

"Sounds like you're going to be a busy little lady, sweetheart," interjected Helen, admiring her daughter and still marveling at the fact they would be leaving the hospital for good in a few hours.

"I sure will miss your daughter," said Abby. "I've enjoyed being her nurse. She's a special little girl and lucky to have such devoted parents. Take care of yourselves. And whenever possible, let us know about Marsha's progress."

"Abby, thank you for everything, for your help," said Helen, smiling. Her tired face had a shine this morning. "I think we should let Marsha rest awhile. We can go get the records and we'll be one step ahead," she suggested to her husband.

"Oh, Mrs. Walsch, they won't be downstairs until Marsha's discharged."

"Oh, OK. Then we'll, we'll just go get a cup of coffee."

"How about some lunch? Will Marsha get lunch?" questioned Sam, concerned.

"Yes sir. One last meal of hospital food for you," Abby teased Marsha as she left the room.

"OK, we'll be back in awhile, honey. You get some rest before lunch and then we'll go home," Sam said as they left the room.

"Everything takes so long, Sam. I thought we'd be home for lunch and could go for a walk this afternoon," Helen was saddened by this little setback.

"Maybe I can call the office and stay home an extra day so I can spend it with my ladies tomorrow."

"Oh yes! That'd be nice. Marsha would be happy, I'm sure, and Bob and Liz are coming in the next day," Helen sighed at all of the work that lay ahead, and the realization that she couldn't just spend time with Marsha all day.

"The Christmas holidays will certainly be hectic this year, Helen. I really do want to give Marsha the opportunity to see the festivities. Even if she doesn't understand completely."

"Yah, I know, me too. But remember we have to watch, not to ove- tax her."

"Yes, I know. At least Santa at the mall and maybe drive around the neighborhood and see the Christmas lights should be fine. What do you think?"

"I guess that's OK. We'll just have to watch her closely, and it'll be so nice to have an extra pair of hands over the holidays while Bob and Liz are here."

"Sweetheart, I'm sorry. I know you're gonna have your hands full with Marsha's care and all. I'll do whatever I can to help. You know that, right?"

Helen walked over to her husband and put her arms around him, "I know our life will be busier and more strenuous from now on, but I'm just so glad our little girl is coming home. Marsha's recuperating. She'll make big strides, Sam. You'll see. And we'll be OK!" Helen was doing the best to reassure herself.

"Yes, Marsha is definitely our little miracle!" gasped Sam and hugged Helen who slumped in his arms somewhat and shed a tear of relief and thanks.

"Oh Sam, do you realize how fortunate we are? I feel like the luckiest mother on earth. Our child survived. She is making progress, and now our baby will be home!"

"I know, honey, shhhh, it's OK, and Marsha will overcome the difficulties she still has to face. We'll get through it, together. Now shhhh, cry your tears of joy. It's OK."

"B-b-but she has such extreme difficulties to overcome, honey. A-and I still feel such pain for her—I mean she's come so far, but..."

"I know, babe—but she'll make it. One day at a time. Now let's get her and go home, at last."

The happy couple left the cafeteria for the last time, hand in hand. They went joyfully to their little girl's room to help with lunch and start taking items to the car. In what seemed like no time, Helen was following the wheelchair to the front entrance where Sam had the car waiting for them to take his family home.

"Sam, let me sit with her in back so she'll feel more comfortable in the car. Is that OK, honey?" Helen looked at Marsha who nodded as her Mother sat behind her for physical and emotional support.

"Ya, Ma-ma. Pa—d-i fa-a-st—."

"Does that bother you, Marsha? I mean how Papa is driving?" Helen asked, worried at what Marsha was attempting to say.

"Ma-ma—pe-se," Marsha leaned into her Mother's

side as she felt the loving arms encircle her to protect her from her fears.

"I got you, sweetie. It's OK. Don't be scared. It only seems like Papa's driving fast. We'll be home soon. Just let Mama hold you!" Helen looked at her husband's eyes in the rear view mirror and they both understood how simple things, things taken for granted, were traumatic for Marsha.

"I'm going the speed limit. I can't go much slower on this highway, Helen."

"Don't worry, I have my arms around her and she's not going anywhere," Helen said into Marsha's hair as she kissed the top of her daughter's head for support and comforting. I suppose the motions of the car are upsetting her equilibrium.

"You just hang in there, angel, Papa's gonna get us home, OK?"

"O-K, Pa-pa," Marsha said with her eyes closed and snuggled as close to her mother as she could manage.

The drive home was without further incident. Sam secretly said a prayer that he wouldn't have to make that trip again, except on rare occasions. I can't bear seeing Marsha in desperation like that, he thought to himself. To distract Marsha, once Sam got into the residential area, he slowed the car almost to a crawl and pointed out the Christmas decorations fronting most homes.

"This is the perfect homecoming for Marsha," Sam declared to Helen. "Everyone is celebrating the birth of Christ and we are bringing our angel home for good."

"Marsha, honey, Santa will be arriving to leave you presents under our pretty Christmas tree," Helen explained. "You are Mama and Papa's Christmas present this year and Uncle Bob's and Aunt Liz's, too."

Helen took every opportunity to explain different Christmas characters and decorations.

"That's it, honey, this is Christmas time," she soothed.

Before she knew it, Sam was pulling into the driveway, and Helen had to let go of her little girl. She just then realized that she was holding her little girl in her arms for the entire trip. She had been wanting to do that for so long, and now it was over. Oh, well, she thought to herself, now that Marsha's home for good, I will have plenty of opportunities to hold my baby. Sam put the car in park and turned off the engine. He got out and opened Helen's door for her.

"Now, let's get you out of this car, little lady, and to your wheelchair. One, two, three, and here we go—good job. Now that wasn't so bad, was it?"

"Pa-pa, I h-um?" Marsha struggled to ask.

"Yes you are, princess, and this time you're home for good. You don't have to go back to the hospital anymore," Sam stated, then secretly wished he hadn't because Marsha would have to go back for her surgery in a few weeks. Too late now, he thought, we'll have to cross that bridge when we come to it.

"I think she's happy, Sam!" Helen looked on as her daughter was smiling from ear to ear.

"Help me get the wheelchair up these stairs, Helen," Sam grunted.

"OK, and then I've got to start dinner, and can you throw in laundry and watch Marsha so I can go grocery shopping?" Helen asked as she realized the rat race had begun.

Another day went by and Helen and Sam marveled at the strides Marsha had made, the progress she had made since she first woke up. Even though Marsha obviously still required constant help and supervision, she started showing signs of independence.

"Little lady, I don't know where you get your strength from," and Sam and Helen helped their daughter into bed for the night, after another long and exhausting day. "We should really turn in ourselves," yawned Sam. "It's more of the same tomorrow."

"Oh Sam, I have a feeling something special will happen soon," and Sam's wife put her arms around him. "But yes, I agree, we should go to bed."

"Sweetheart?"

"Yes, Sam?"

"I love you, and Marsha's going to be OK," and he hugged her and they both fell fast asleep, cradled like spoons.

"Mama, Mama—I can do it—I can walk—look."

Marsha's crutches were floating away and Marsha was walking, first slowly, one step, then two, then three. She was balancing all by herself.

"Look, Mama—no crutches, no crutches, Mama!"

Her walk started shaky and Helen moved to help Marsha.

Marsha screeched, "No—I can d- do it," and Helen held herself back.

Pained beyond what she thought she could bear, Mama watched her little girl struggle. Then, all of a sudden, her equilibrium improved. It was not instant, but slow motion until it was normal.

"Marsha!! My baby!! Look at you!!" Helen saw the transformation of her daughter's recovery before her. "It's a miracle. Oh my God, it's a miracle," and Marsha ran into her mother's arms as if her injuries had never been there.

"Mama, I love you," she cried, arms around her mother.

Helen instinctively hugged what was in her grasp, her husband, and woke up with a start. "Oh, honey," she mumbled as she realized it was a dream, and soon returned to sleep and dream a second time.

Unknown to Helen, her husband was dreaming with her, the same message, at the same time.

"You need to encourage your little one as much as possible the next couple days. Marsha's doing the very best she can. She's looking for praise to keep her going, Sam."

"Praise? That's nonsense! She knows we're proud of her accomplishments!"

"Listen to me. Marsha wants confirmation from you she's doing well. Her conscious zest for life is in direct correlation with the praise and encouragement she

receives from you and her inner voice. By the way, that's me, Brisa."

"OK, OK, I'll do whatever you say, whatever is in my power to help Marsha."

"Oh, another thing, just so you're aware. Marsha will be exposed to negative outside pressure, and you need to stand by your daughter and explain why the world is the way it is."

"I don't understand what you mean?"

"Marsha will experience undesirable, obnoxious, offensive harassment, and sometimes you won't even know it. She'll be crushed at something, anything directed at her, because she is handicapped. That's what I mean, it's a cruel world, and you need to be cognizant of that fact."

"Like teasing?"

"Yes, like teasing, and Marsha is bound to get lots of it, throughout her life."

Brisa floated into thin air, out of the dream both Sam and Helen just experienced simultaneously.

Sam stretched and reached next to him for his wife but she wasn't in their bed anymore. The realization startled him momentarily, but then he smelled the aroma of coffee permeating the air from downstairs. Sam kicked off the covers, made his way to the bathroom and, in his robe, strode down to Marsha's room.

"Good morning, princess, what do you say we surprise Mama for breakfast?" Marsha beamed up at her father and stretched out her little hand.

Sam picked Marsha up into his strong arms and she nuzzled into his broad chest.

Helen let out a soft gasp as she turned and saw Marsha and Sam in the doorway.

Papa placed her into their breakfast nook. Papa seated himself next to her.

"I am making French toast," informed Helen, and hurried back to her post. "I'll be with you shortly, with the French toast," she teased.

As she stood there, preparing and cooking one of

Marsha's favorites, Helen's mind wandered, could my dream have had meaning to what happened here this morning?

"Helen? Helen, I think I smell something burning," shouted Sam.

Brought back to reality, Helen stood erect with a start. "I guess maybe Sam's right and everything will work out," she mumbled to herself. "God, I hope so!" she breathed silently as she placed the slightly crisp French toast on their plates. "Here we go. They're not that bad, only a tiny bit crisp."

"Just right, honey, not soggy," encouraged Sam with a mouth full.

"Mmmm—Ma-ma, go-o-d," replied Marsha, licking her lips.

Helen delighted in seeing her little girl enjoying her meals again. She realized that the sense of taste is also a function of the brain, and it was obviously returning, bringing evidence of further recovery.

"Oh, sweetheart, enjoy your French toast. Can I make you more?"

"N-o, Ma-ma."

"OK, honey, eat as much as you want and we'll decorate for Christmas after breakfast," encouraged Helen and smiled at her husband with heart felt satisfaction.

Sam detected a new hint of determination in his wife's composure, "Yah, good idea, and maybe I'll start putting up the Christmas tree."

"That would be great. Marsha can watch you while I go to the store this afternoon."

The couple tried to coordinate daily activities between the two of them as much as possible to ensure their daughter would never be alone.

"OK, and after she's asleep we can decorate the tree."

"Yah, if we still have energy. I'm glad you'll be here tomorrow because I still have so much to do before Bob and Liz get here," sighed Helen.

"You don't have to have everything perfect. They

understand, honey, really! We knew this wouldn't be easy, right? You're doing your best and that's all you can do!"

"Yah, I remember—, I know," Helen sighed, because she wanted everything to be perfect for the holidays, and their guests, but knew that it couldn't be, before zipping her jacket to battle the winter elements.

"Please be careful," Sam cautioned his wife, because the snow was starting to fall. "The roads may get slick."

"I'll hurry back and I'll be careful," Helen answered as she was halfway out the door.

"OK, Marsha, Papa's gonna put the laundry in the washer. I'll be right back. Wait here!" Sam said as he checked that Marsha could not fall and get hurt before leaving the room for the moment.

"O-K, Pa-pa," Marsha said as her Papa left the room. She then looked around that the somewhat familiar surroundings.

"Brisa, are you there?"

"Yes.

"Look at all these things around here. This is much more interesting than that hospital room. Look at all the pictures. In that one stuff is moving and look, little thingies are flying in and out."

"That's a picture window and the wind is blowing through the tree branches. Those are birds flying around the tree."

"Oh—, will that picture, I mean window, always move?"

"Yes, and behind that window is outside. Remember how you and your mama used to play in the garden and you picked flowers for her. Papa saw you doing that through that window."

"OK. I think I remember."

"See, you're remembering and that's good. You're making progress."

"Will I play outside with Mama again?"

"I think so. You just need to stay focused on getting better and keep doing your exercises. The harder you work on your exercises, the sooner you'll be up and

around. But remember, you need to be patient. Your recovery will be little by little."

"You mean, it's gonna take a long time?"

"Yes, I'm afraid it will. But the harder you work, the faster you will recover. Always remember to be patient."

"I'll do my best and try not to get mad."

"Hey, Marsha, what do you think if we surprise Mama and have the Christmas tree up when she gets back from the store?" Sam questioned his daydreaming daughter.

"Yah—OK," Marsha replied, and gave Papa her full attention from the love seat Sam situated her in before. Marsha hadn't moved. She was snuggled in an almost fetal position with her little scarred head on its wide armrest.

"Here we go. Let's move the chair over here so you can watch Papa," as Sam effortlessly positioned their love seat to where he would be placing their Christmas tree.

"Oh Pa-pa—o b-b-ig," and Marsha's eyes opened wide with excitement and anticipation.

"Yah, it's big all right and heavy, too. Wait until we put lights and decorations on it—and put an angel at the top. It's gonna be beautiful, baby—just like you!" Sam smiled at his Christmas angel.

All Marsha said was "Papa," but Sam thought he saw a little twinkle, previously not there, in Marsha's puffy, tired, blue eyes. He thought he saw a little excitement building in his daughter's physique. Oh, how Sam wished the power of Christmas could bring happiness to his little girl, his own special little angel. I will do what I can to make you happy, he thought, as he twisted the tree to get the best side forward.

"Hello—I'm home," said Mama as she passed through the living room with a bunch of groceries. "Well, well—the tree looks exceptional. Is Marsha OK?"

"She's here watching me. We've been having fun, haven't we, honey?" Sam inquired as he looked at his tired little girl.

"Yah..." Marsha said with a yawn.

"That's great. Why don't you take a little nap, sweetheart? I think you might need one before dinner is ready. Afterwards maybe we can finish some decorating."

Sam nodded and started carrying Marsha to her room. He put her in the little bed and adjusted the side railings. Before he was finished, Marsha was asleep.

Helen called to her husband as he left Marsha's room. "Would you like to me make a fresh pot of coffee and get out some cookies for us? Marsha can have some cookies and milk when she wakes up, or for dessert."

"That sounds wonderful, honey. I'll string up the lights in the meantime."

"Sounds like a plan," sang Helen doing her best to bring the most Christmas spirit and cheer out for Marsha's sake.

A little later, Marsha joined them.

"OK, princess, why don't you hold some tinsel. Let me drape it across your arm, then I'll take it, and put it on the tree. Mama can put the box of ornaments in your lap," instructed Marsha's father. He and Helen were having fun watching as their daughter enjoyed watching them. She was thriving on the participation.

"Just to be in the midst of what we're doing is brightening her spirits I think, Sam. Look at her," and Marsha beamed, gazing at the lighted Christmas tree and watching intently as her mother and father covered it with ornaments. "Marsha's thriving on feeling useful, Sam," Helen whispered in Sam's ear. "Baby, can you open your fist and let me put it in your hand—? That's it—Look, Sam she's opening her hand a little."

"Angel, that's wonderful. Steady now—it's OK!" Sam instructed his daughter.

"Look how she's concentrating—how she's focusing, trying so hard," Helen whispered excitedly, almost in tears. Her heart was pounding rapidly. "It's the first time I've seen her do that, Sam! How about you?"

"Yup, she's fighting all right, and she'll continue recovering if we continue our love and devotion to her. Just look how far she's come, the steps she's taken since she was home at Thanksgiving, even though they're minuscule."

"How can she not keep flourishing with the attention we're giving her, Sam? Good for you, sweetheart—," and Helen hugged the little girl, who welcomed the affection, like always.

"You are doing terrific, sweetheart. They're huge steps for you, honey, and you're going to continue making progress, aren't you? You're happy and comfortable here, right, baby?" Helen said as she hugged her little girl again, with a feeling of even more love and appreciation.

"Yah, Ma-ma," Marsha answered, not really sure what all the fuss was about.

The evening of togetherness passed quickly. The family enjoyed their time together, decorating their Christmas tree for a Christmas that only weeks earlier they were not sure they would spend with their daughter.

"Let's get our angel ready for bed and we can read *The Night Before Christmas* together," Helen said, watching Marsha yawn for a second time.

"I'll be there in a minute, just a few more decorations for the tree," Sam protested playfully. "I'll help you in a minute, Helen. OK, up we go."

Sam carried his little girl with Helen following in tow.

"Sleeping Beauty tonight?" inquired Marsha's mother from her dresser.

"Aha—" Marsha nodded and let her Mother drape the white, pink, and light blue nightgown over her head and little body.

"'Twas the night before Christmas. And all through the house. Not a creature was stirring. Not even a mou—. Look Helen, she's already asleep. The evening excitement must have really tired our little angel out," commented Sam, lovingly, and with some concern. "I hope it wasn't too much for her."

"Oh, I think it's a natural tired. We didn't, or rather, she didn't, do much and she did take a nap. Just her being out of bed is hard work for her, I imagine, and she's still taking in her new surroundings. Decorating our tree was the only thing she actively participated in today, the only thing that was more strenuous," explained Helen as she yawned herself.

After straightening boxes from the decorations distributed throughout the house, largely for Marsha's benefit, Sam and Helen retired for the evening. Tomorrow was going to be another busy, but wonderful, day. They needed all the rest they could get.

"Don't forget her accomplishing to open her fist a bit. That was wonderful!" Sam smiled. "Did you catch the expression on her face? I think she was surprised and even amazed herself."

"Yes! I can understand how delightful it is to do something you've not been able to for so long. I mean, for her it's like a miracle. Oh Sam, hold me, I'm so overwhelmed with what's happening and everything ahead of us."

"I know, baby, we'll get through it, one day at a time," consoled Sam and before he put his arm around her for comfort, Helen was asleep. Sam wondered how he could be so lucky to have such a devoted wife. Helen is doing everything she possibly can to keep Marsha and our family together and happy.

Helen stirred, heard birds chirping outside their bedroom window, looked at the alarm clock and moaned, "I swear we just fell asleep."

"I'm with you. I could sleep for a week," Sam moaned in answer.

"Can't do that today. Bob and Liz are coming."

"Oh, yah," Sam moaned again.

"OK, on the count of three we'll both get up."

"No, wait. I'll check on Marsha on the way down to get coffee. Stay in bed and I'll be right back. We have a long day ahead of us and we deserve this."

"You mean a few minutes together, in bed, and with a cup of coffee?"

"Yah, just you and me—before another storm."

"Oh honey, you're so wonderful, thank you," Helen said sweetly and beamed at her loving husband.

"Rise and shine, my sweet—. Mama's got breakfast

waiting and Uncle Bob and Aunt Liz are coming today," Papa said as he gave his little angel a kiss on her forehead. Marsha's still sleepy eyes focused to the brightness of the early morning sun shining through her bedroom window.

"Ooo, Pa, I t-id," Marsha closed her eyes and turned her face from the sun coming in the window.

"You can't still be tired. It's Christmas Eve and we are going to visit Santa today. Let's wash that sleepiness right out of your eyes and start our busy day," Sam said as he got his daughter's clothes from the dresser.

"O-K, Pa-pa!" Marsha said, opening her eyes and watching her papa pick out a pair of pants and a warm pullover sweatshirt.

"Wait, we need fresh underwear, an undershirt, and socks, don't we, honey?" Marsha nodded slowly. She was unsure about all the commotion she had to endure, all the new sights and sounds and movements of home. On the other hand, every day new adventures and Marsha's thirst for comprehension, although she had frequent problems with headaches. She was apparently on information overload. Her little mind couldn't handle all the new information at once. Marsha needed time and repetition to grasp and understand her surroundings.

"Brisa, watch Papa. He's going to get me ready for another busy day. I want to help with everything and listen to Mama and Papa, but everything gets to be so much. My head hurts and I get so tired, Brisa."

"I know, Marsha, it's something you'll have to deal with for a long time, I'm afraid. But like everything else, the more you try, the better it will get, and the faster too. Your mom and dad know this and work with you to teach you as much as they can. They also realize what a toll the learning process is for you, and comfort you to make it a bit easier to handle."

"Is that why Mama puts me to bed, Brisa?"

"Yes, dear, you get sleepy easily, and naps help your headaches, don't they?"

"Yes. Oh, and you mean the more I use my mind and

try to talk and do things, the quicker I'll get better?"

"That's right."

"Here we go, little lady, now how about starting this Christmas Eve off with the nice breakfast that I'm sure Mama has waiting for us downstairs?"

The Walsch's were like any young busy family over the holidays, except they had a severely handicapped child. There were many things to do and preparations to make. But Sam and Helen wanted to make the most of this holiday for their little girl.

"Oh Sam, do you remember last Christmas, Marsha's excitement when she saw the Christmas tree all lit up? Remember her first two dolls and how she played with them for hours?" Helen said as she watched Marsha look at the tree from the love seat.

"Yes, I don't think we heard another word out of her until she almost fell asleep. I wonder if she'll like the doll house we bought her for Christmas. I'll put it right in front of the fireplace, on the hearth, so she can lay or sit in front of it to play."

Sam and Helen found themselves consciously and unconsciously rearranging their lives to best accommodate their daughter.

"Maybe we can find a sofa for the doll house at the mall. I sewed a pretty little blanket with matching cushions for the living room," and Sam felt his wife's dedication for making their little girl as happy as she possibly could.

Later that morning, they proudly wheeled Marsha through the mall, and relished in the smile that became broader and broader on her face. The place was decorated to the rafters for the holidays and Helen could only imagine how magical it felt to Marsha. She imagined Marsha couldn't remember past Christmases.

"What an impact this must be making," she whispered to Sam, "this winter wonderland, with all its miniature animals and characters."

They went towards the Santa train ride and Helen pointed out all the characters and decorations.

"Look at Santa's train. See the little elves. Those are Santa's helpers. They make all the presents for all the good little boys and girls. Would you like to ride the train, honey?" Marsha, mesmerized, nodded her little blonde head.

Sam spoke to the person in charge of the Santa's train and waved to his wife to proceed to the front of the line, and special care was taken to remove Marsha from her wheelchair and into a secured train seat.

"OK, here we go. You're all strapped in and safe," Sam said after double-checking the safety harness.

The little train started to move and Mama watched closely. Marsha started screaming. Papa ran to the man at the train's control bellowing, "Stop! Stop! Stop that train!"

Immediately the train stopped, and Mama ran to Marsha's side. She sobbed in her mother's outstretched arms, and Sam gently took her in his arms and eventually, after consoling, placed her back into her wheelchair.

"What happened, honey? What's wrong?" Helen soothed her scared baby girl.

All little Marsha could do was shake and cry more.

"I suppose the motion scared her. We should have realized her equilibrium couldn't handle it yet. I'm so sorry, angel," Sam said beside Helen, who squatted and hugged their little princess to comfort her.

"Sweetheart, it's OK. Mama and Papa didn't realize, sssssshhhhh, it's OK, baby. It's all over now. You're safe."

"Mama's right, It's OK now, princess. You're safe."

"I think we should probably go home and come back to see Santa later maybe, if she's up for it. She's too traumatized now to do anything, don't you think?" said Helen with Marsha nuzzled, still in her arms.

"Yah, you're probably right. Marsha, honey, we'll get some play dough we can play with, you and me. OK, honey?" Papa Sam said to take his daughter's mind off of the scare she just experienced.

Tears still not completely gone, Marsha just sat there, confused.

"Sweetheart, I'm sorry. We didn't know," soothed Mama. "Baby, we didn't think. It's OK," Mama said, taking her small, trembling hand and gently caressing it.

When they pulled into the driveway at home, Helen peered in the back seat at Marsha hunched over, sleeping with her seat belt around her. "Oh dear, that looks uncomfortable. How are we going to get her out without waking her?"

"I'll carry her to her room if you can kinda help me maneuver her out of the back seat."

Sam and Helen gently moved the fragile, sleeping bundle from the car.

Sam carried the little sleeper as Helen hurried ahead to unlock the door. "OK, here we go."

After Sam came back from Marsha's bedroom, Mama had made some coffee and was sitting at their kitchen table, a bit disturbed.

"What a morning, huh? I can't believe that happened. We should've known better, Sam."

"I know, Helen, but we're new at this and I guess we're going to make mistakes, but she's all right, not hurt at all, just scared, and now we know. There's nothing else we can do."

"Is she still sleeping?"

"Yes."

"OK, let me start some of the cooking and finish cleaning."

"Yah, and I'll finish the bills and get some firewood. Doesn't Bob and Liz's plane get in at three?"

"That's what you told me."

"Then I had better hurry."

Time flew and soon Sam kissed his wife before heading for the airport. Holiday traffic and last minute shoppers made the drive a nightmare and he was late. Bob and Liz saw him before he saw them as he hurried through baggage claim to their luggage carousel.

"Hey, young man," bellowed Uncle Bob at his worn nephew.

"Good to see you. I thought I'd never make it," Sam said as he hugged Liz hello.

"Oh, after what you've been through I'm sure you can do anything," Bob said as he extended a comforting arm around his nephew's shoulder.

"OK, let's go, because I have no idea how long it's gonna take to get back, and with rush hour starting soon, it'll get even worse," said Sam.

On the drive home Bob and Liz tried to get an idea of life at the Walsch's since Marsha came home. They asked lots of questions and Sam tried to provide as much information as possible. No matter what, they weren't sure that they were properly prepared for what they were about to face.

"How's Helen holding up? I'm sure it's been very hard on her. She's so devoted to that child," praised Liz.

"She's coping—best she can—wonderful, actually. I really have to give her credit. The doctor told us Marsha's progress is due a lot to the attention she's been getting. We've given her all the help we could from the start and that's giving her a good possibility for recovery."

"Oh thank God, that's wonderful," said Bob and Liz in unison.

The three made their way to the Walsch's and Uncle Bob and Aunt Liz wanted to know everything about their great-niece.

"If there's anything we can do, we'll do it, you can count on us," said Bob, "you should know that already. Dr. Hanks was a friend of an acquaintance and his book on reconstructive surgery is just amazing, and that's what prompted me to tell you about him. "

"Thanks, Bob, it means a lot. We're so unsure of the future, the help Marsha will need for therapy, school, everything!"

"Yah, that's a scary thought," Liz agreed.

"Whatever it is, it doesn't matter, we'll help!" Bob announced again.

"Well, here we are," and Sam pulled into the driveway and parked in the garage. It was dusk and the Christmas tree lights in the picture window sent a glow outside. Liz gasped at the spectacle. "Oh, how beautiful!"

"Where's my favorite niece?" Uncle Bob called playfully but quietly as he made his way into the house with bags and presents. "Oh, baby, there you are. Look at you," he gasped, trying his best to mask the pain he felt as his niece came into view.

Uncle Bob dropped his load and quickly embraced the frail, quivering being, so pitiful in front of him.

"Oh, sweetheart, my sweet, let me hold my little favorite doll," came Aunt Liz's voice as she hugged the child and tears welled from her eyes. "Oh baby, Auntie Liz has missed you so!"

Mama joined the joyous, yet painfully emotional reunion of the triad and couldn't help shedding a tear herself. She watched as her daughter, obviously laboriously and painfully, tried returning her dear Aunt's hug and put her head on her shoulder and yes, those were tears Mama saw in Marsha's eyes.

"Sam, look, Marsha's crying. She's showing emotion. This was a sign of improvement the doctor had said. Any further development of emotion is improvement, he said."

Sam rushed to his distraught wife's side, held her and watched, with increasing distress, at the poignant site before them. "It's OK, honey. It's OK," is all he could manage to say as he struggled with his composure.

How can I keep it all together? How a-am I gonna handle the struggle? he thought, feeling a dull pounding headache coming on once again.

"It's a nightmare seeing her like this," Sam muttered softly under his breath.

"Yah, and it's wonderful to know she's improved so much already!" Helen whispered back.

"Yes, we'll make it. She'll make it."

"She's fighting, Sam," and tears streamed down Helen's face. She was so tired, stressed, and helpless.

"I know and look how marvelously she's responding to Bob and Liz."

"They were always her favorite, remember?"

"Yah!" Sam nodded.

"I'm so glad they're here for a few days. Maybe it'll do Marsha good, get her out of her shell, you know."

"A change of pace for us, too."

"Hey, sport, how about going for a walk around the neighborhood with your favorite aunt and uncle, if that's OK with your mom and dad?" Bob said before taking his coat off. The fresh air will do her good.

"Fine, I'll get her wheelchair," Sam said.

"Her coat and a blanket are in the closet by the front door. Liz, can you get them?" Helen asked, glad to have help for a few days.

"Sure will, Helen," Liz said, already heading for the closet.

"I'll put the finishing touches on dinner."

"Sounds good. We'll be back in a bit."

Sam carried Marsha outside and placed her in the wheelchair that Bob had carried out. Liz gently placed a warm blanket over her lap and pulled one corner up over her chest so that no drafts could sneak in. Once everything seemed in order, Sam went back inside and left his daughter in Bob and Liz's care.

"OK, little one. How about I pretend to be Santa and you be Rudolf and guide me through the neighborhood?" Uncle Bob asked as they started down the driveway.

"Re-dd no-ssse—," Marsha stated as best she could.

"Yes, I suppose so. Rudolf had a red nose," Uncle Bob thought out loud as he slowly pushed the wheelchair.

"Here, Marsha, I'll put some of my red lipstick on your nose," offered Aunt Liz.

"There—now you look like Rudolf," exclaimed Uncle Bob out loud and started singing *Rudolf The Red Nose Reindeer* as he carefully pushed Marsha's wheelchair onto the sidewalk and down the snow-dusted street.

"Oh honey, look at that Santa and his eight reindeer over there," said Aunt Liz excitedly, pointing towards one of the neighbor's houses. "Everything looks so much more magical when it's snowing, don't you think, Bob?"

"I'm not Bob, I'm Santa," retorted Bob in a hoarse voice.

"Oh! Sorry, Santa!" Liz giggled to lighten the mood.

"I re-e-d-ee," Marsha interjected with slight emotion in her voice, obviously enjoying their play. Liz had no idea the importance of the slight outburst, but decided it might be just that.

"And you're the best reindeer Santa has," Uncle Bob assured her.

They walked in silence for a bit and Marsha gazed, in amazement, at all the Christmas lights on and around the houses. She watched, mesmerized, as the snowflakes fell onto her jacket. First Bob and Liz observed as Marsha stuck out her tongue to taste the white crystals. Then, laboriously, she moved her right arm to brush snow with her mitten-clad hand.

"Bob, did you see that? She's curious. Did you see her move? I can't wait to tell Helen and Sam," Liz said excitedly. She hoped that this was yet another step forward for her damaged niece.

"Yes, seeing Marsha move at all is a miracle and I'm sure we will see more miracles happen the next few days. I just have a feeling..." whispered Uncle Bob quietly, so as not to break the beautiful moment, the tranquility.

Keeping with German tradition, the Walsch's celebrated Christmas on Christmas Eve. After a special holiday dinner, gifts would be opened, and the families celebrated togetherness and their blessings. This evening would be no exception. Sam and Helen wanted this Christmas to be memorable, an extra special one, just for Marsha.

While the trio was out on their adventure, Helen and Sam worked franticly to finish last-minute details and get the presents under the tree. They wanted to tell Marsha that in her absence the Kriskind had appeared and left presents under the Christmas tree.

"Sam, can you set up Marsha's doll house at the fireplace and put the little furniture in it—and don't forget the little pillows I made. Just put them on the living room floor since we couldn't get a sofa at the toy store today."

"I'm working on it! I've got the sheet to put over it, too."

"Good—and I'm fixing a plate of Christmas cookies and treats. Maybe a few pillows so Marsha'll be comfortable lying in front of her new doll house," reminded Helen. Her head was spinning a bit, trying to remember everything. "I want everything to be perfect, a perfect Christmas for our angel!"

"Yah, honey, you're right, this'll probably be her favorite."

"I think so. Let me turn off the lights so the Christmas tree is the focus of attention," Helen said, turning off the overhead light and one of the table lamps.

"OK, come and sit a minute by the Christmas tree, honey. Relax and enjoy the little time we have, just you and me," Sam held his hand out to his tired wife.

"OK—thanks—I love you, Sam!" Helen was thinking of the many chores yet to do, but welcomed a minute to sit and put her feet up, be alone with her husband, the man she loved and cherished.

"I love you too, babe! We're gonna have a wonderful Christmas, you'll see," Sam said as he lovingly nuzzled his wife's neck.

Helen sat and enjoyed for a few minutes. Then she had a thought, "I know...let's put on some Christmas music. The 'jingle bells' album Marsha likes!"

"Good idea... and I think I hear Bob. They're singing Christmas carols. No wonder Marsha likes them so much. They're kids themselves, especially Bob!" Sam said as he went to the window to look out at the street.

"Yah, he certainly is. He does his best to amuse Marsha, make her smile and giggle," Helen said, putting the album on the phonograph player.

Bob pushed the wheelchair up to the front steps and effortlessly carried Marsha through the front door, leaving Liz to tend with her wheelchair.

"Hello! We're home! Sam, could you come help me

carry Marsha in?" Bob called from the front door. Sam was already halfway to the door to help.

Sam took Marsha from Bob at the front door and waited as Bob carried the wheelchair in. Liz was in charge of holding the door. It was a team effort, accomplished without a word, each fulfilling their duty.

"Marsha is the best Rudolf ever—you know. I think she should get the job permanently," Uncle Bob exclaimed to Sam as he put Marsha back in her wheelchair in the living room, and little Marsha beamed from ear to ear. She gazed at the lighted Christmas tree and the colorful presents underneath without a word.

"Look, honey," Helen exclaimed excitedly, yet quietly as she entered with the last of the serving trays for dinner. "Kriskind has been here and left you presents. Papa, let's seat Marsha over here so she can see the Christmas tree."

Sam moved Marsha's wheelchair to the position directly diagonal of the tree.

"Hey, sweetie, ready for some yummy roast and mashed potatoes? Your mama fixed some very good Christmas goodies," Uncle Bob said as he entered the room.

"Ooooo y-um!" answered Marsha, and Liz noticed her hand curling a little around her napkin.

"Oh, yes, smells wonderful," cooed Liz, following close behind as she pointed and mouthed the word look to Marsha's hand. Helen and Sam both heeded Liz's gesture and smiled happily.

"Did you have a nice walk, sweetie? Did you see Santa?" Papa asked his little angel.

"Li-ts, Pa-pa," Marsha said.

"I bet you saw lots of lights. Kriskind needs all those lights to see where she's going. Let's eat, honey, then we can open all the presents she left."

The sight of Marsha's hand gripping her napkin was a gift of itself and a totally unexpected one! Could the Christmas Angel have dropped some of her magic onto Marsha, their little angel?

"O-K, Pa-pa," Marsha nodded, and Sam thought he saw a twinkle in his daughter's eyes.

"Are you hungry?" Aunt Liz asked. "I sure am!"

"Mmmmmmm..." Marsha smiled and looked at the table full of yummy food.

"Bob, can you make sure the stops are down on Marsha's wheelchair so she doesn't move, and I'll fix her a plate. What would you like, dear? A little roast, potatoes, some cranberries 'n apples?" Helen asked, although she was serving everything anyway.

"Yah!" Marsha nodded.

"Thank you Father for this food and for letting us share this Christmas together," began Uncle Bob.

"And thank you Father for watching over our little Marsha," added Aunt Liz.

"Amen," they said together and, there was silence.

"OK, let's eat," Bob finally interrupted.

"Yes, please. Let's eat and enjoy," said Helen, ready for some good times.

"Here, honey, I'll help you. I'll cut everything up nice and small for you," Liz told Marsha as she served her niece.

Helen couldn't help but watch her little girl eat. Actually, then, Marsha pretty much couldn't even hold a spoon. Now, at least, she was able to hold the napkin. Oh, she had a tough time not helping her daughter. But she knew that Marsha had to do it on her own, at least for a while, until she gets frustrated. After a while Helen did ask, "Can I help you, sweetheart? Can Mama feed you?" and Marsha just kept concentrating on her chore at hand, oblivious to Mama's question.

"Helen, I'll help her," interjected Liz. "You go ahead and enjoy your meal. You've really been outdoing yourself...and this is really good. You need to eat before it all gets cold."

"Mmmmm, I agree, this is good," agreed Sam, and took a second helping of roast.

"Thanks, it's really nothing extravagant, really," Helen said, taking another bite.

"Oh, listen to you, with everything that's been going on, this is marvelous, Helen!" Liz teased and praised at the same time.

"I agree whole heartedly! Helen's amazing!" praised her husband.

As the family finished their meal, Uncle Bob spoke slowly and softly, "Well, little one, what do you think Kriskind brought you? Did you have any wishes for Christmas? Did you ask Kriskind for anything special?"

"Yah," Marsha nodded.

"What did you want Santa to bring you?" Uncle Bob asked, trying to get the little girl to answer with more than a nod. He was trying to get her to use her words. To practice speaking, like Sam had told him the doctors suggested.

"Do-l-l-ee," said Marsha.

It had worked. She said a new word. Helen and Sam smiled brightly at each other. The entire group then smiled at Marsha.

"Helen, I noticed on our walk earlier, Marsha's language skills and movement is improving," assured Liz. "What a Christmas gift that is!"

"Oh, I'm sure there's a baby doll under the Christmas tree. Let's go look, OK?" Uncle Bob said.

The little family went into the family room to enjoy the upcoming scene. Helen turned the table lamp back on so that they could all see Marsha's expressions.

"O-K," Marsha said, motioning with her arms to be picked up from her wheelchair. Sam and Helen, simultaneously, gazed at their daughter's apparent burst of energy and strength to propel her arms in a fashion communicating her desire.

"Here, sweetie, let Papa pick you up and we'll all sit around the pretty tree and you can open your presents."

Uncle Bob, Aunt Liz and Helen sat in a semicircle around Marsha, and Sam positioned himself behind his daughter, for support, so she wouldn't lose her balance.

"Sam, why don't we get a picture of the Christmas tree with the presents under it so Marsha can always remember this Christmas," Bob suggested.

"OK, maybe we'll take one of Marsha with her favorite gift, and that's all, because she really does still look so sick and I don't want memories of that. It's just too painful."

"Oh Sam, I'm sorry. I understand your pain. Please take one with our camera too, though," commented Uncle Bob. "Maybe we can get a few of her from behind, at least that won't show the scars, but will convey the Christmas magic."

"Good idea."

"Oh Pa-pa—" came Marsha's voice.

Obviously she was taken by the vibrant colors of wrapping paper, ribbons, and bows under the Christmas tree decorations and lights. Our tree must look very big to Marsha, suddenly flashed through Helen's mind. She didn't know why this would suddenly be a concern to her.

"Yes, baby, look at all these presents, and I think most of them are for you," Sam whispered in his daughter's ear.

There were teddy bears, dolls, and books wrapped and placed within reach of the little girl. Although they were wrapped, Helen had used the tape sparingly, so as to make the packages easier to open.

"Let me cut the ribbon and you can see if you can manage from there, sweetheart," said Mama as she sat back observing, with pain in her heart, watching as Marsha laboriously worked to unwrap her first present. Although she cherished every moment of her child's happiness, she cried inside. "What are we going to do? How will we go on? How can we make life bearable for Marsha…for all of us?" was all she could think at the moment.

"Ma-ma... bi on," brought Helen back to her senses and she smiled at her daughter lovingly.

"Ma-ma, bi on," repeated Marsha with more excitement.

"OK, honey, Mama's made a little bed for you in front of the big present. Sam, can you help me?"

"Oh, precious, here, let Uncle Bob get you. Let's all gather round while Marsha opens this one."

"Ooooo, hou-s bi…" Marsha said through a giant smile.

"Yes, honey, it's a doll house!" Helen said.

"Yah!" Marsha sighed and Mama, Sam, Uncle Bob and

Aunt Liz watched as little Marsha's eyes lit up in amazement and appreciation, and she strained herself to touch and handle the little dolls and furnishings.

"Baby, let me see if we can't position you a little better," said Sam, obviously also pained by the sight of his little girl's condition. "You go ahead and play, little one. I love you, baby," he said, almost in a whisper into Marsha's ear before turning and seeing Uncle Bob with both Helen and Liz on either side, shedding tears. He was sure these were tears of both joy and anguish. Everyone in this room, celebrating Christmas together, loved this little girl so very much. The four sat together, watching their little angel play before them.

Sam and Bob each took a couple of pictures of Marsha playing at the doll house. They carefully selected angles that showed her and the doll house, but didn't show her damaged leg or scars.

"At least she can have the memory of getting the doll house, without the memory of how bad she looked," Bob whispered to Sam as they finished the pictures.

"Ba-bee hun-gwy? O-K. Ma-ma fee yo. Na-p ti. Pa-pa p-se he-p," Marsha was playing with the mama, baby, and papa doll, as best she could. The four observers noticed Marsha's role-playing with her new dolls, lovingly and nurturing, as her parents did with her.

"Oh, Sam, look, look at her. Let's take another picture of our happy little girl, Sam. Even in her state, this will leave happy memories."

"Yes, I agree. She seems to be putting her challenges behind her, and just using her imagination, the one she's just recently started rebuilding. It's amazing, really!" and Sam positioned himself and clicked yet another picture of their entranced little girl.

"The doll house was the best idea we had, Sam," cooed Helen dreamily, and sat back and just observed again, and Aunt Liz and Uncle Bob nodded in agreement. There was complete silence amongst them as they watched and listened to Ella Fitzgerald singing *Silent Night*. Unknown to the grown-ups, there was another presence in the living room.

"Marsha—Marsha—do you notice you're doing better, your condition is improving? I've been fighting your injuries with you, you know? You're doing very well and everybody is very proud of you. Including me! Your mom is over there crying because she's so amazed at what you've done, your progress since your accident. Look at you. You couldn't curl your fingers, let alone pick up anything a month ago."

"Oh, Brisa, I'm so frustrated. Really. Although I'm happy, too. I mean, being home is the best, instead of in that hospital. And Mama and Papa are so nice to me. I feel so safe here, Brisa."

"You should, I mean, your mom and dad are gonna help you get better."

"How—, how're they gonna do that?"

"Well—think of how they've helped so far. They're not gonna give up on you. They'll work with you to get you better. It's gonna take a long time, remember? But they know that and they'll do what they can for you."

"Like when Papa plays ball with me?"

"Yah, like when he rolls the ball to you—and you'll get better and better, the more you practice."

"How long, Brisa? How long will I have to practice? How long will it take me to learn?"

"Oh Marsha, I can't answer that. It'll take years for your challenges to dwindle. That's all I know for sure. But you're strong and I know you can do this. You have the willpower. I know you do."

"You have lots of faith in me, Brisa."

"Of course I do, because I am your will and I know you're a survivor."

"OK, you're right. It's just so hard. I mean, I have to work so hard at everything, things that used to be so easy."

"I know, persistence pays, remember that, Marsha, and you'll go far."

"Yah, OK, I kinda got it now."

"That's a girl. Never give up, OK?"

"OK."

"Ou heer 'sat do-l-l-ee? Nev gi-ve up."

"Sam, did you hear what Marsha just said?" asked Helen excitedly. "She told her doll not to give up! Oh my God, did you see that? I'm amazed at Marsha's willpower."

Papa Sam, conversing with Liz and Bob, sat up with a start at the announcement. He was astonished, sat in silence, in amazement, continuing to watch his daughter play, hoping for a rerun of what he just missed. But Marsha continued playing in silence.

"I wonder how she got that concept, not to give up?"

"I am sorry we missed it, honey. It really is so hard to understand her sometimes. I'm glad you caught it, babe! But, my God, that's wonderful!"

"Oh, she's coming back. I'm telling you. Her play is showing her positive attitude," chimed Liz.

"Marsha's our little trooper," continued Uncle Bob with pride.

"Her brain is functioning. Isn't it wonderful? Oh, come here, baby. Let Aunt Liz hold you," and little Marsha melted in her arms. "You've obviously been very affectionate with her because she seems to enjoy affection and the attention she's been getting from all of us."

"She's always been a tender and passionate child, but yes, we've been told our unrelenting attention made a big difference, in her recovery," Helen smiled.

"It's a good thing she's home, because you can spend so much time with her. Even if you're doing your things around here, you can talk to her and interact somehow. Even when you're not directly working with her she's learning," Liz said.

"Yah, and Marsha feels safe and comfortable and the doctor says that's important, too."

"Everything will just take a little, or a lot, longer. But I have to remember that she doesn't understand much right now, but she will, in time. I mean, even taking Marsha to the grocery store is a learning experience for her."

"Oh Helen, we know you'll have your hands full and I wish we lived closer so we could help out."

"Well, there are organizations where you can get help." (Appendix 2)

By this time little Marsha was soundly asleep in Aunt Liz's arms and Helen couldn't help sitting back and daydreaming about spending every day with her daughter, encouraging her, coaxing her, maybe even bribing her to keep going. She knew she had to be strong, strong for Marsha, especially in the absence of Sam, when he went for business all over the country.

"Sam, can you help me take Marsha to bed? She's really had a long day!" Helen called.

"Actually I'm amazed at the hours she's been up today. She's only had four or five short naps, right?" Sam said as he lifted Marsha from Liz's side.

"About that, I think," Helen thought aloud.

"I'd guess that's improvement, wouldn't you say, Bob?" Sam asked as he carried Marsha through the living room to her bedroom for the night.

"Absolutely!" Bob agreed as he smiled at the little sleeping girl as she was carried out of the room.

Liz yawned, "I'm beat. What do you say we call it a night?"

"I agree, it's been a long day for all of us," and they simultaneously cleared the Christmas wrappings and nummies from the table and the surrounding area. Helen stood by the picture window when all was done and gazed at the flurries falling outside. It looked magical outside and Helen made a wish. She wished for a miracle, a miracle for Christmas.

Moments later, Sam joined his wife, in silence. They were alone. The only sound was water running in the upstairs bathroom. Sam put his arm around Helen's waist and both parents stood, transfixed on the falling snow.

"Isn't it beautiful?" Sam whispered.

"God—, please help our baby," whispered Helen.

Sam's grip tightened as he nuzzled her to comfort her. "I am sorry. I never meant for this to happen to us—I would do anything to change things. I'd do anything for Marsha—anything."

"M-me too, Sam..." Helen sighed and they stood together in silence on this magical Christmas Eve, praying for the recovery of their little girl.

XII. Premonitions: Can Dreams Become Reality?

Helen had problems falling asleep. "Sam—Sam, are you asleep?" she whispered into the darkness of their bedroom.

There was no sound except her husband's rhythmic breathing. Finally she could stand it no longer. Kicking off covers, in frustration, Helen made her way to the bathroom and found a sleeping pill.

"I desperately need—sleep, and tomorrow's another strenuous day, like all the rest, really. I am just so t-tired," she whispered to no one but her reflection. After climbing back into bed she looked towards the ceiling as she rested her throbbing head back on her pillow. When she finally nodded off, close to midnight, she was restless.

Immediately she had a feeling that a part of her was missing. It was the realization that Marsha was gone. She had no idea where or how; she only felt that her baby was missing.

Now, in a mist, Helen saw visions of little girls passing by her. All were obviously disabled, others less so. Some were in beds, some in wheelchairs and still others on crutches. Helen didn't know them. They were of all ethnic backgrounds. They ranged from ages five to six. Some were chubby, others skinny, and still others of average weight. But they all had one similar characteristic, blonde hair, cut just like Marsha's.

Helen found herself searching, searching for her baby, her child, her daughter. "Where is she? Marsha, where are you?" The children kept passing her by like on a conveyer belt as she sat in her wicker chair on the patio. Strangely, she was stuck to the chair. She couldn't move. Helen had no choice but watch these children pass her by, some smiling at her, others even beckoning to her. But there was nothing she could do. She was stuck, frozen to her chair.

Oh my God, what is this? What does this mean? Where is my child? Helen thought. "This is driving me crazy...insane...I can't handle anymore...please," she sobbed. "Please... I can't see anymore. Oh dear God, where's my baby?"

Then, suddenly, a small, frail little girl appeared.

"I can see you in the distance, my love. You're a blur. Come closer, baby. Come to Mama...please...darling, come to me."

Slowly, Marsha fully materialized in front of Helen, just beyond her reach. Her image was vivid. Her pink nightgown draped loosely over the white cast on her right leg, extending towards her waist. She lay on a canopy bed clad in white, asleep.

"You look beautiful, honey," Helen breathed. "You are OK. Thank God you are OK!" As she gazed at the vision before her she noticed the details of her daughter's face. Her eyelashes and brows, though not dark by nature, stood out prominently against her pale complexion. Her pale pink lips were so chapped it hurt her to look at them. Marsha lay so still.

"Is she even alive?" questioned Mama, as her gaze fell to the rise and fall of her small chest.

Her very pale, fragile looking arms were strewn with punctures from what Helen guessed was from countless medical procedures.

"Oh, little one, you've been through so much! How much more can your little body handle? How much more will it handle? Will you ever be the same? Will you be able to walk and play like you did before your accident? Before our tragedy? When your world, our world, was shattered?" Questions and doubt raced through Helen's mind, as she looked at the sleeping child, her daughter.

Then slowly, little Marsha faded away and a mist appeared, giving way to another apparition. This time Marsha, still clad in her girly pink gown, was aloof. Her eyes searched the ceiling and Helen observed Marsha moving her head, then her thin arms hugged her chest as if to say I'm cold.

"Sweetie...Baby, can you hear me? Anything I can do for you? Anything? What can I do? How can I help you?" There was no response.

The vision was just that, a vision, no communication possible between mother and daughter. Helen felt herself perspiring. She was still stuck to her chair. Helen couldn't move. She felt her dress starting to dampen, stick to her slim figure. Are these hallucinations or premonitions? Still, with deep concentration, she hung on to the anticipation of seeing more visions of her daughter.

"Oh, baby, there has to be a reason for this, for me seeing you like this. Are you trying to tell me you'll be OK? What do you want me to learn? Could these be your stages of recovery? Could this be a sign that my baby will recover?" she wondered, her excitement growing, without the promise of any answers.

Again, Marsha faded away and a new image of the same little girl slowly materialized. This time she was in a wheel chair, playing with red, blue, and green blocks on a hospital roll-away table. Marsha curled her little hands around the blocks, successfully picked them up and put them one on top of the other.

"Amazing," Helen shuddered as tears rolled down her already swollen face. She felt like she was at the premier, a movie, of Marsha's recovery and she was the sole attendee.

"Can this really be the preview of what will happen with Marsha," she wondered, while her blurry eyes hurt and her head throbbed.

Marsha's nurse came into view, extending her hand. Marsha took her hand and pulled herself out of the wheelchair.

"She is walking! Oh m-my G-God, she's w-walking...or is she floating?"

Helen turned away with a jerk and sat upright in her

bed, drenched. "What a d-d-dream... so r-real! Sam. Sam!" she sobbed and shook her husband awake.

"Oh honey...yes? What is it? You've been restless for hours, what's wrong?" Sam asked franticly.

Still mesmerized, she replied, "This dream was so—real Sam. I saw Marsha, our baby, Sam—I saw her injuries. I saw her recovery. It was like a movie, Sam. It was so real. She's gonna be OK. I know she is! I saw it," and Helen started crying from exhaustion and realization of what she witnessed.

"It's OK, my love. It's OK. Everything will be OK," and Sam lovingly hugged his distraught wife as she collapsed in his arms, still sobbing.

Moments passed and Helen fell asleep in the comfort of her husband's arms and Sam gently placed her beside himself. He looked at her in the darkness and caressed her hairline. "You're an amazing woman—," and he caressed her lightly before falling asleep.

"Marsha—Marsha—it's me, Brisa. Can you hear me?"

"I'm here."

"You know you've done an excellent job so far—I mean, you've really worked hard at getting better and I'm so very proud of you, everyone is."

"It's s so h-h-hard, Brisa and sometimes I just wanna give up, I don't wanna fight anymore, you know?"

"I know, but you can't give up. Everyone is helping you, including me. You're strong remember? You can't give up."

"I know b-but..."

"Listen to me. Your mom just had a dream and she saw your recovery. You're gonna make it and she knows that now. She also knows that it's gonna take lots of work and pain."

"What do you mean, pain?"

"Well, for one, your parents will see you struggling, and that's painful for them."

"And I have to give it all I've got, right?"

"How did you get so smart? Now, let me tell you what we're gonna do, what you're going to do with my help. You're

gonna really start working your hands. Your mom will give you blocks and play dough to work with. She saw you lifting and building with blocks in her dream. She's empowered now. She's been given extra energy to help you. Your mom was shown the light at the end of the tunnel. Your mother saw your future. She saw your recovery."

"Wow, you're right. I've got to go on now. I c-can't let Mama down."

"That's right. Now you're talking. You need to think positive and keep going, keep pushing..."

"OK, OK, I will. But keep telling me—reminding me—cause it's so hard for me to keep trying to make my body work and nothing happens."

"Oh, but it is. You just don't know it. But you will, in time, everyone will. Just keep trying, Marsha and believe me, I'm one of your biggest fans."

"Are you always gonna be my cheerleader, Brisa?"

"Yup, the one only you can hear."

"Forever and always?"

"Forever and always."

A few days after Christmas Uncle Bob and Aunt Liz returned home. Sam went back to work, and life started a normal routine. Helen's will and determination for her daughter, strengthened by her recent dream, caused her to work even harder with Marsha. Her special attention, and something else, Marsha's inner strength, fueled by herself and Brisa, caused Marsha to make strides every day. It almost seemed like Marsha's last conversation with Brisa really made an impact.

"Nobody knows why Marsha is progressing as rapidly, or diligently, the results are obvious and appreciated undoubtedly by all. Marsha doesn't give up. She'll keep trying until she reaches her goal, from picking up a glass to trying to dress herself," Helen reported to Aunt Liz only weeks after she and Uncle Bob visited for Christmas. We are so proud of her, Liz. We really are," exclaimed Helen, with tears escaping her eyes because she felt so blessed her baby was mentally recuperating so beautifully, and so quickly. "Now we're hoping and praying the operation results in Marsha being able to stand and walk again. It is only a few days away. I'm both excited and nervous!"

"Bob and I have our fingers crossed, and we know Dr. Hanks is Marsha's one and only chance to ever walk again."

"Yes, he is, Liz. No other doctor wants to do this kind of operation, and it's the only way."

"Helen, we'll be waiting by the phone to hear how the operation went and her prognosis."

"OK, Liz, and thank you again for your help over Christmas!" Helen laid down the receiver quietly and went to watch her daughter sleep.

The next two days flew by and it was the day of the operation. Everything was riding on this. This was the turning point in Marsha's future. This determined if she would be handicapped or have a chance at normalcy.

Helen finished getting her things together and grabbed a book as she went out the door. Sam was already waiting for her in the car for the trip back to St. Francis Hospital where the operation was to take place later this morning.

This was the second trip in two days. Yesterday Sam and Helen had taken a confused little girl to pre-op for the surgery today. Both Helen and Sam tried explaining how, after this hospital stay, this operation, Marsha's right leg would be straight and she could walk again.

All Marsha heard was the word "hospital" and that frightened her.

She instantly became teary eyed and clung to her mother. "N-no, Ma-ma, no. Me st-ay ho-m, Ma-ma," she cried.

"Oh sweetheart, you will come back home in just a few days. You'll come home with a new leg. You'll come home with a better leg, baby."

"You and I can practice walking and soon we'll be playing ball," chimed Papa Sam. "Wouldn't you like that? Wouldn't that be fun, angel?"

Sam tried to brighten her, as well as his and Helen's spirits, get their mind off where they were and the ensuing operation.

The night was long for the Walsch's, but they did manage to get a little sleep.

This morning Marsha was very groggy. She had been given something to relax her for the operation. Helen held her daughter's small hand until the orderly came to take the small child to surgery.

"Marsha, honey, Mama and Papa will be right here when you get back. You'll be just fine, sweetheart," Helen said as much to soothe her daughter as to soothe herself.

"You'll be OK, baby. I'll see you when you wake up and we'll work hard together; you, Mama, and me. We'll be waiting for you, here in your room, sweetheart. Papa loves you!" said Sam, stroking Marsha's tiny brow.

"Mama loves you too, sweetheart," said Helen almost in a whisper, and she wondered if her daughter knew what she was facing, as a tear rolled from her right eye.

Marsha lay loosely strapped to the gurney to prevent her from sliding off. Helen lightly kissed her cheek and Papa gently squeezed her small pale hand before the gurney rolled away from them, down the corridor, towards the operating room. As it rolled away, they could just hear little Marsha murmuring from time to time. Her parents watched as their little girl disappeared down the hall and around the corner, praying for her safe return...hours from now.

Will our daughter be OK? Will she have the ability to walk again? They both wondered to themselves.

"OK, sweetheart, I am Dr. Hanks. Do you remember me?" Dr. Hanks pulled down the white surgical mask covering his nose and mouth. Marsha nodded. "Good. I understand you are feeling better since the last time I saw you. That is great. Now close your eyes and I'll take care of you. When you wake up we'll have your bad leg all fixed."

Another man was sitting by Marsha's head. He leaned over and whispered in her ear, "Let's put this little mask over your nose. It won't hurt at all, honey. Breathe deep and think about playing on the beach... In...the...sand..."

Helen had waited all that she could without losing her mind. It had been a very long morning. She had tried to eat when the couple went to the all too familiar cafeteria for lunch. She just couldn't! She felt like she was going to scream! She was too worried, and had to ask, "Sam, what do you suppose is going on? Marsha's been down there five hours."

"Dr. Hanks said it's a complicated operation, remember? He guessed it would take about eight hours," Sam said, looking up from his book.

"I know, but it seems so long! I can't help worrying!"

"I know, baby. I'll go check with the nurses' desk to see if they've heard anything," he patted her knee for support as he got up and walked out of the room.

"OK!" Helen sighed, putting her sewing project down in her lap to get up and stretch.

"Mr. Walsch, this is a new procedure. I'm not sure how long it could be. But I'm sure Marsha is fine. Think of it as no news is good news. We'll let you know if we hear anything at all," the nurse reassured the pensive father.

"There's no word yet. We just have to be patient. There's nothing we can do but wait, honey..." Sam announced as he walked back into the waiting room.

"And pray!" Helen added.

"I'm sure the operation is just not finished yet. Remember, Dr. Hanks said that the femur has to be broken, reset, the pin put through it and then everything closed up again. I'm sure they'll have to do some blood transfusions maybe.... Lots to do. They are going to work slowly to make sure every detail is right."

"Oh, Sam...I hope she's OK." Sam took his despairing wife into his arms and rocked her as he buried his face into her blonde hair to try and hide his anxiety from her.

"You're trembling too, honey. You're also w-worried aren't you?" Helen's concern began to grow knowing he was worried too.

"Yah, I am...of course I am. Our baby's under the knife and we have no idea how this will work. Hell, nobody really does."

Sweat beads ran down Sam's face as he spoke and

he wiped himself with a handkerchief. "She just has to come out of this. She just has to!"

"Oh honey, I'm sorry!" sobbed Helen as she grasped her husband's sweaty hand.

They peered at his watch and shed tears of desperation together.

Another hour past as the worried couple waited.

"Is there anything I can get you Mr. and Mrs. Walsch?" asked one of the nurses. Helen nearly jumped out of her skin at the sound of the woman's voice.

"No thanks, we're OK," answered Sam. "Let's walk a bit, Helen. As long as we have a view of this room we'll see when Marsha comes back."

"OK," Helen reluctantly agreed.

Another hour passed and Helen and Sam walked up and down the hall enough to wear a path down the middle, or so it seemed.

"There's nothing we can do, honey," Sam repeated.

"Yes, dear. I know. There's nothing we can do. But I'm going crazy, Sam! What's happening down there?" she cried in a desperate whisper. "Why won't they let us know *anything*, Sam?

"Come sit beside me and try to relax," soothed Sam, putting his arm protectively around his distraught better half, increasingly worried himself. The couple sat side by side, comforting each other as best they could.

"Marsha's been in the operating room seven hours n-now," and she began sobbing. "Oh, Sam, why is it taking so long? Maybe they found something else wrong. Maybe the bones are too shattered and Dr. Hanks can't fix her leg. She'll never s-stand or w-w-walk again. O-o-oh, my baby..." Helen sobbed.

"Honey, please don't s-say that," snapped her husband at the very idea. "Dr. Hanks is a good doctor! He's our last hope. Remember, Marsha's s-strong. She *will* be okay. She *will* pull through. And she *will* be normal again!"

Sam got up abruptly and made his way to the nurses' station, again....

Part Two: Marsha's Difficult Road

XIII. Stress Of Surgery: Nothing Is Ever Certain

Sam left the room with his visibly distraught wife sitting beside Marsha's empty bed and entered the hallway just across from the nurses' station desk. "O.R. just called," said the nurse at the station, as she hung up the phone. "There were unexpected complications. But the operation is going well," and she paused for inevitable questions.

Helen overheard and came rushing from the room with tears instantaneously pouring from her eyes, "Oh my gosh! How much longer? When will we see her?"

"The operation is still in progress. That's all I know, ma'am," repeated the nurse before she turned to another task, visibly concerned. The pediatric staff was aware that the operation performed in the St. Francis Operating Room was the first of its kind, and everyone seemed concerned and on their toes. Every nurse was secretly saying a little prayer for the little blonde patient in room 24A. Although Dr. Hanks had performed these procedures since the 1940s, during WWII, this was the first time on a patient so young.

"Oh Sam, what could have gone wrong? When will this nightmare end, Sam?"

"Helen, honey, the nurse said she's OK. You heard her. We'll have to ask later what happened, what the complications were... We've got to focus on the positive right now, remember? It's the only way, babe! Believe me, I'm having a difficult time too... Come here and let's say a prayer together."

"Y-yes Sam, hold m-me. Dear Father, who art in Heaven, please watch over..."

After the prayer, Helen and Sam sat huddled together calming each other's fears. Sam, noticing that Helen had visibly calmed, suggested, "Honey, let's go to the cafeteria, get something to eat, coffee maybe."

"I have no appetite, Sam!" Helen sighed.

"Honey, we need to keep our strength for Marsha. We have each other to lean on and you and I must keep our sanity!"

"Yes dear, I know. Let's go for a walk. Maybe we can find a little something for Marsha in the gift shop."

"Then we'll get a bite to eat, OK?" Sam prodded.

"Oh, all right!" Helen agreed. She knew that when Sam had an idea, there was no changing his mind, so arguing was pointless.

"That's my girl," Sam praised as he helped his wife to her feet and together, hand in hand, they walked to the elevator.

Sam couldn't help imagine his little angel lying helplessly on the operating table, doctors and nurses surrounding her. This time there was a different level and degree of hope. This time, Marsha was alive, she wasn't on the brink of death, and Sam recognized their absolute gift. Their daughter was alive. These hours alone, waiting for Marsha to return from the O.R., getting the chance, the ability to overcome yet other inconceivable obstacles, made him come to terms with a lot that had happened and the extremely hard road ahead for all of them.

"Do you know how lucky I am? How lucky we are?" he asked Helen as he gave her a loving squeeze in the elevator.

"I know, honey," and she returned his affection with a hug and kiss. They left the elevator and went into the gift shop. "Look, isn't this little teddy bear with the nurse's uniform cute? And look, she even has a nurse's cap. Look at those brown button eyes, Sam. I think they're saying, 'Please get better.' The little one is not as expensive as the bigger, plain teddy bear. Do you think we can afford to get Marsha this one?"

"If you think it'll make her happy," and Sam watched Helen caressing the bear lovingly. "Yes, dear, get her the little one," Sam pulled out his wallet.

With the little bag securely tucked in her purse, Helen looked into Sam's eyes and kissed him again. "Thank you," she whispered and smiled, "Marsha will love Nurse Teddy. Can we get some coffee to stay awake now?"

"By all means, and some food too. OK? Even if you're

not hungry," coaxed Sam. Maybe that bear gave her the extra sense of comfort she needed, he thought.

They walked to the cafeteria and got sandwiches and coffee. They found an empty table away from the other occupied tables, which could still be seen if someone, such as a nurse, came to find them.

As they settled into their seats, Helen spotted her husband glancing at his watch. "What time is it? How long has it been now?"

"It's going on eight hours, honey."

"Sam, what are we going to do—?"

"Have your coffee and sandwich. There's nothing else *we* can do," and the two clutched each other's free hand as they ate. "Baby, don't worry, she'll make it," Sam reassured again, although he also felt queasy.

Eight hours in the operating room seemed a very long time, unimaginable. They didn't talk much as they ate. The little they did talk was of topics other than the one foremost on their minds. Idle chitchat was just what they needed. They soon finished their lunch and left the cafeteria.

"Let's sit in the hospital lobby and wait, for a change of pace," Sam suggested.

"OK, but it makes no difference really, honey," Helen sighed.

"I know. I just thought..."

"Oh Sam, the time, the waiting, for hours. It's just so hard. The not knowing..."

"At least we know that she's going to make it out alive, Helen!" Sam commented a little too abruptly and Helen fell into tears. "I'm sorry, baby. Please understand. I'm also on the brink of insanity, just like you. Let's go see if there's any word on Marsha."

He put his strong arm around Helen's shoulders and led her to the elevator.

Both parents were so exhausted; they were running on pure adrenaline. "Some good news would help both of us, I think," said Sam out loud to no one in particular.

"Oh God, yes! That would be wonderful," and Helen

streaked her fingers through her now unkempt blonde hair. Her head was pounding from worry, sleep depravation, and thoughts about Marsha. "What time is it, Sam? How long has it been now?"

"It's been about ten minutes since the last time you asked!" replied Sam with a cracking voice.

"The nurses have to have some news for us. They just have to..." Helen said as the elevator doors opened to the hall where Marsha's room was. They started walking to the room when they heard a familiar voice calling them.

"Oh, Mr. and Mrs. Walsch, they're finishing up with your daughter now. Everything's OK," said the tired nurse with a hint of relief in her voice. Abby had been Marsha's nurse since she came to St. Francis Hospital Pediatrics Unit and had obviously become attached to her.

"How long will it be, Abby?" asked Helen.

"I honestly don't know. All they told me is they were finishing the operation. I've been a pest calling them every hour for updates."

"That's good news," interjected Sam with encouragement in his voice. "Our Marsha is a little trooper!"

"She sure is," interjected Helen with a sense of relief in her voice.

"We sure are lucky, Helen," and some of the stress had visibly been released from Sam's composure.

Another hour passed and Helen and Sam sat side by side, almost in oblivion, as they listened to song after song of Carol King, Dionne Warwick, Dusty Springfield, Christopher Cross, and others. In the back of both their minds one voice, one picture, still remained, one of horror and pain: screams of horror when little Marsha fell off her horse, laying on the rocky dirt path, motionless, unconscious, barely alive. Time seemed to stand still and when Sam looked onto his wife, he noticed she had finally fallen asleep. He settled her more comfortably in his arms and soon also nodded off to Dionne Warwick's song *So Far Away.*

"Mr. and Mrs. Walsch? Mr. and Mrs. Walsch? Your

daughter is in recovery. The operation is finished. Marsha is OK!" said Abby to Marsha's still groggy parents, with a smile and a wink. "She should be up here in an hour or so. As soon as she wakes up!"

Sam sat up with a start and welcomed the news with a stretch of his shoulders and Helen still rubbed her eyes. "What happened, Sam?"

"Marsha's in recovery and should be brought up to her room in about another hour," smiling as he repeated what Abby had told them.

"Oh thank God! Marsha's OK! Sam," and Helen hugged her husband. "She made it, Sam... The operation was a success!"

"Yes, dear," and Sam smiled at her enthusiasm.

"Our baby's going to walk again," and Helen's face visibly lit up, and a tear or two escaped her, a mixture of pent-up worry, anxiety, and gratitude. The couple still clung to each other and Sam unsuccessfully held his manly composure, as tears of joy also escaped him, his wife now weeping openly in his arms.

"Yes, honey—thank God. This is what we'd hoped for! It's fantastic! Dr. Hanks was right after all. It could be done," said Sam out loud to no one in particular, as he couldn't help remembering all the doctors he and Helen had seen with Marsha. He couldn't help but recollect the agony of hearing doctor after doctor saying nothing could be done for their little girl.

Doctors said there was absolutely nothing they could do to reconstruct Marsha's right leg. Their six-year-old little girl would live with a deformed leg the rest of her life, without the chance of standing or walking again. Now, a year after the terrible day of Marsha's accident, when their lives were turned upside down, the impossible seemed possible. Marsha might, one day, lead a normal life. At least she would have that chance, that opportunity, with hard work and perseverance from her and those close to her.

"We're living a miracle, honey," exclaimed Sam as he gently pulled Helen towards his side and hugged her.

"I know! It's a miracle! We are so blessed! I can't wait to see her!" answered Helen with the voice of relief; excitement and anticipation all rolled into one.

"I feel almost like I felt when Marsha was born," she thought. "Our baby is being reborn. I can't believe we're getting a second chance. The operation was successful. It opens so many opportunities—."

Helen's mind was racing through the many wonderful turns Marsha's recovery had taken and she could feel herself recovering from the intense gloom within her the past year. Helen imagined her daughter walking to her in a pretty red dress. She and Marsha were going to have lunch together. Marsha was happy and there were no signs of the tragedy she had suffered.

"Oh Helen, we have a long road ahead of us," exclaimed Sam, bringing his wife back to reality. "We will have to encourage every opportunity for Marsha to practice walking, using her fine motor skills on top of her outside therapy. It'll be busy and hard, Helen, for a long time..."

"I know, and that's OK. I don't mind. We'll do the best we can, Sam. And we have to try and explain to Marsha that she needs to help us make her better... Oh Sam, where is she? What time is it? It's been an hour, hasn't it?" Helen began to pace in the small room.

"Just about. I'm sure Marsha will be brought up from the recovery room soon. Remember that she has to wake up from the anesthesia. They don't know how long that will take for sure. They were guessing at an hour."

Helen was pacing the room, stopping to look out the hall every time she was by the door. Movement caught her eye and she leaned out the door looking toward the elevator.

"Look, I think there's a gurney coming up the hall now... That might be her, Sam!" and she stretched and strained her eyes to get a better view. "I think it is her!"

The gurney kept coming closer.

"It is Marsha!" Helen whispered and both parents cleared the doorway.

Marsha, lying still, limp, eyes closed, was wheeled past them into her room. Sam and Helen followed close behind and watched as their little girl was gently transferred from the gurney to her bed. No one said a word. Only the sounds of Anne Murray's, *A Little Good News,* over the hospital sound system filled the room.

The recovery room nurse positioned Marsha's IV and finally broke the silence. "She woke in recovery. She'll be in and out for a while until the anesthesia wears off completely."

"That's fine. We'll be here with her now," said Sam as Helen was marveling at their sleeping daughter, their sleeping angel. She couldn't keep her eyes off her and slowly the tears of pent-up worry, fatigue, and now, joy, trickled down her face again, with Jackie DeShannon's *What The World Needs Now Is Love,* playing in the background.

Sam, too, was captivated by his sleeping little girl, his angel, and looked upon her with pride. "You are truly a fighter, little one," he whispered and both parents stood in silence for a long time.

Gratified that all their endless, countless sacrifices in fighting for their child's survival had finally paid off. Never losing faith and recognizing the need for direct and complete involvement in their daughter's recovery process were the crucial elements for success.

"Sweetie, what we did for you was out of love, and we'll continue to fight your battles with you," and Helen placed her hand gently on Marsha's chest. She felt her heart beating; thump, thump, thump.

"Ma-ma—?" Marsha mumbled, trying to open her eyes.

"Yes, sweetie, I'm right here," Helen leaned close.

"Uuummm... I ti-red, Ma-ma..." Marsha mumbled again.

"I know, dear, you just relax and rest. Mama and Papa are right here," Helen said, stroking Marsha's forehead.

"And we're not going anywhere!" Papa continued, squeezing her tiny hand for reassurance.

"Oh Sam, do you really think she'll walk in a month?

She looks so weak," Helen whispered when Marsha had fallen asleep again.

"Dr. Hanks seems to think so. Of course she looks weak, she just came out of surgery."

Both parents stood side by side, touching for comfort, speechless, admiring their child, their miracle. Were there more miracles to come? Mama and Papa had every intention of making that happen. Cognizant of tough times ahead, they committed to working with their daughter. Both parents understood Marsha would need constant attention and support. Their lives would be forever changed.

Their marriage became stronger. The depth of commitment between Helen and Sam strengthened considerably, resulting from their common interest: the rehabilitation of their daughter. Emotions ran rampant, from pure despair and bewilderment at Marsha's injuries to sheer astonishment and amazement with each little progress. Though they spared no efforts or pains where Marsha was concerned, Helen and Sam quickly became aware of exhaustion and the need to take small breaks between the two of them and accept favors from friends and neighbors when possible. The mere shock of Marsha's young life, radiance reduced to barely flickering in an instant, took it's toll, and now the sun was rejuvenating that wilted, dying flower and returning the possibility of vitality.

"It just seems so impossible after what Marsha's gone through," Helen said, slumping in her chair from exhaustion and sheer relief at Marsha's bedside.

"Yes, it does!" Sam agreed.

They sat in silence watching their little girl sleep. Thinking of the tough road ahead for them all. Not much time had passed when Dr. Hanks entered the room. He looked surprisingly fresh for having spent over 8 hours operating on Marsha that morning.

"Good afternoon, how's the little lady? She did very well this morning," he said, reading her chart and making additional notes.

"Thirteen hours, and we were so worried. What took so long, doctor?" Sam inquired.

"Yes, it took a little longer than we expected," said Dr. Hanks. "The bones at the fracture were very badly broken and had grown together very firmly. The re-breaking and setting was very tricky. But we got it."

"Thank God!!" was all Helen could manage to say. "Will Marsha really be able to walk again?"

"Physical therapy will have her standing in a week. We'll get her on her feet in a day or so. She'll get six weeks of intensive PT and we'll go from there," continued Dr. Hanks as he studied Marsha's chart. "You'll be a busy little lady, won't you?" and he looked at his little patient, still lying groggily in her bed. "Remember to encourage your daughter. It'll help her recovery."

"Thank you so much, Dr. Hanks!" Sam said.

"I wonder if he knows how thankful we are, Sam?" Helen whispered to her husband as the doctor checked his patient.

Dr. Hanks looked up from Marsha's chart and smiled with affirmation before taking his leave, leaving another happy family to carry on.

"Oh, I'm sure he does. Imagine knowing that you made it possible for a child to walk again when everyone else, every other surgeon, refused to operate, refused to touch her, because they thought there was no hope!"

"You're right. It's just amazing—!" Helen agreed, turning toward her daughter who was beginning to stir.

"Pa-pa, whr a-m I?" Marsha mumbled.

"You're in your room at the hospital, baby," answered Papa, bending over his little girl. "Everything will be OK, sweetheart. Don't you worry about anything."

Sam's amazement and sheer exhilaration at hearing his daughter's voice clearly showed in his face.

"Mama and Papa will help you get better," added Helen, lightly grasping Marsha's hand as she thought she saw a faint smile. "Did you see that, Sam? Did you see that smile? She responded, Sam!"

"I think you're right," said Sam, moving closer to share the moment. "We'll be with you every step of the way, honey!"

Marsha closed her tired eyes and drifted off to sleep again.

"Boy, Brisa, I feel so strange. My leg feels heavy kind-of and I'm so tired."

"Of course, you just had surgery, and the anesthesia is still wearing off. You'll feel better soon and you'll be able to use that leg of yours soon, too."

"How?"

"With lots of hard work. Didn't you hear the doctor saying physical therapy will have you standing in a week and walking in a month?"

"I guess I missed that. I'm so tired."

"Remember, Marsha, you need to do your very best and keep your strength up, do what the doctors, the nurses, and your parents tell you, and keep practicing. I'll be doing my part if you do yours."

"Yes, Brisa. Isn't it called persistence or something?"

"Yup. You got it,"

With that Marsha's angel faded from her conscience again, like so many times before, but a little message blew in and settled into her conscience, like a puff of fresh air.

"True survivors direct themselves elsewhere and take a big step forward over time."

"I wonder what that means," thought Marsha.

Marsha had learned to trust Brisa and her disappearance didn't frighten her anymore. With Brisa's advice and encouragement, Marsha didn't feel alone anymore. She felt stronger with her presence. Although what just happened she didn't quite understand.

"Brisa, you told me I would understand everything, and I-I just don't get it. What do you mean?"

"You're mistaken, Marsha. If you had chosen Heaven instead of to fight and stay alive, you would be immortal now, with unlimited understanding. You chose life, and now you must learn, make decisions, and persevere."

"Oh, OK—, good night then."

Brisa drifted away again as fast as she had reappeared to answer Marsha's question.

The night brought much needed sleep for the Walsch family. Helen slept better than she had in almost a year. The morning was fresh and bright. The sun seemed to shine brighter and the birds seemed to sing more beautifully. The extra something that seemed to be present gave Helen hope. It seemed to be the start of a new chapter in their lives. It was like God was giving her a sign.

It wasn't long before the couple made their way to the hospital, as they had done countless times before. Only this morning the sunshine seemed a little brighter. Marsha was still asleep and the couple quietly sat by their daughter's bedside while the little girl awoke from her nighttime slumber. Our baby must be so tired after what she went through yesterday, and I can't imagine her having the strength to get up, out of bed, so soon, like Dr. Hanks suggested, Helen thought.

"I know Marsha has the strength and persistence to get through her difficult rehabilitation," offered Sam, breaking the silence. "I'm sure the love, devotion and determination we're showing is giving her the desire to persevere—. Oh, and Helen—, we need to ask the nurses what they're doing to motivate and encourage Marsha when we're not here."

"Yah, you're right," Helen said as she made a mental note.

"Good morning, let's get the young lady ready!" Abby announced as she busied herself with Marsha.

"Excuse me, what's being done for stimulation by the nurses? Dr. Hanks mentioned its importance to us yesterday," Helen asked Abby.

"I think he meant physical movement, Helen."

"Marsha has her scheduled times for grooming and we check in from time to time as you know. Other than that we're not authorized to do anything out of the routine. Whenever possible we talk to her, which we do with all our patients," Abby answered.

"What do you talk about?"

"We let her know what we're doing with her. That's all we can do, all we are authorized to do. Marsha does have her PT and speech therapy appointments every day, remember?"

"We're grateful for the progress Marsha's made since she's been here and it's the continuous attention and care that's made the difference, I'm sure. But there's got to be more that can be done."

"Yes, we'll do the best we can! I've observed you and your husband devote so much time to your daughter, talking, reading, and singing to her and even stroking her and otherwise touching her lovingly, continuously. Marsha really is a lucky little girl. She gets more stimulation than most patients do. I will ask the doctors if there's anything else we can do to help her."

The day was fairly uneventful. The parents sat by their daughter's bedside and Marsha vacillated between sleep and consciousness. There wasn't much they could do, but to let her know they were by her side.

"Oh Sam, do you think we're overreacting?" Helen wondered out loud.

"Not when it comes to the welfare of our daughter. I want to know we're doing everything we possibly can."

"You're right, Sam! We need to do everything. I'm so tired... but, we need to do whatever we can," murmured Mama as she lovingly, painfully gazed down at Marsha, stroking her covered form. "Honey, there is positive energy in touch, especially in your mama and papa's touch. I hope you feel our love and devotion. We will get through this too, you, me, and Papa."

"I know and I'm worn out too," agreed Sam and weariness was evident in his eyes. We'll see you in the morning sweet pea. Sleep well and Mama and Papa will too," whispered Papa to his sleeping little angel before he guided his wilting Helen out the door and down the hall to the elevators. "Everything will look brighter in the morning after we get some sleep," he told her as calmly as he could muster.

"I know. It has to. Marsha was always so persistent and strong! She never gave up, Sam."

"She's not going to this time either, Helen, you'll see..."

They went home for another night of much needed sleep, only to return to the hospital and Marsha's bedside the next morning.

"Rise and shine little lady. This morning you're having your first Physical Therapy session," announced Abby brightly, but gently, to her little patient. "Let's get you washed up for breakfast first. Here we go..."

Abby gently moved the little girl and washed her with a washcloth, and she was surprised to hear a little hushed, quivering voice.

"C-a-re, I ca-n-t mo-o-ov su-o-gh!" Marsha struggled with the words, but managed to get her point across.

"Oh honey, you will after Physical Therapy works with you a bit. Your doctor said so."

"Oh?" Marsha replied, remembering that Brisa had told her to listen to the doctors and nurses and to do what they told her to do.

"Yes-sir-ee! Now give me your right arm and let me wash it. No honey, the other right. That's it... Oh, look! Here comes breakfast. What do we have today? It looks like oatmeal and strawberries to start, and scrambled eggs. Let me go get rid of this and I'll be back in just a minute to feed you. Don't go anywhere, OK?"

"Oh Brisa, this is so boring being in bed and not being able to go anywhere. I can't even move. I can't even pick up my spoon and feed myself. I can't do anything by myself, Brisa. What am I going to do? I'm so sad and so lonely."

"Marsha hang-in there. You'll get better. You need to focus on that. Strain yourself to go forward and don't give up. Remember you're stubborn."

"OK, I think I can do that."

"I know you can. Just don't give in."

Abby came back in the room. "Are we hungry yet?"

"Haaa..." Marsha smiled and opened her mouth like a baby bird.

"Are you hungry?"

"Y-Y-Y-is," Marsha stammered.

"That's what I like to hear. I'm sure these luscious strawberries will give you extra energy for your PT today. We better hurry—they'll be here for you soon."

A year after life was changed forever, and a week after the strenuous thirteen-hour operation, Marsha's right leg lay motionless in a white, plaster cast for initial healing to commence. The seven days of anticipation, of wondering whether their daughter would stand on day eight, were hell for mother and father alike. How could they be so lucky? How was it possible Mr. and Mrs. Walsch had found the one doctor who would make the difference in their daughter's life? Dr. Hanks had turned a hopeless situation into one with possibilities, a one hundred and eighty degree turn from never being able to even stand without assistance to great possibilities of being able to, one day soon, have ability to walk, run and jump again.

The day had finally arrived. Marsha's cast came off. It was almost six months since Marsha stood on her own two feet without a lift or assistance of some sort and now she would have ability to stand and walk on her own.

After breakfast, Abby repositioned Marsha back to a comfortable position so she could rest until physical therapy called for her. Her right leg lay bare, motionless, covered only by the weight of the hospital sheet and blanket.

Marsha looked outside her window, daydreaming. Her eyes focused on the single cumulous cloud, encircled by deep blue sky, and she thought, there is me, imperfection in a perfect world.

"Oh nonsense, you are as perfect as the rest of the clouds!"

"Brisa? Brisa, is that you?"

"Yes ma'am, and don't put yourself down, Marsha! You're strong, stronger than most people are. Even some adults."

"Oh, how so?"

"You decided to survive instead of giving up, for one

thing, and now you are going to challenge yourself with your difficult road to recovery. Your cumulous cloud will fade slowly, over time, as your disabilities diminish."

"Will I really overcome my handicaps, Brisa? Will I be normal again?"

"With dedication and persistence, Marsha."

"OK, Brisa, I promise I will work as hard as I can on my recovery."

"That's my girl. You have the winning attitude now and do you realize you just gave me your commitment, your promise not to give up?"

"I know. And I won't."

Driving to the hospital, Sam and Helen's anticipation mounted. Their daily route to St. Francis Hospital was routine now and both parents made extra effort to focus on direction, the road, and other vehicles as they made their way to their destination, especially this morning.

"I think this drive will stay with me forever, Helen!" Sam groaned.

"I know what you mean. I won't forget it either, this whole nightmare!"

"Just think, all this time, and then today, finally, Marsha's getting out of that wheelchair. I don't think I'll ever forget her struggles. It's haunting, really."

"It puts everything into perspective, doesn't it?" and Helen saw her husband silently choking back tears. She kept quiet, reaching for his right hand, squeezing it to comfort him. Helen and Sam rode the remaining few miles in silence, as they were delayed again by the inability to find parking.

XIV. Rehabilitation: A Long Journey

Marsha was ready. She didn't quite understand, but anything was better than lying in that hospital bed all day, unable to do anything. She did get the idea that this was going to help her and that it was hard work. She made a promise to Brisa and she was going to try her best. The doctors, the nurses, and her parents had all told her that it was important, so it must be.

When the young man with the pretty, sparkling green eyes came to get her, Marsha thought that this might be easier than she thought. Then, she saw the PT room. All of the equipment was large and scary. The young man introduced himself as Stefan and explained all of the things they would be doing in words that the young girl's mind would understand.

"Whenever you are ready, honey, we'll get started," Stefan said with a smile and a wink.

"I do qo-od t-d-ay," Marsha stammered. She wanted the young man to know that she was going to try her best.

"Oh sweetie, I know you will. Soon you'll be walking between those parallel bars, you just wait and see."

He lifted her to a standing position as if she were a rag doll. He held her by the waist after he placed her hands on the bars.

"Bu I-I ca-n –t!! I ca-n-t do it!!" and Marsha had fear in her eyes all of a sudden.

"The longer you sit in that wheelchair, sweetie, the more your body breaks down. The more you resist now, the longer and harder your recovery will be, Marsha. Is that what you want? We had a deal, remember?"

"I s-s-tan-ing—!!!" Marsha cried with a huge grin on her face. She couldn't believe it. She was so happy and proud.

"Yes, you are. Now balance. Squeeze the bars with your hands when you need to. See if you can steady yourself first though. I'm right here, sweetie. Nothing will happen. I'm right here," Stefan said in a soothing and reassuring tone from directly behind her.

"Li-ke sis?" Marsha asked through her Cheshire cat smile.

"That's right. You've got it!" Stefan had let go of Marsha's waist and she was standing on her own.

"Ooo..." Marsha was feeling unsteady.

"Keep trying. Keep practicing. You'll be balancing

longer every day and soon you'll be standing all by yourself."

"S-o ha-rd," Marsha said, gripping the bars as best she could.

"I know. Let's do some other exercises and we'll come back to the bars in a bit, OK?" Stefan said, pulling the wheelchair closer with his foot, and lowering his little patient back into her chair.

"O—OK," Marsha nodded.

The next thing was some leg lifts on the big table. Stefan was moving her legs for her, but he explained that soon she would be doing this herself. He massaged her legs and helped her back to the parallel bars for a final shot at balancing.

"Good job, Marsha. Keep that good attitude and you'll be running down the hall in no time. Let's go for a ride back to your room now and I'm sure you'll have company soon."

"Ma-ma n Pa—oooh?" and Marsha lost her balance and fell backwards.

"Careful..." and the tall, brunette caught his patient before she had fallen even a little ways backward. He had his strong muscular arms around her and he gently placed Marsha into her wheelchair again. "You need to be careful, young lady. We still have lots of work to do before you can join the circus, OK? That's my girl," and he winked at her.

Marsha was dizzy from the sudden loss of balance, the shock, or was it the grasp of her therapist? That hug felt nice, she thought secretly. "I ti-r-d. Ca-n I go se-ep?" she asked shyly.

"Of course, cutie. We'll get you back to your room for a nap right away," and a candy striper quickly took the little patient back to her room.

Sam and Helen had left earlier this morning to avoid rush hour. Their plan was to be at Marsha's bedside when she returned from her physical therapy session. They wanted to be among the first to congratulate their daughter. Sam dropped Helen off at the front door and went to park.

Helen greeted the all-too-familiar faces on her trek to Marsha's room. When she walked into Marsha's room, she found her sleeping soundly. Her wheelchair stood in the corner, supporting a small pair of crutches.

"I'm afraid we're too late. I am so sorry, angel. You look so peaceful sleeping. You must have had a big morning," and Helen thought how lonely and sad Marsha must have felt with neither of them there when she returned from her big accomplishment.

"Ooooohhhhh, MA-MA!" Marsha opened her eyes at the sound of her Mother's voice.

"Yes, dear!" Helen leaned over her daughter, nearly dropping her coat on the floor rather than the chair that was its original destination.

"Ma-ma...I d-di-d go-o-o-d to-o-da-ay!" Marsha said through a wide smile.

"Oh sweetie, I'm so glad to hear that! I knew you would!" Mama smiled back and kissed her baby on the forehead.

"Mrs. Walsch, good morning. I heard Marsha stood up this morning. She's already making big strides and I'm sure she'll be walking in no time. We keep telling her she needs to focus and keep pushing onward," said the nurse coming in to check on Marsha.

"Oh baby, I'm so proud of you! Papa's going to be so happy and so proud of you too. He'll be in any minute, sweetheart. He is just parking the car," Helen said, hugging the girl again.

"I ti-r-d, MA-MA!" Marsha said, yawning.

"I'm sure you are after all that hard work. Here, let me make you comfy," Helen said, fluffing and rearranging the pillows behind and under Marsha's legs. "Oh look, you're bending your right knee. That's wonderful!" and Helen gently caressed the newly-uncast leg. She noticed a faint, but proud smile in her daughter's face.

"O-K, MA-MA. I w-u-v uu," Marsha said, settling back into her new nest of pillows.

"Sweetheart, I love you too!" responded Helen, kissing

her daughter on her forehead. "You rest now, baby, and I'm sure lunch'll be here soon."

At that moment Sam walked into the room with a bundle of colorful balloons. "These are for our little trooper," he announced and looked at his sleepy daughter. Marsha smiled at the sound of her father's voice and Sam saw her acknowledge the balloons before she closed her eyes and fell fast asleep.

"Wherever did you get those, Sam?"

"My office sent these for Marsha. They were just delivered. They stopped me at the front desk to give them to me. That's why it took me so long to get up here."

"Put them here by the TV, Sam, so Marsha can look at them when she wakes up."

"Look, they're swaying in the breeze of the vent, like they're dancing, Marsha would say," Sam said with a half chuckle.

"Oh, Sam, Marsha's making great strides, just like the doctor said! She was standing and balancing today!" Helen announced proudly.

"I'm sure her doctor's forecast is correct. She'll be walking in a month. Just think how great that'll be!" Sam said, taking off his coat and hanging it on the back of the door.

"Yes, and maybe she can come home soon... Forever! Wouldn't that be wonderful?" Helen said with a dreamy look in her eyes.

"Yes! And it will happen soon. Think positively, remember?"

"Oh Sam, we've got to be the luckiest parents!"

"Yes—we are honey," and Papa reached for his sleeping daughter's outstretched little skinny bruised hand.

Helen cringed at the sight of the little purple-blue skin on her daughter's hand. "Do you think they could do something against the bruising of the IV's? I mean, look—it looks so painful."

"Helen, I don't think it hurts her. It's just unsightly and I don't think they can do anything about it. It's certainly the least of our worries, wouldn't you agree?"

"You're right. She probably still has a few plastic surgeries to go to repair her face too. Do you think she'll ever look like she did before—?" Helen said, starting to work herself up again.

"Dr. Wei is here to talk to us about that right now, honey," responded Sam as he saw the physician enter the room.

"Good afternoon, I'd like to look at this young lady's face to see what I can do," said Dr. Wei, diligently examining Marsha's uneven, scarred face. "Oh, I think we can improve upon this. It'll take a few dermabrasions, spread over a few months, but we'll have her good as new," and he smiled at the still sleeping frail child and then at her parents. "I'll start with dermabrasion on her nose, and in a few months, the forehead. From what I can tell from my notes, Marsha's nose was hastily tended to, without cosmetic regard, approximately five months ago and nothing was done to her forehead."

"That's correct. The doctors told us rehabilitation and her leg took priority," answered Sam.

Dr. Wei looked at Marsha's chart again. Flipping pages to find the information he was looking for, "Surgery is scheduled for Monday morning and should take a few hours."

"Will it be risky and could there be complications, doctor?" and Helen moved towards her husband for the added comfort of his touch.

"I don't foresee any complications. There will be irritation and discoloration for some time as tissue heals in about six weeks or so. It is important to refrain from manipulation of the area as much as possible. Other than that, our little patient should be just fine."

"Of course she will," chimed Sam. "Time will heal all those nasty scars—and remember—we have to let her know that she's a beautiful little girl, no matter what!"

"You're so correct," replied Dr. Wei. "Dermabrasion takes time and the emotional scars she'll likely have definitely need attention. You might remove mirrors in your house when she goes home, for example."

"Helen, we have to do our best she doesn't become self-conscious. For now at least, we can protect her, at least until she becomes a little stronger. She'll get lots of ridicule soon enough because she's different in so many ways," Sam sighed.

"That's true, but she seems like a fighter. What I can do is help her look more normal so that people won't judge her so harshly. You will have to help her deal with the rest. If you have any more questions, please let me know. Otherwise, I will see you all on Monday morning."

Dr. Wei then left the room, leaving Marsha's parents to think about what he had said.

"Yes, Sam, she'll have so many ch-challenges."

"I know—and the first is her coordination and motor skills."

"Yes, Dr. Davis said to keep working with her using her hands, like having her manipulate objects, playing with clay or merely picking up a ball. Sam—I saw her—she can't do that... it's, it's so..."

"I know, I know and she'll get better. Marsha will get all the special help she needs, honey, I promise. Dr. Davis prescribed outside physical therapy for when she comes home."

"Oh Sam, what are we going to do? Her world will be so hard and cruel. But you're right. We have to anticipate what's going to happen and try to protect her. At least for now."

"Ya, don't forget we have to listen, too. She might not open up to us, so we will have to listen to her for clues."

"It will be s-so hard for her, Sam. I mean, Marsha's starting over. She's learning everything we take for granted—and—it hurts me just to..."

"I know, Helen, it's going to be a long tough road—for all of us."

"Uh-huh, we'll do the best we can, huh? What else is there? We have to leave the bandages behind and look forward."

Marsha's parents were beside themselves with anticipation for bringing their child home. There were so many details to think about in making their home handicap friendly. Both Sam and Helen couldn't help but think of the implications of their daughter being out of reach of immediate medical care, either.

Lunch arrived shortly thereafter, and Marsha ate with gusto, as she had worked up an appetite with the excitement and hard work of this morning. Later that afternoon Dr. Hanks came by to check on her progress.

"Good day. Marsha is progressing better than expected," said Dr. Hanks. "It looks like she'll be able to go home in a couple weeks."

"Oh my heavens!! Did you hear that, Sam? Our angel will be home soon!" Helen almost sang, she was so happy.

"That's wonderful news! Sweetheart, did you hear what Dr. Hanks just said? You'll come home for good."

Dr. Hanks was now smiling at his little patient as he continued talking. "This little lady is working hard and her progress will be rewarded. She's going to be balancing more and longer every day and has even taken little steps this week. I envision you'll be walking out of here on crutches."

Marsha's attention focused on the doctor, and she stayed silent. Her pale, uneven little face turned slightly and her blue eyes seemed to twinkle.

I wonder if she understands or maybe she doesn't believe it herself, thought Helen as she watched her daughter lying there listening, motionless, quiet, with only occasional blinking eyes.

"What about her equilibrium? There's no way that will allow her to walk in two weeks," exclaimed Sam, a little abruptly, and his wife broke down in tears, overwhelmed with emotions.

"Mr. Walsch, your daughter's equilibrium will be affected for a long time. Because she's so young she's more likely to recover in time. However, for the foreseeable future, her crutches will help her unstableness. Otherwise, you will have to help her, and be careful with her as well."

"OK, but you said she'll walk," repeated Helen.

"Yes, slowly and carefully, with crutches," repeated the doctor.

"As long as she has the capability, we'll work with her."

"Yes," answered Helen with a forced smile between lingering sobs.

"Well, let's let Marsha get some rest after her stressful day and we'll conquer more tomorrow, won't we, angel?" and Papa looked lovingly at his attentive daughter.

"M-e g-o h-om-e, Pa-pa?" asked Marsha.

"You did understand, sweetheart! She did comprehend, Sam!" Helen was smiling with tears still wet on her cheeks.

"No, angel, not tonight. You have to stay here for a bit longer, while your leg heals more and you get stronger. You're going to have another operation, to make you prettier. You need to focus and take your recovery one step at a time, one day at a time, as we do. Now close those beautiful eyes and rest, and Mama and Papa will see you in the morning."

More days of intense therapy and observation passed and Marsha continued making strides forward. Even with the first plastic surgery, she only missed two days of therapy. She was trying as hard as she could to please everyone.

"Be careful, Marsha. Your legs are becoming stronger, but you can't trust them yet. You could still hurt yourself very easily. No silly stuff, OK, cutie?" Stefan said with a serious tone and a smile.

Marsha looked up at the young, tall, brunette physical therapist beside her, while she grabbed hold of the parallel bars. "I sor-ry," and she stood still to catch her breath. Unassisted standing and walking took the most concentration and energy out of Marsha.

"Oh, Brisa, this is both so hard and so boring. I have to keep standing, and walking back and forth, over and over again, Brisa. My legs don't want to do this!"

"Hang in there, Marsha. I know it's hard for you. Your legs haven't been walking in almost six months, longer than

that really, and the right one just had major reconstructive surgery. Your muscles, bones, and joints have to learn to work again. Your therapist is right; you need to keep practicing, but focus. It's the only way, Marsha, and it's the only way you'll get to go home."

Marsha's sea blue eyes filled with tears and they trickled down her still scarred, exceedingly pale face. She wanted to walk, but she didn't want to be in the hospital any more.

"Pa-pa, I go to-o?" and Helen was by her side holding onto her daughter's outstretched little fragile hand. Day after day, whenever Marsha's parents prepared to leave, tears rolled down Marsha's face.

"Oh baby—Sam, how can we make her understand? How can we make Marsha understand she needs to stay here at the hospital to get better, to get stronger?"

"Oh, I think she knows, honey. She just doesn't want us to leave her. She doesn't want to be alone. Sweetie, we'll be back early tomorrow morning, like always. You need your rest to get better. You need to go to sleep, and we'll be back before you know it" Sam explained.

Marsha looked at her mother and father, tears in her eyes, and nodded, "I s-ee-p-y n-oo-w," she uttered between sobs.

"That's a girl," responded Sam softly and Helen breathed a sigh of relief. "You really are a bright, sensible little girl, aren't you? Of course you are and that's what's going to get you onto your feet again, angel. Do you realize how much Mama and I love you? How proud we are of you?" Papa praised.

There was no verbal answer from Marsha, just a little smile. She lay there snuggling the nurse-dressed teddy bear Mama had bought in the gift shop, and both parents could tell their daughter was fighting sleep. Helen walked around the bed making sure Marsha's bed rails were secured and her covers proper. When she was finally satisfied she kissed Marsha's forehead and found her already asleep.

"Mama will see you in the morning and Papa will be here after work. Sweet dreams, honey," and Papa also kissed their little girl good-bye.

Sam and Helen strode down the hospital hallway to the elevators arm in arm with a lighter heart than ever before in the past year. Compared to the early days, since the accident, both parents felt the pressure of their immediate worries for their daughter's mere existence fading. Yet new concerns replaced them almost immediately. From now on everything would be a chore for Marsha, The Walsch's life would be focused on caring for their handicapped child. Every day would be geared to optimize their daughter's recovery. Marsha's parents vowed to give her every opportunity to overcome her handicaps. Life took on new meaning.

"Helen, I believe there are organizations that can help us help Marsha. She faces many obstacles, and we just don't have the knowledge or resources to do it ourselves," Sam said with resolve. (Appendix 2) "Sweetheart, would you like to go out to dinner on our way home? I thought that little Italian place close to home. It's not extravagant. But it's all we can afford right now."

"Oh Sam, I'd love to! We still think of each other and that's important. I love you so much!" Helen said with a smile as the young couple made their way to the car, arm in arm.

As Helen and Sam were seated in the dimly lit restaurant, the two counted their blessings once again and looked ahead to their future. They openly credited each other for their daughter's recovery and continued to foresee what it would require to bring about further success.

"Helen, you deserve so much credit for Marsha's recovery. You were the one who spent most of the time with her, coaxing her back to life. I'll never forget that!" Sam said proudly.

"Oh Sam, come on. You would have done the same in my position. The work you were doing was equally important. Without it, we'd have no income coming in. But thank you, I appreciate your acknowledgment," Helen said with a smile.

"Again, in Marsha's recovery at home, you'll be the primary caregiver, the one she'll depend on, and I want you to know that I'll do whatever I can to help you."

"I know, Sam, you always do and I love you for it."

"I'm going to talk to my boss about flex time when possible, so I can help, help you take care of Marsha. I'm sure Hal won't mind, especially under the circumstances."

"Oh Sam, I realize we'll have to change our way of life, honey, but don't go jeopardizing your career. It's our only money supply!" Helen said with a look of concern on her face.

"Oh baby, it won't come to that, don't worry," assured Sam. "I'm sure you can ask our neighbors for help, when you're tired, I mean, to help with Marsha and the cooking maybe?"

"I'm really not good at accepting help and really not good at asking for it. You know that."

"I know, but remember, you can't do everything, honey, and we can't afford for you to get sick either."

"Yah, you're right. It'll be hard though, to ask for help, I mean," Helen sighed.

"I think our neighbors will come calling and ask if they can assist you in any way, and all you'll have to do is agree, and you really should, baby. It's important. I'm worried about you! You can't carry the burden of everything, even with me helping. It's just too much!"

"Yes, dear, OK, I'll accept help!"

"Good. You can't wear yourself out because the extra care that Marsha will require will be endless. If you are out of the picture where will Marsha be? You must accept help and rest, for Marsha's sake if no one else."

"I know," whispered Helen in a sad voice.

"Honey, think positive. The harder we work with her now, the more we apply ourselves, the quicker we'll see progress. That's what she is doing. Just think of the miraculous advances that she's shown us so far. Each little step brings progress and hope for her too, I'm sure."

"Oh yes, progress gives her the will to go on, to struggle, to get even better. Sam, do you think she understands we're trying to help her when we're pushing her?"

"Somehow I think she does, Helen. We have to keep reminding her, though, and it never hurts to explain why we do the things we do. This will help in learning both language and life lessons. It's also a way of encouraging Marsha to help herself."

"Yah, Sam, and we're not only teaching communication skills, but setting an example of how to treat others, how to work together," commented Helen with the teacher in her coming out. "Do you realize we are modeling behavior for Marsha. How she sees us interact with her and between ourselves will form the basis for her behavior."

"It's amazing how the two of us are emulating the role of new parents, isn't it, honey? If you think about it, we are starting over, Marsha's starting over. She's starting life a second time," stated Sam, a bit dazed.

"Yah, you're right, and we're going to make her the best we can, you and I. It'll seem impossible at times, and so difficult, I'm sure. But we'll do it, you'll see. We did it the first time, we can do it again!" said Helen triumphantly.

"I don't doubt you. You'll find unique ways to help Marsha, to teach her. You'll make it happen. You always do. When you put your mind to something, nothing stops you, Helen. That's one of the qualities I've loved about you for so long!" Sam beamed at his wife.

"Oh, sweetheart, I couldn't do it without your love and support," responded Helen with a smile. "Do you think we should get a tutor for Marsha, Sam?"

"I think you've done very well with her so far, and you were a certified teacher a few years ago. But it might be a good idea to give you a break and also to keep up with the system. That will be a little while yet until she will be ready. Don't you agree?"

"Maybe we can find a tutor who can come in twice a

week to fill in what I'm not doing. Remember, we have to look at the cost of everything, honey. I don't think Marsha will have many problems learning, do you? I mean, she picks up pretty quickly with us," Helen was starting to sound excited again.

"You're to thank for that, you know," praised Sam yet again.

"How so?"

"Well, all the time you spent with her, the music, the stories, the building of our daughter's brain from the very beginning."

"Yah, you're right. I keep taking all that for granted and it really does make a phenomenal difference," Helen said with a sigh. She and her husband sat across from each other in the little booth, silent.

The sounds of the busy restaurant filled the air. They had a quiet meal and went home to rest for the next set of challenges, all the while their minds raced with unanswerable questions. They individually thought about their daughter's situation, and their situation overall. How would circumstances play out? What else could they do for a positive turnout?

Their questions and doubt about their daughter's future lingered well into their slumber that night and Sam awoke the next morning, stirring, and exclaimed, still half asleep, "Your parents want you to succeed and can't help wonder if handicaps from your accident will hinder you forever."

His dream, once again, had ridden him with guilt. "Oh Helen, we have to stop blaming ourselves. You and I need to stop feeling sorry for ourselves. We need to move on. There's nothing we can do about the past. I know that. So why can't I let go?"

"Honey, you're in pain. Marsha's coming home and you have no idea what the future will hold for our little girl. Of course you're scared. So am I," Helen reminded her husband. "Do you remember how Marsha was always the eternal optimist and we encouraged her enthusiasm to learn and prosper?"

"Yes, but now she'll face so many disappointments because of her disabilities."

Both parents were disillusioned by the fear of failure.

"How will we pick her up from major disappointment?" she stammered.

Helen and Sam had great concern that if Marsha didn't succeed, she would give up. Neither wanted their child to be disillusioned or disappointed over and over again. Sam and Helen never before dealt with fear of failure and didn't know how to handle it, especially for their offspring.

"Marsha—Marsha, I wish your parents would understand that disappointment and fear is tempered by the will to go on. Your persistence and perseverance will make you succeed. I really hope you understand because that's the only way to succeed, especially for someone who is challenged."

"Thanks for reminding me, Brisa. I've always been very positive and taken on life's challenges. I suppose I'll have to work a little harder now though."

"Yes, and you'll have to be a lot more patient with yourself. Like I told you so many times before, life won't be easy for you."

"I remember."

"You will have many obstacles and hurdles to overcome, and don't be surprised if you hear people repeatedly saying you can't do it, that you'll never amount to anything."

"But why, Brisa? Why would someone say that to me?"

"Because they only see the frail, damaged little girl from the outside. They have no idea of the special power within you. They have no idea of the strong person you are, and some people are just cruel. That's just the way it is, Marsha."

"OK, you are really preparing me, aren't you?"

"Marsha, it's best to be prepared for the future. Being prepared can help make a difference in how we succeed, and I want to help you as much as I can since you made the decision to live and persevere. This is my job, Marsha,

and it is the job of your parents. The only difference is that your mom and dad will love and support you in a special way."

"How's that, Brisa?"

"You're special, Marsha. Your parents came close to losing you and they'll never forget it! You'll need extra help from them and they're going to do everything they can for you, forever."

"Mama and Papa must really love me. I've felt the power of their love from the beginning, Brisa."

"Yes, and it's definitely helped your recovery. Your parents will be on top of your doctors and caregivers and you too, Marsha. At times it may seem too much to the observer, and as you progress, to you too. Your parents will continue to support you in every little step you take. Always remember that they are doing this out of love for you. Your mom and dad want you to succeed and can't help but wonder if your handicaps will limit you. Remember too, you're their only one, their only child, and they are in so much pain because of what happened to you and, deep down, are still filled with guilt, Marsha.

"Wow, Brisa, Mama and Papa really have a lot to handle. I will certainly do the best I can, to recover, I mean. Thank you for explaining all this to me."

"You're welcome, and I'll keep reminding you from time to time so you'll continue fighting your injuries and disabilities when times get tough, when you're so frustrated you don't want to go on."

"Thanks, Brisa. I'll need all the help I can get. I'm sure. I'm beginning to realize the long, hard road ahead of me."

"*Oh, sweetheart, you have no idea. Sometimes your parents will want to shield you from disappointment. They'll have this worry that if you fail the first time you'll give up forever and they wouldn't be able to handle that, Marsha!"*

"You mean Mama and Papa are afraid they won't be able to help me if I feel bad from my disappointments? Is that it, Brisa?"

"That's it, Marsha. You're smart, and don't ever forget

that. Also, remember to keep moving forward and don't look back. Keep going, keep struggling and don't take no for an answer. Your condition will improve only if you are positive and persistent. Everything, your recovery and future, are up to you."

"I understand."

"Oh, one more thing, and I'll let you rest.

"Yes, Brisa."

"There is a bonus for you if you try, try, try, and succeed."

"What's that?"

"You will not only recover better physically. You'll also be building self-esteem to help you along and further your recovery even more."

"You mean my parents can help me help myself, right? That's pretty neat, Brisa."

"OK, we've had a long day today. Get some rest and work on your recovery, Marsha, OK?"

"OK. Good night, Brisa"

"Good night and sweet dreams, Marsha."

XV. The Long Road To Recovery: Every Step Is A Step Forward

Sam, since we have Marsha home now we certainly have special obstacles ahead of us, and we need to accept the fact that Marsha is physically challenged," Helen stated over her breakfast of eggs, toast, and coffee.

"Of course she is, Helen, in many ways. Don't worry though, we'll stick together, you and I, and work with her to accept her challenges and overcome them, all of them, in time."

"Sam, thank you for being positive and accepting the responsibilities we have now. I'm sure if Marsha could understand, she'd be very thankful her parents are standing by her in these times of difficulty."

"I'm sure Marsha will react better if we tend to her with a smile," Sam said, smiling and getting up from the table to gather Helen's breakfast dishes so she could sit quietly a few minutes longer.

"Oh Sam, just thinking about how much I want to help her get well and the work it's going to take gives me a headache. I guess the not knowing how to handle our situation or what lies ahead, adds to my frustrations," Helen bowed her head slightly, putting her right hand to her forehead to ease her emerging headache.

"I know. I'm as concerned as you are, honey. What we need to do is watch and listen to Marsha's physical therapists very closely and help them by doing what we can at home to help Marsha. We'll get a better idea every day. Medical treatment is a partnership between the professionals and the patient to make it most successful," Sam said while loading the dishwasher with the breakfast dishes.

"You mean like getting Marsha to want to help herself walk again, Sam?" Helen asked while refilling the coffee cups.

"Exactly, honey, and get her so she'll want to learn."

"Oh Sam, I know. I will have her be by my side as much as possible while I'm still doing what needs to be done around here. I will let her watch and let her participate when possible. Observation is one of the best ways for her to learn. I'll also talk as much as possible to teach her, tell her what Mama's doing. Marsha's vocabulary needs broadening, and all of this will help. Watching me and helping me will make her proud of herself, on top of it. Small accomplishments will be big, especially at first. I'm sure of it, Sam! I'm confident!" Helen said looking renewed and proud.

"That's a great idea. But it'll slow you down so much and you're going to have your hands so full. You're describing yourself as superwoman and I'm worried about you!" Sam said as he sat at the kitchen table and took his wife's hand.

"I'm just thinking about everything, Sam. I realize we'll need to prioritize things. We need to do whatever we can! You and I have to show our daughter an extra abundance of love and patience. Remember what Dr. Davis said, 'Marsha's handicaps will only improve the more she learns, the more she's taught and the more she's challenged.' It's right, it has to be."

"Progress will be slow, sometimes even unnoticeable. We need to set goals for ourselves and for Marsha, don't you agree? Make little goals, and realistic ones, and please don't overwhelm yourself!"

"Oh Sam, I'll be OK. This is our baby, our child. Please don't worry about me too much, honey. I want to do this... I need to do this!"

Like any mother, Helen wanted to do the very best for her child. Both parents committed themselves to the special care and dedication their offspring would require, in varying degrees, for years to come. They came to accept their daughter's physical and mental challenges. Only then were they able to overcome their inner pain and move forward with their daughter's recovery.

"I know, we have no choice really, and yes, Marsha will get the care she needs, the best we can give her. I read *dis-ABILITY* by Linda Lee Ratto[2] and learned we must learn to accept Marsha's challenges as normal. This way she will grow with a positive attitude. I also learned that you are actually working through your pain, Helen, sweetheart. You're directing your painful energy constructively. Ratto does point out though, that your Super Mom tendencies will take their toll both physically and mentally," Sam said, finishing his coffee.

He kissed his wife good-bye for the day and headed out the door and off to the office. Helen sat for a few minutes in the quiet kitchen gathering her thoughts and preparing for the day's challenges. It was going to be tough. But somehow, she had to make it work. She had to make Marsha want to recover. She had to make it fun. With a final sip of coffee, she gathered her bearings and went to wake her sleeping miracle.

"Wake up, Marsha. Time to go to physical therapy," Helen gently nuzzled Marsha. The sleeping girl opened her eyes and smiled up at her mama.

Helen walked to the window, drew Marsha's dark green curtains, and rays of sunshine shone through the open window into the little girl's bedroom. Helen turned and saw as her daughter released a sigh of contentment and closed her eyes again. She does look like an angel, Helen thought. There's a heavenly glow surrounding her. Maybe there's an angel watching over our precious little girl, giving her the extra strength she needs. You are so amazing little one!

"I love you so much! You have no idea, little one!"

"Ma-ma? Ha-v Ted-dy?" Marsha exclaimed suddenly, awakening her mother back to reality. Marsha held out her arms towards her Mr. Teddy and repeated, "Ma-ma. Ha-v Ted-dy?"

"Yes, dear, we can take Mr. Teddy to therapy with us today. He'll watch you get your massage and do your exercises. You can bring him to breakfast so we don't forget him, OK? Now here's my hand. Can you sit up? Good girl. How about standing up? I have your wheelchair right here. Be careful, sweetie—. Mama's right here, Marsha."

Days, weeks, and finally months passed and little Marsha struggled daily on her long and tedious road of recovery. Helen set up a schedule for herself and Marsha to try and optimize the days. She kept her promise to teach Marsha as she did chores and encouraged participation whenever possible.

"The wet, clean laundry goes in the dryer. Can you help me put it in the dryer, Marsha? Oh, look, here are dry clothes. Let's take them out first and put them on the kitchen table. Can you help Mama fold? First the left, then the right side."

Helen was also conscious of speaking slowly and clearly so Marsha would recognize and associate words.

"Mama, food, cook, eat," Marsha declared pointing at bags of groceries. Helen put the grocery bags on the counter after their shopping trip another day.

"Yes, dear, very good! We cook food before we eat it," Helen instructed.

Inconsequential ideas and most anything, things taken for granted, suddenly became monumental. Helen's dream about all the recovering handicapped little girls and her search for Marsha among them, so long ago, was becoming reality, ever so slowly. Since Marsha's return home, she showed signs of improvement almost daily. After the amazing operation on her femur, Marsha learned to stand and walk with the assistance of crutches quickly and her coordination also continued improving dramatically over time. She could feed herself with a spoon, although she still had problems brushing her own hair and threading block-sized beads. Friends and family made special efforts to assist Marsha with her special circumstances and time and time again she would acquire different developmental toys, which Helen incorporated into their daily schedule. She soon recognized Marsha's eagerness to learn, although recognizing extreme frustration very quickly.

"Sam, we must help her by showing her over and over again, without doing for her. She has to learn that she can do for herself and by herself. We need to be careful to help only when she asks."

Marsha's parents made every effort to help their child physically and mentally.

Sam heard his wife sobbing as they retired that night and all he could do to comfort her was reach for her and hug her.

"Oh Sam, we are trying so hard. Marsha's trying so hard, and I'm so tired. I can't help her any more ..." Helen sobbed.

Sam wished there was something he could do to make the pain stop, but knew there was nothing. "Baby—honey, shhhh. You are helping her more than you or I know. Please don't think you're useless. You're the one Marsha depends on, the one I depend on. Cry all you want. You'll feel better—I know how hard it must be for you day in and day out. I hurt too, you know, not knowing exactly what to do next or expect next, for that matter. Maybe it's time to enroll Marsha in the handicap school, honey. It probably wouldn't be a bad idea for her to have social interaction either. What do you think?"

"I'm reluctant to let her out of my nurturing arms, but I'm willing to try if you think it's OK, Sam."

"I know what you mean, honey. Marsha's so fragile and still recovering, but we need to let her grow in more ways than we can provide at home. In Linda Lee Ratto's[2] book, *dis-Ability,* I also read that a physically challenged child should be challenged, based on their abilities, of course, but nevertheless challenged. Ratto brings up lots of issues that make good sense. You really should read it when you get the chance.

"Oh, I *have* read it. Ratto stresses how important it is to challenge a challenged child because not challenging them is taking away from their capacity to and for learning. Challenges and repetition is part of the learning process."

"Helen, you're so amazing! How do you find the time?"

"Marsha is my sole focus, Sam. My goal is helping our daughter overcome her handicaps and if it means reading a book to help me do that, so be it. I generally read all that I can while Marsha's napping. Although she is getting stronger every day, her naps are still desperately important."

"Like I said, you're amazing! And I love you for it!" Sam adoringly took Helen into his arms and kissed her. "Why don't you take a break, a hot bath maybe? I'll check on Marsha and get the breakfast things out, and even fix my lunch. You two probably have another busy day tomorrow."

Sam gently pushed his tired wife out of bed and toward the bathroom.

"Yes, you're right, Sam. I thought we'd go to the handicap school tomorrow and I'll sign Marsha up for the fall. It is in a new building and the school itself came highly recommended," Helen said, starting the water in the tub.

Helen made every effort to find out everything she could about Marsha's new school. She was introduced to Mrs. Long, Marsha's teacher, whom she found to be a very nice and caring person.

"My two assistants and I busy the children with what their interests are. For example, we may have play dough on one table, blocks on another, and colored paper and crayons on yet another table for the children," and Mrs. Long showed Marsha materials she and her assistants used to educate the children.

Marsha looked interested yet apprehensive. She quietly observed the teacher and the room. She didn't smile a lot, but nodded when asked questions by both the teacher and her mother. Although she didn't understand what this was, she got the idea that it was a place for children her age to go and learn.

Helen explained to Marsha all the way home, and for the remainder of the afternoon, about how nice the school was and how much fun it would be to be with children her own age. She wondered if in the process she was also trying to convince herself.

Marsha was quiet most of the afternoon and seemed to be in thought about the new place that she might be attending soon. Although she nodded when her mother asked her questions like 'Did you like the school this morning, honey?' and 'Do you think you will make lots of new friends there?' She was apprehensive. Weren't there supposed to be other children there? "Where were other children, Mama?"

"School hasn't started yet, baby. It's still summer vacation. But soon, and you're right, school will have children to play and learn with. You are so smart," and Helen beamed at her daughter's emerging inquisitiveness.

"I thought the school itself was very nice, Sam. Marsha's classroom, I noticed, had soft hues of yellow and orange on the walls, soothing colors. One of them had a mural of a little boy and girl in a garden. Mrs. Long explained they use it to identify objects in nature, and that it soothes the children," Helen was very excited at the prospect of getting help with Marsha.

"That's a good idea, a mural for teaching purposes," Sam nodded.

"I also noticed numerous art supplies and a variety of books. I think this may very well be a good thing, Sam. I feel comfortable, Sam, and their bus will pick Marsha up and bring her home right here at our house," Helen said with resolve. "Marsha seemed comfortable with Mrs. Long. And she curiously played with some of the toys too. Do you think we, as her parents, should tell her that she is going to go to school, just so that she is prepared? I tried my best to point out things that I saw and told her that she will have fun with kids her own age there. I tried to be positive, without pushing."

"I would want to be informed instead of surprised by a monumental change," Sam finally answered.

"I think so too!" Helen smiled.

"When is our big girl's first day of school?" Papa announced proudly, smiling at Marsha as he entered the family room.

Marsha sat quietly and thought pensively for a few moments before continuing to play with Mr. Teddy and her doll.

"Sweetheart, you'll do great! You'll meet other children just like you and Mama says your teacher is really nice," Papa said as he sat by his little girl.

"Mama will put you on the bus right in front of our house and I'll be waiting for you when you come home," Mama chimed in as she entered the room.

Marsha continued sitting quietly in the corner, hugging Mr. Teddy.

"I'm not sure what Mama and Papa are saying. But I think they want to send me somewhere and that scares me. I've never been away from Mama and Papa and I'm afraid of being by myself. I'm afraid of being alone," she thought to herself. "Brisa—Brisa, can you hear me? Can you help me? I'm confused. How can I do this, be away from home, all by myself?"

"Calm down, sweetie. You need to do this. It's kind of a next step for you and you won't be alone, remember? I'll be with you and besides, you're strong, remember?"

"Oh, Brisa, I know I'm strong. But I'm not sure I can do this! I've tried to be brave, but a new place, and without Mama there? I don't know."

"Marsha, You have to. It's another step in your recovery. We talked about this, remember?"

"Uh huh, I remember."

HANGING ON

I'm not sure about this kitten,
Tho it's as cute as can be.
I wonder what it is thinking,
Hanging to a clothes line so
Perr-fectly.
Its eyes are wide and open
Just what's intended is not clear.
Is there a message for us humans?
To have hope in spite of fear?
Yes, the kitten could suffer a fall.
How far is it to the ground?
In the meantime it keeps hanging on
'Til a rescue person comes around.
****

No matter the problem, hang on!

Helen Parker Steele
June 2002

Sam and Helen looked at their little girl and knew she wasn't happy.

"I don't think she likes our idea, Sam. What are we going to do? I can't bear to see her like this, Sam," Helen said, working herself up again.

"Sweetheart, I know it's hard, but we need to go forward. Marsha needs to grow outside of this little bubble we've created for her. She needs to experience life, other people around her. It's been about nine months since she's experienced the outside world," Sam reassured.

"Yes, Sam, I know. We need to focus on moving ahead and not wallow in pity for her. It's not healthy for Marsha or us. You're right!" she said, smiling up at her husband.

But Sam couldn't mistake the pain in his wife's eyes. Without realizing, Marsha's parents were accepting their daughter's challenges as normal and helping Marsha accept them, and accept herself.

That night Marsha was quiet throughout dinner and afterwards, with realization something life changing loomed ahead, but fell asleep quickly nonetheless. The anticipation drained Marsha's energy. The following morning was as confusing, as Mama got her up early, and got her dressed quickly. She had a nice, but quick, breakfast, and went outside to the end of the driveway and stood there. Marsha was puzzled and looked at her mother from time to time, questioningly, as Mama stood behind her, stroking her shoulders lovingly. Soon, a small van-like bus came and took Marsha away.

When Marsha was brought home by the van hours later, her mother asked her a lot of questions. Marsha nodded, but didn't say much. She wanted her Papa.

"How was your first day of school, sweet pea?" asked Papa encouragingly as he swooped Marsha into his arms.

"Marsha cried when I left her on the bus this morning. Oh, Sam, I could hardly bear it!" Helen started sobbing.

"Oh baby, it must have been scary to ride that big bus all by yourself, huh? You did it though and you know what? Papa is very proud of you!" Sam tried to sound strong and encouraging, but was very sad inside for his scared little girl.

Marsha just clung to her father and didn't say a word.

"How was she when you got her off the bus, Helen?"

"She wasn't crying. But she was glad to see me and clung to me much like she's doing to you right now."

"Well, it was a big day for you, wasn't it, sweet pea? What did you do in school? Can you tell me?" Papa asked, trying to encourage Marsha to speak.

Marsha stayed quiet, still clinging to her father and he rocked her gently to comfort her. "This was obviously a traumatic experience for her today," he thought. "I suppose something new, whatever it is, is monumental for a child, especially a handicapped child."

As the days passed, little Marsha seemed to get even quieter and withdrawn into her own world. Despite all the efforts of her loving parents, Marsha was just not happy.

"Oh Brisa, I really don't like being away from home. Mrs. Long is nice to me. But the other children are so noisy. They yell and scream. They're all over the place, Brisa. I hate being there. I can't handle it. What can I do, Brisa? Help me, pl-ease."

"Hang on, Marsha. Hang in there a little longer. Your mom and dad will realize your pain and come to your rescue. They love you, remember?"

"Y-es, Bri-s-a, I know and I l-ove them."

Helen and Sam sat in the living room after dinner the week after Marsha started school. They both noticed Marsha was very quiet and played by herself in her favorite spot. She had turned down Helen's attempts to play and had even chosen the solitude over sitting with Papa and reading the paper. The sight of her solitude made Helen worry.

"What else can we do, Sam?"

"Nothing but talk to her, try to get her to talk to us, reveal her feelings, and keep showering her with unconditional love. A few days and she'll fall into the routine, the swing of things, Helen, I'm sure."

"It's an adjustment, a huge adjustment for her, for all of us. But you're probably right. We should just be patient, she'll get into the routine."

Another day went by and then another, and every morning little Marsha battled with tears and Helen was stressed beyond belief. "How can I continue this, putting my baby through this," she thought. She had thought her dire stress about Marsha a thing of the past, and here it was yet again. Daily, she was practically in tears as the small van with the handicapped student plaque on either side rolled away from the Walsch's driveway and Marsha, greeting her in silence, clung to her day after day.

Marsha's teacher recognized her unresponsiveness and lack of enthusiasm, and brought it to the Walsch's attention. She gave Marsha the customary three weeks to adjust and since there had been little, if no change, she thought it best to speak with the girl's mother.

"Mrs. Walsch, there are fifteen handicapped students in Marsha's class. We try to give each student as much attention as possible, and Marsha is not very responsive to any of the activities at all."

"Sam, I took Marsha to school this morning and sat in class to observe. I thought that maybe I could ease Marsha's fears by understanding them. Now I understand Marsha's anxieties. I understand! It looked like Marsha sat in confusion the entire morning. She looked sad and confused. Oh, honey, it broke my heart to see her that way!" Helen said sadly.

"What do you mean? Did something specific happen, Helen?" Sam asked, concerned.

"The children, God bless them, are primarily either mentally handicapped or autistic. Only two others are physically handicapped. Sam, it was chaos! The confusion and noise was unbelievable. I understand it now. Marsha's little, recovering mind can't handle it. Then, I went to the office and they told me, 'Mrs. Walsch, this is not for every handicapped student. Not every student can handle our curriculum.' They said it like it was Marsha's fault, not theirs," Helen said in a tone mocking the head of the school's tone.

"Really?" Sam was shocked.

"Oh Sam, when she told me that I almost flipped! She was implying Marsha doesn't have the ability to learn. I felt this woman was discarding our child. I felt she was inferring Marsha is worthless," Helen said indignantly.

"Oh, Helen, I'm sure she didn't mean that. Maybe you're overreacting? Did they tell you if there's been any improvement in Marsha's attitude or abilities in the last two weeks?"

"There hasn't, Sam. How can there be? I wouldn't expect her to improve. I think she's worse. At least she is at home! What are we going to do? Marsha can't handle the environment and to tell you the truth, I couldn't either! Marsha's so unhappy and I'm sure that has something to do with her withdrawn attitude here at home. How she could learn there is beyond me. It's not for her, Sam! I know it!" Helen began to sob.

"OK, that does it. Marsha's coming back home and we'll see about a tutor for the rest of this school year," Sam announced after quietly thinking things over.

"Maybe Marsha is just not emotionally ready for a public environment to begin with, Sam. Maybe it's just too much for her. That school, specifically, is definitely too much!"

"I'm sure it was something like that. Don't let what that woman said bother you though. We have a very strong and bright little girl! We both know that!" Sam continued in his matter-of-fact tone.

"You are right!" Helen nodded her head. "To know what she's overcome, what she's learned and the desire to learn we've seen in her. How can anyone imply she's hopeless? The nerve and insensitivity, with her record, and that from a school administrator!" Helen went from sobbing to fuming with every word as she realized it wasn't anything but insensitivity on the woman's part.

"Put it out of your mind, Helen. We need to focus on the positive, be positive and move forward, for Marsha's sake. She needs to keep moving onward and upward and she needs our positive guidance and encouragement to make that happen!"

"We've seen that accomplishments take her a little longer, but she can handle anything. Her mind is hungry to learn."

"You're absolutely right, Helen, and we're not going to let anyone tell us differently," Sam stated in a tone that announced the end of that discussion.

Marsha's parents spent extra time consoling their daughter over the weekend, due to Marsha's traumatic experience that Helen had become privy to. On their walk in the nearby park Sunday afternoon, Helen thought she would broach the subject of the school with Marsha.

"Mama is so glad she went to school with you, honey. Why didn't you tell us that it was so scary and loud? Sweetheart, next time please tell us when something is bothering you!" Mama gently instructed.

"Maybe she didn't know how, Helen," Sam whispered.

Marsha seemed to be deep in thought. So her parents thought it best to drop the subject, at least for a little while.

"Brisa, why can't they see I'm trying my best? I don't know why I don't fit in. I realize Mama and Papa are doing their best for me, to help me get better, and I don't want to disappoint them, Brisa. But I just don't fit in anywhere."

"Marsha, nobody ever knows what's best. All we can do is try different things and be persistent. Your parents tried what they thought would be good for you and make you happy. You gave it your best shot too, didn't you?"

"Yes."

"Now it's time to move on, try something else, OK? It's part of the learning process, Marsha."

Marsha was happy when she woke up late the next morning. Mama hadn't awakened her early to go on the van to the noisy school. Mother and daughter had a nice breakfast and did their usual morning exercises. Marsha wasn't quite sure what was going on, but she liked the fact that she didn't have to go away today. The next couple of days went the same, with Marsha smiling more and more everyday, and Helen was relieved that she seemed to be less stressed each day, confirming the decision to have Marsha tutored at home.

Thursday morning brought a new surprise to the Walsch house. Marsha was just beginning to feel like herself again, when somebody came to the back door of the house. She could hear a strange lady's voice, but she sounded happy. Mama sounded happy too. Marsha wondered who it was.

"Your teacher, Mrs. Baker, is here, Marsha. Come say hello," Mama called from the kitchen to Marsha in the family room.

In a few minutes, while Mrs. Baker was setting up, Marsha walked stiffly and slowly into the kitchen on her crutches.

"He-llo, Mis-us B-a-er," she stammered, obviously out of breath."

"Well hello, Marsha, don't you look pretty today, with your pink sweater?" Mrs. Baker was careful to pronounce every word and enunciate every letter.

Her mannerisms told Helen she was obviously drawing Marsha into her world. She was being very careful not to upset Marsha. Mrs. Baker wanted Marsha to feel comfortable with her as she eased her into a teaching and learning curriculum. She had already instructed Helen they should do the same to encourage Marsha's vocabulary, without the knowledge that Helen, a former teacher, already enforced the practice.

"Are you ready to learn more about colors and the ABC's today?" Mrs. Baker asked.

"Y-es," replied Marsha, already making her way to the kitchen table.

Helen had a hard time watching as her little girl struggled to get from place to place, and the time and energy it took her. She remembered her physical therapist had advised to let her make her own way, that it would be worth the pain and her aggravation in the long run and only this refrained her from helping her child. As she stood observing, she marveled, once again, at Marsha's turnaround from about six months ago. Helen found herself doing that more and more these days, as her daughter progressed beyond anyone's beliefs.

Marsha seemed to have fun learning with Mrs. Baker. She loved the picture cards brought for learning colors, numbers, and letters, and how she made learning fun. Helen had the feeling that Marsha didn't even know she was learning because she was so enthralled and fascinated with Mrs. Baker's antics.

"Sam, you should see them together. Marsha is almost mesmerized by this lady. She adores her, idolizes her and wants to emulate her!" Helen beamed.

"That's wonderful. We're lucky our neighbor knew her and she volunteered to help us, honey. Do you get the chance to review, with Marsha, what she's learned in her lesson today?" asked Sam.

"Oh yes, I try the best I can, while we were playing with play dough and doing dishes, for example. I plan to do things like singing the ABC's or counting while we are doing physical therapy and taking a bath? It worked real well this afternoon and she's enjoying herself too. Oh, honey, I think this was the right thing to do!" Helen said, starting to shed some happy tears.

"Oh honey, you're such a good mother, you know that, right? Marsha's a lucky girl and I'm a lucky man," Sam whispered in her ear softly as he took his tired yet encouraged wife into his arms. "We're going to make it, babe. Marsha's gonna make it."

Helen closed her eyes and snuggled into his chest.

Sam gave his wife multitudes of encouragement. Every day he knew the situation was tougher on her than him. Sam thought to himself, I have such respect for her and what she's doing.

He kept reminding her, "Look at what Marsha's accomplished because of you."

He often thought, when looking at his lovely wife, I love her so much and there's nothing that could make me stop loving her!

One morning Helen stirred and said, for no particular reason, "Honey, I need to go check on Marsha."

She always had their child on her mind, first and foremost. To an observer, a fly on the wall, it was an obsession. To Helen, it came natural. Although she ran herself ragged at times, there was nothing else she could fathom herself doing, but helping and taking care of her child. Helen saw it as her job. No, it was more than that. It was her duty.

"God doesn't give you more than you can handle," and smiled into her husband's eyes before turning to find Marsha.

"Oh honey, I read about some programs for parents with handicapped children taking place this weekend and there are different organizations out there we can contact for help," he called after her. (Appendix 2)

Stress and fatigue showed itself on Sam also. "How can I not be out of my mind," Sam thought. Every effort, every step, every business decision is made with little Marsha on my mind. Every spare minute was spent thinking about his little girl. Some days Sam spent his lunch hour researching for avenues for further rehabilitation. He was consumed, as his wife, and kept pressing on for the benefit of their daughter.

When Mama came into Marsha's room the little girl was standing at the window loosely hanging on her crutches. She was apparently looking out the window at something. She turned when she heard her mother enter and stared toward her.

"Marsha, look at you. You're walking wonderfully with your crutches. Keep up the good work. Keep practicing, honey," Mama said as she clapped her hands in praise.

"I ca-n wa-k, Ma-m-a, lo-ok, I c-an w-alk," Marsha declared.

Helen called to Sam, who came down the hall at a dead run. He stopped at the doorway and his look of concern immediately turned to a beaming smile. Helen and Sam were very proud of what Marsha was accomplishing and with such willingness. They were amazed at their daughter's stamina and had no idea where it came from.

The couple helped the little girl down the stairs and they followed her to the kitchen where they had a nice egg and toast breakfast. Marsha finished and made her way into the family room to play with her doll house.

"Mrs. Baker told me that because we're stimulating and encouraging Marsha, she wants to learn as much as possible. We're the reason she is the way she is. It's so important to give Marsha positive reinforcement, says Mrs. Baker. Marsha wants to please us and is thereby advancing in every aspect, Sam. Mrs. Baker will be here tomorrow and suggested an outing for the afternoon. The three of us will go to the park and look at the beauty of nature. She felt it would be a good diversion to the trauma Marsha's experienced and be a fun way to start a series of lessons on nature. She's good, Sam. I really like her," Helen said as she put the breakfast dishes in the dishwasher.

"It sounds like it, and the most important thing is Marsha's comfortable and she's enthusiastically learning with her."

"The woman makes learning fun and that's what works with Marsha, besides the calm, quiet, and familiar environment of home."

The family spent a nice day together and Marsha's parents took advantage of every opportunity to help teach their little girl. Although everything took longer, Marsha's slower speed was becoming "normal" to the Walsch family. They were beginning to feel like a "normal" family again. They were beginning to enjoy life again.

The next morning Helen answered the knock at the door. Mrs. Baker was there, right on schedule.

"Good morning, Mrs. Walsch!" Mrs. Baker said as she entered the kitchen.

"Oh please, call me Helen."

"OK, Helen, then you call me Grace from now on."

"Very well," and both women smiled at one another.

Grace resumed, "As time goes on I plan to introduce Marsha more and more to what she can expect when she goes to school next year."

"How do you mean?

"Colors, color combinations, pictures, and stories will get more complex and busier, more involved, I mean, as our time together progresses. Marsha will be able to handle more materials and situations before she enters school next year. She'll be better prepared, you'll see."

"I am so glad we have you, Grace! Marsha loves you and I am confident that what you say will come to pass. I have a feeling that Marsha will persevere with the proper guidance, education, and patience, and I believe you. She'll be ready for school in the fall," Helen was at the end of her rope. She swayed slightly to one side, felt a migraine setting in hard, and reached for the aspirin in the upper cabinet. My child is not a freak, she thought defiantly!

A brilliant blue sky and spring-like temperatures promised a beautiful excursion the following morning and Marsha was so excited to be going on a field trip to the park.

"Marsha, see the ducks on the lake? Shall we count them? Watch them—one, two, three, four. Just watch them, honey, and relax. Breathe deep and listen to the sounds of nature," Grace instructed as she walked with her.

"Mama and I are right here behind you, pushing your wheelchair. You're safe, honey. Don't worry, just relax."

"Uh huh. Pretty lellow flowers in zee grass," and Marsha's face brightened as she continued to relax and feel more and more at ease.

"See the purple ones too, honey?" No verbal answer came from the little girl in the wheelchair, only a continuous content smile, which spoke volumes.

"At least Marsha feels comfortable, so the transition to tutoring her won't take long. I need to ease her into a routine of playing and learning, and I think she'll do just fine. Look at the boat, Marsha."

"Red boat," said Marsha and pointed to the boat and Helen lovingly caressed her daughter's shoulders, bent down beside her wheelchair and gently kissed Marsha's glowing cheek for praise and encouragement.

"Marsha's vocabulary and pronunciation are really excellent from what you've told me she's been through," whispered Grace. "I know you've worked with her, Helen, and it really does show. I will reinforce your efforts, as I'm sure you will mine. Repetition really is the key."

Helen and Marsha's teacher continued quietly discussing Marsha's progress and what lay head.

"In a few weeks you may want to start taking her to the grocery store and the mall, for example. This way she'll get exposed to other environments and learn to deal with them while you're still by her side to give her comfort."

"I tried that. It's hard, but so worth it, Grace."

"Hard? Yes, Helen, in more ways than one! It's tremendously evident you've worked with her."

"Oh yes, we certainly have!"

"It's really amazing how much we take for granted to educate. You and I can experience or notice several things at once and Marsha needs to focus on one at a time, for example. One really has to stop and think how lucky we are and how amazing the brain really is. I think in time, Marsha's abilities will improve just based on what you've told me and what I've experienced so far. We really have to be educated about what to do, and to what degree a handicapped child can handle different environments. I really think Marsha is capable of learning and she'll flourish over the years. Repetition really is the key. It's hard, but so worth it."

"Thank you. I couldn't agree more. We are confident, patient and optimistic!" Helen said with confidence.

"Yes, and it requires patience and persistence," agreed Mrs. Baker. "Helen, I can see your dedication to Marsha, to help her eventually overcome all her difficulties. It is also quite obvious you and your husband are in great pain. May I suggest you read, *The Road Less Traveled*, by M. Scott Peck, MD[1]? It is a book about problems, suffering, challenges, and the choices we make. I think it may shed some light, be of some help."

"Thank you, Grace, I really could use some guidance. I feel like I'm the only one in the world going through this sort of tragedy, the only one who has a child with challenges, and no one else understands," Helen said, sounding frazzled.

"Oh, that's not true. Just think about how many children were in the handicap school where Marsha was, and that's only a very small percentage of the children in this area alone. That school could probably refer you to a parenting or support group."

"Like I have time to go to a meeting, and I really don't

want to return to that school or talk to anyone there, after they referred to Marsha as hopeless," Helen sounded indignant again.

"I understand, Helen. No one wants to have their child referred to as useless," Grace responded sympathetically.

"Have you contacted your church, your pastor? I'm sure a church member would come visit occasionally, maybe even one who has been through a somewhat similar situation."

"Mama?" Marsha turned in her wheelchair and was looking at the two ladies sitting on the park bench.

"Yes, dear?" Helen said, getting up and returning to her daughter's side.

"Mama, I tired, Mama!" Marsha said with a yawn.

"OK, sweetie, we have been here for about an hour," and she looked at Grace, who nodded, and said, "honey, we'll return to the car and go home."

"She still gets tired so easily," Helen told Grace, motioning to her daughter with motherly concern in her eyes.

"Of course she does. It's a lot for a little girl to go out into the world isn't it sweetheart?" commented Grace with reassurance. "But in time Marsha will be able to handle more and more. It's all part of the healing process, Helen."

As they drove home Marsha fell asleep in the back seat. Helen carried her daughter into the house with Grace's assistance. Helen hugged Grace good-bye and sat at the kitchen table with a cup of coffee, thinking about the things Grace had said. Marsha took a long nap and awoke full of vitality. They did her exercises as they did every day, but this time Marsha had a little more resolve and seemed to try harder.

The fresh air must have done her a lot of good, thought Helen.

Marsha helped Mama with dinner by placing the biscuits on the baking sheet. She took her time, and put them in straight rows. Helen was happy at the progress of Marsha's motor skills and let her "best little helper" arrange the silverware on the table. It warmed Helen's heart to see Marsha succeeding at these types of tasks.

"Marsha really is making progress in leaps and bounds, Sam," Helen relayed to her husband when they had finally retired for the evening. "I am so glad we have Grace for her tutor. She's so kind and knowledgeable and Marsha really responds to her. Grace instructs me on how to best reinforce her teachings, so there's maximum repetition for Marsha. I'm really seeing progress, Sam, both mentally and physically. Marsha picks everything up so quickly, more than before even. I mean, just look at her. She's becoming more alert and is happy, Sam! Aren't you noticing the change?"

"I do, honey. It may just be the extra attention, from someone outside the home. Maybe she has turned another corner in her recovery. Either way, I am very proud of her. Of both of you, actually," Sam said, beaming at his wife.

"Yes, it could be as simple as that. We are so lucky she is regaining her strength and full potential. I am proud of her too, and she really responds when I tell her that! It seems to give her renewed strength. Like I said, we are very luck parents to have such a special little girl," Helen repeated proudly.

"We certainly are, honey," and he hugged his wife who willingly snuggled in his arms like a playful kitten. "I am so happy to see you back on your way to your normal self too, dear. It's been a difficult, long road, for both of us!"

"Yes, and it seems Marsha is well on her way to recovering and to being happy again. Do you think she resents being different?" Helen asked, looking up into her husband's steel gray eyes.

"I'm sure she realizes it. How can she not. I'm sure she struggles with it too, Helen. I guess we'll never know the extent of her inner pain. What we need to do is keep encouraging her and letting her know she's special, asking about her feelings."

"Yes, you're right. We need to encourage her to tell us how she feels. I try to get her to talk about her feelings with me. I know she hurts. I can see it in her eyes when she's looking at the neighborhood kids running and playing outside. It hurts me too, Sam. I just don't know how to help her. I just don't..." Helen began to sob yet again.

"Helen, Helen, slow down. Sssshhhh... Marsha will be OK. We just have to be patient with her. She needs..."

"Oh Sam, I know she needs!!!" and Sam took his distraught wife into his arms.

XVI. Determination:
Little Steps Lead To Monumental Changes

Helen, sweetheart, you know you have to think of yourself a bit every once in a while. Let me make you feel better. I have a secret to tell you," Sam whispered into her ear.

"What is it, honey?" Helen asked, her curiosity showing.

"I've been offered a transfer to Brussels, Belgium and it's a really good opportunity. We can start fresh and it could be healthy for Marsha too. I already found out they have a private American School in the suburbs," he said proudly, smiling at the news.

"WHAT?!?!?!" Helen almost screamed.

"Honey calm down!" Sam didn't expect that she wouldn't be as excited as he was.

"You want me to move our handicapped daughter to Europe??? We just found Grace and Marsha is doing so well. And besides all of that, when do you think I have the time to pack up and move?" Helen was in full stage panic mode.

"I found out about it last week, and immediately looked into help for Marsha's schooling and into moving companies that take care of everything. I set everything up so you won't have any worries before I surprised you. I promise that this will not be an additional burden on you, sweetheart!" Sam soothed as best he could.

"Oh? I guess you've already made up your mind?"

Helen suddenly felt squashed.

"Well yes, sort of, and this would put distance between us and what happened to our family. I think it will be a good move for all of us," Sam was still trying to soothe his wife's sudden attack of fears.

"When are we moving?" Helen asked with a new set of anxieties sounding in her quivering voice. She was on the brink of tears.

"I have to be in the Brussels Office next month," replied Sam confidently. "I thought we'd move you and Marsha into an apartment until summer so that Marsha can finish the school year with Mrs. Baker. Then you two come join me in Brussels, and I'll have a house for us by then."

"That way Marsha can start fresh at the private school in fall. That actually makes sense!" Helen said, absorbing the information about the new situation.

"I can help you get into the apartment before I have to leave and you won't have as much work as with this house, and I'll feel better about leaving you behind for a while, Helen."

"Oh Sam, you take good care of us. That would make it much easier on us. I was imagining having to pack up the house and Marsha and having to be there in a few weeks. There are moving companies that actually do the packing for you?" Helen was beginning to sound a little curious and a little less stressed.

"Yes, several actually. I can help you pack and move the things you'll need at the apartment, and the moving company can take care of the rest. Like I said, I don't want this to be an additional burden for you. I want this to be the start of a new adventure for our family. A fresh start, as it were." Sam was carefully watching Helen.

She was beginning to breathe more normally. He had hoped not to upset his wife, but it may turn out all right yet, he thought to himself. He climbed into bed beside her.

"Well, I guess this does sound pretty good. I love you so much!" Helen hugged him and nestled into his shoulder.

"I love you too, baby. Now let's get some sleep so that

tomorrow we can look at some of the possible apartments I found, and start packing, maybe, too."

"You think of everything, Sam."

"Well, you take care of everything relating to Marsha, so this balances things out," Sam said as they curled up like spoons in bed.

"Yah, I guess. So tell me about your new job," Helen urged, with interest.

As he told her the details, she quickly fell asleep, more content and happier than she had been in many months.

The next morning the family went out looking at apartments for the ladies. They had a nice lunch then stopped by the liquor store for some empty boxes and headed home.

"Mama, why my dollies going in boxes?" Marsha asked as Helen put dolls and doll clothes in a box and taped it shut.

"Sweetheart, we're moving to our new home. Remember? And it's far, far away. We don't need all our things for the next few months, do we? We have to send some ahead. Remember that we will be staying at that nice little apartment that is close to the mall. There isn't room for ALL of your dollies and teddies. We'll keep your favorite ones with us, and the others will meet us at the new house. Also, remember that the apartment has a pool. Mama will take you swimming and shopping. We'll like it there, honey."

"Will Mrs. Baker come see me still?" Marsha asked, a little concerned. She understood a little of what Mama and Papa were talking about. It sounded hectic, and busy stuff made Marsha confused and scared. Mama said they would be together, though, and that made things better. Marsha was going to do her best to be strong and help with the move, even though she was not sure exactly what that meant.

"Oh yes, Mrs. Baker will continue to be your teacher until we go on the airplane and go to Brussels, Belgium, our new home."

"Good," responded Marsha, and it was apparent she wasn't quite sure about all these new and strange things to come.

Helen and Sam saw this as more of a positive sign that their little girl was returning to the child they remembered, inquisitive and adventurous. But although she was starting to process information and ask questions, there was a long way to go. Every tiny recognizable step was reason to celebrate in the minds of Marsha's parents.

A few weeks later, when Helen was taking a load of house-stuff to the apartment, she decided to show Marsha the mall. Helen parked, and was helping the girl from the back seat when Marsha grabbed her crutches and started toward the door, before Helen stopped her.

"Marsha? Honey? I think it might be better for us to take your wheelchair to the mall. It is a big place and you might get tired on your crutches, dear."

"OK, Mama, but can I take them?"

"Oh yes, sweetie, by all means! You can start off on your crutches and I'll push the wheelchair."

Helen made a point to always encourage physical activity, per recommendation of Dr. Hanks, and Marsha's past and present physical therapists. Helen was amazed at her daughter's tenacity and iron will.

"Oh Mama, look—, the halls are endless!" Marsha was like a kid in a candy store. There was a lot more room to roam than at home or at the new apartment. She was a seven-year-old intrigued with exploration and inquisitiveness, just like other kids.

"Yes, they are. Now be careful and stay with me. Those crutches are dangerous things if you don't use them correctly, remember?" Helen lectured, again.

"Yes, Mama, I know, and no silly stuff."

Helen stood still for a moment, watching Marsha easily and fearlessly hopping down the mall corridor on her crutches. Children are amazing, she thought, and joined Marsha in stride.

"Slow down, little lady, so Mama can keep up with you."

"Oh Mama, I'm having fun."

"I know, honey. Just be careful and tell me when you get tired."

"OK." Marsha concentrated on walking with her crutches and only when she stopped to catch her breath did she look at the store windows and her surroundings.

Helen was amazed at Marsha's concentration. The little girl visually grasped all the sights and colors on either side of her. Marsha's exuberance showed on her face, in her eyes, as they danced and shone with excitement. Helen was filled with pride as she watched, breathlessly, as her little girl enjoyed her first mall excursion, free of wheelchair assistance. Marsha appeared fearless on her crutches, and Helen was sure she had no idea of how easily she could get hurt.

"Marsha, honey, why don't we sit on this bench and you can look around a bit?" Helen said as she heard Grace's voice in her head, "Let Marsha take in her surroundings."

"OK, I tired now, Mama," and Helen helped Marsha into the wheelchair and draped the crutches along either side, with their bottoms resting on the foot rests. "Honey, do you have enough room for your tootsies?"

"Yah, Mama, I OK. Oh Mama, look at all the stores. We have a book about a food store and a shoe store. Mrs. Baker is helping me read it."

"There are many different kinds of stores here, Marsha. Remember when Papa and I brought you here at Christmas?" Mama asked, checking to see what the little girl remembered.

"Yes, lots of lights," Marsha responded after a pause.

"The mall was all decorated for Christmas then and yes, there were lots and lots of lights, you're right!" and Helen was amazed at Marsha's memory, and she then sighed to herself that Marsha didn't remember the incident with the Santa train. Marsha's voice finally returned her from her thoughts.

"Can we go in a store, Mama?"

"We'll go to JC Penney's and find a pretty sweater for you. You can pick it out all by yourself," Mama said, trying to encourage thought and decision-making.

"What's JC Penney's, Mama?" Marsha asked.

"Penney's is a big department store. It's called that because they have a different department for everything," Mama explained. "You can find just about anything for you or your house there."

"OK, wet's go. Wait till I tell Papa about the mall."

Helen enjoyed spending time with her little girl again. Doing things they used to do together. She marveled at how happy Marsha was, marveled at her very spirit. The incredible spirit of a child, one she thought Marsha had lost forever! All my hard work has paid off, she thought to herself as she pushed Marsha past the colorful shop windows and she sat quietly, intensely taking it all in.

"Mama, so many things to pick from."

"I know, honey. Let me help you. Do you prefer the red or the green sweater to match your jeans?" Helen was giving Marsha little opportunities to make decisions of her own to further her development.

"Red, Mama! Red!" replied Marsha, holding out her arm to touch the red sweater.

"Let's pull it on over your t-shirt to make sure it fits. Here, let me help you."

"What's the paper hanging from the sleeve for, Mama?"

"It's a price tag. It tells you how much money you have to give the store in order to take the sweater home with you. This one is on sale, honey. See the reduced price," and Helen showed her daughter the two price tags.

Helen took the sweater to the counter and paid for it. She was careful to explain what they were doing since Marsha couldn't see everything from her wheelchair. The sales clerk gave Marsha a big smile and a sticker for her hand, and Marsha grinned up at her friendly face.

"On our way back to the car, would you like an ice cream?"

Helen felt people looking at her and Marsha, and wondered if Marsha noticed. She wondered if Marsha noticed, if it bothered her. She knew she was one of the few people that chose not to shelter her child just because she had handicaps. Helen knew that exposing Marsha to the outside world would give her added advantage for recovery, full recovery, hopefully. This was the dream Helen kept in the back at her mind. She kept telling herself she had to bear burdens now and always continue for the sake of her child. "The time spent with Marsha is priceless," Helen thought, and gently shook her head to clear her head and deal with getting Marsha back into her car to return home.

That evening Marsha was bubbly with enthusiasm as she told her father about the mall.

"It was so big, Papa!" and she demonstrated with arms outstretched. "I walked some, Papa, and then Mama drove me in my wheelchair, and there were so many stores. I got a red sweater at Penn-ey's and Mama bought me an ice cream and..." She was starting to stammer with her mind racing to catch up with her words.

"I'm so glad you had fun today, angel," Papa said as he embraced his little girl who responded willingly. "Now why don't we play together for a while, because Papa has to go away tomorrow."

Sam sat a couple feet away and he and Marsha rolled her red ball back and forth.

"Papa, why are you leaving?" asked Marsha sadly.

"I have to go far away to work, honey. You and Mama will join me in about three months. Remember, you are living at the apartment near the mall," Papa explained.

Marsha thought for a minute, and then asked, "Where will you live?"

"I'm going to find a new home for all of us, with a yard for you to play in. Mama will show you on the map where Brussels, Belgium is, tomorrow. Until I find the perfect house for our little family, I will be living in an apartment too, very far away."

Marsha continued to think for a while and still rolled the ball without looking at it. Then, suddenly she said, "Papa?"

"Yes, angel."

"Can I have a pet in our new house?"

The question surprised Sam. Marsha had never mentioned anything like this before. Helen hadn't either. "Oh, I think so. What kind of pet?"

"A bunny rabbit," Marsha said without hesitating.

"We'll see, OK?" Papa said with a smile and a wink.

Marsha smiled at her papa, then fell silent again and concentrated on rolling the ball, as straight as possible, to her father.

"Your aim is really improving, sweetheart! You and Mama must really be practicing!" Papa praised.

Marsha nodded and smiled at her accomplishment, or was it the possibility of getting a pet rabbit? Sam wasn't quite sure.

"Helen, if you need help, you can always count on Bob and Liz. If you want to talk to me, you can always call, honey. Anytime, day or night," said Sam, with concern. "I feel uneasy about leaving you tomorrow morning. Is there anything else you can think of that you need? Or that I need to help with or do for you?"

"No, not really. Oh Sam, I'll miss you so much. But I'll be all right. I'm more worried about Marsha. She doesn't understand!" Helen said, looking sad.

"Like everything else, explain it to her over and over. Explain where I am and why, the way you always do. So brilliantly, I must add! You're such a good mother and you'll get through this too!"

"Thanks, honey. The only thing is, this is going to be more difficult when we don't see you for three months."

"I know, but it will be over before you know it," Sam tried to reassure his worried wife.

The couple went to bed, after checking on Marsha – together. They each tossed and turned, their minds racing with thought of what the next three months would hold.

The following morning Sam stood looking down at his little angel sleeping quietly and contently and soon, Helen joined him. They stood arm in arm as Sam said, "We have a beautiful little girl."

Helen added, "And we are a lucky little family."

Then Sam took his wife's hand and led her out into the hallway and then outside to the waiting taxi that would take him to the airport.

"I love you, sweetheart. Take care of yourself," Sam whispered in Helen's ear. "I'll call you when I get to Brussels," and he took her into his arms and kissed her lusciously.

The taxi driver waited patiently as the couple exchanged good-byes in the predawn hour of five A.M. He was not foreign to the show of affection and only checked his watch to make sure his passenger didn't run too late.

"Honey, you better go. Don't worry too much. We'll be OK," Helen said, catching her breath.

"I love you, Helen!" Sam said with a final hug.

"I love you, Sam!" and she watched as her husband got into the yellow taxicab. The cab backed out of the driveway and drove down the street.

Helen's eyes hurt from the strain of holding back tears. She knew if she started crying, she wouldn't be able to stop for a long time, her face would get flushed and Marsha would know that she had been crying. At least that was what she was telling herself. Helen had to be strong for her daughter and she knew she would have to console Marsha about her papa's absence for a long time to come. Helen had to find the words to make it less painful for their daughter. She went inside and fixed herself her second cup of coffee and sat in their breakfast nook, coming to grips with herself and gathering her thoughts.

Approaching seven o'clock in the morning, Mama still sat in the comfort of the kitchen, with her fourth cup of coffee. It was light outside now. The sun was shining bright, with promises of a beautiful day. Funny, Helen thought, I don't feel cheery at all, and then she thought she heard something stirring outside the kitchen. She forced a smile and met Marsha at the kitchen door, on her crutches. This was the first time Marsha had come downstairs in the morning by herself. She usually waited for Helen or Sam to carry her to breakfast. How Helen wished she could just pick up the telephone and call Sam at work and tell him of another little step, a big step actually, in Marsha's progress.

"Mama, I walked all the way h-ere!" Marsha announced proudly.

"Yes, baby, that's wonderful!" and Mama gave her a big hug as Marsha nuzzled her face in her mother's chest.

"I love you, Mama. Where's Papa?" she asked.

Mama Holon swallowed. "Papa is on an airplane right now, sweetheart."

"Oh, yah, I remember. Papa said you show me where he going."

"Yes, let's go find the atlas and I'll show you," said Helen, a little surprised at Marsha's big girl attitude. I guess she's curious and the pain of not seeing him for so long will come later, she thought to herself. Or, maybe, she doesn't realize the concept of time yet.

They found the big atlas on the bookshelf in the family room, took it into the kitchen and laid it flat on the table. A few minutes and Helen found the page and pointed to the little dot denoting Brussels. She observed as Marsha's gaze wandered the page and finally rested on the little dot.

"Mama, what's this?" Marsha's attention focused on a big blue area.

"That's the Atlantic Ocean. Papa's plane is flying across these states and then over the Atlantic Ocean to Brussels, the capital of Belgium."

"Oh—is that far, Mama? Will we see Papa again?" she asked sheepishly and snuggled in closer to her mother.

"It is certainly a long way, dear. Of course we'll see Papa again in a couple of months. But we have to be without him for a while. We'll consider it our special girl time together, OK?"

"OK," Marsha responded, and thought for a while, quietly. "I miss him, Mama," she exclaimed suddenly.

"I know. I do too. But we have to be strong and show him we can be by ourselves, you and me, OK? We can do this, can't we?" Mama questioned with a smile on the outside and tears on the inside.

Marsha looked up at her mother with glistening blue eyes and said, "Yes, we can, Mama!"

Helen squeezed her little darling daughter. She felt a great weight leave her, almost instantaneously, unrepentantly. In the midst of all this recovering, Helen felt her little girl growing up, in spite of all her difficulties. How did this happen? Marsha's only just seven years old, and the more she thought about it, the more she understood.

"Marsha spends all her time with grown ups and she's learning everything from us. Of course she's going to be a little adult in a child's body," Helen said out loud as she now watched Marsha sitting on their green sofa, dressing her baby dolls. She stood there, in the doorway to their living room, mesmerized by her daughter's play, and she could not help but to once again marvel at how far she had come. Marsha was walking almost normally on her crutches now, her speech was almost back the way it was before the accident, and her motor skills were improving rapidly. She could now string large beads onto a shoelace that only a couple months ago was impossible. The days went by without incident and Helen observed Marsha incorporate her father's departure into her play.

"She's dealing with you being away from home pretty well, Sam. She's acting out her situation the way she sees it, and it's amazing to watch. She'll pretend Mr. Teddy is you and he's leaving her dolls behind, and she pretends Mr. Teddy can fly. Marsha's using her imagination, Sam! She's thinking! It's progress, Sam!" Helen was so happy that her smile showed in her voice.

"That's wonderful!" Sam, too, was smiling on the other end of the telephone, thousands of miles away. "May I talk to our little lady?"

"Hi, Princess, Mama tells me you're doing great!"

"Papa, when are you coming home?"

"Not for a while, baby. But Papa has a surprise for you. You watch the mail for it, OK, honey?" Papa said.

"Oh, Papa, what is it?" Marsha asked curiously.

"It's something special for a little girl who's doing really great with her therapy and listening to Mama and Mrs. Baker. It's a surprise."

"Papa, we're playing with paper dolls, and I get to find house pictures in magazines for my paper dolls," Marsha explained slowly.

"That sounds like fun, sweetheart. Now may I please talk to Mama again? I'll call again soon and you can tell me how you liked your surprise, OK? I love you."

"OK, Papa, I love you too. Here's Mama," Marsha handed the phone to Mama and wandered off to the family room to play dolls some more.

"She sounds really good, Helen. But, more importantly, how are you holding up?"

"We're fine and I'm so thrilled with Marsha's progress! Like I told you the week you left, she got up all by herself and came to the kitchen. She does that every morning if I don't get to her in time. Sam, Marsha accepted you were gone on an airplane, just like that and now she's playing your departure with her dolls. It's amazing! Her imagination is working, Sam! We talk about you often, but there haven't been any tears yet. She is such a resilient child."

"Well that's great, Helen. But, you didn't answer my question. How are you holding up?" Sam repeated.

"Oh, it's hard without you, but I'm fine. Everything will be easier once we move to the apartment next week. I am so tired of living in and amongst boxes! It's Marsha that I am most focused on, as usual, and I'm hoping the move won't upset her too much!" Helen explained.

"Like you said, she's resilient. She'll be fine. I think you both will enjoy the pool and the smaller apartment," Sam said, and there was a long pause, "I find myself thinking about you both a lot. I hope that this is not too much on the both of you. At least you have a friend to help you with Marsha now. How are things going with Grace?"

"Grace is wonderful. She is helping me prepare Marsha for the move to the apartment and for the big move over there, too. Her tutoring is doing wonders. Marsha misses her the days she's not here, and sometimes we call her just to say hello. I think she'll miss Grace the most when we leave. Marsha and I are having fun together just like we used to, Sam. It's so wonderful!" Helen was still smiling, and Sam could tell his wife was more at ease, for the moment anyway.

"That's the best news I've heard. I want my girls happy! Oh, and I sent Marsha a little prize for all the progress she's made. It should arrive in the mail in a couple days. I told her to keep a watch for it."

"OK, we'll watch for it. Sam, she really misses you and so do I."

"I miss you too, honey. I have to go. I'll call again soon. Remember, if you need me, you know where to reach me."

"Yes, honey. I love you."

"I love you too, and I'll talk to you soon."

With Helen being at home by herself and at times noticeably overwhelmed, Grace became more than a tutor. She stayed with Marsha so Helen could go grocery shopping or run errands by herself now and then.

"You need to take a break, think about yourself, too, Helen," Grace would say time and time again.

Sundays, for the most part, Helen invited Grace for coffee or brunch to show her appreciation. The ladies would sit together and chat about lighter subjects, while Marsha usually sat playing within earshot or taking a nap. The discussion always seemed to lead back to what was dear to both women: Marsha. Grace had grown so fond of this little wonder, especially in the past few months. Grace became a part of Marsha's world as she skillfully and playfully developed the will to learn.

This Sunday was different. It was their last together before the big move to Brussels. It had been a wonderful few months, and Marsha was thriving. She was nearly to the point where Grace felt she could handle regular school in the fall. They had done Grace's lessons, gone on walks, swam, shopped, and learned together, and Grace had been there for most of it. The three had become nearly inseparable. The move was going to change all of their lives. Although they knew it was a good move, it didn't help the sadness they were all feeling. They had planned to spend this last day together without tears and sadness, for Marsha's sake. So they planned not to do anything out of the ordinary. The ladies sat in the kitchen area and watched Marsha play on the floor in the family room.

"I miss her the days I am not here," Grace said as she looked at little Marsha playing with the new Barbie she had brought for her that afternoon.

"I really dislike the thought of moving to Europe, because we'll lose you, Grace."

"I can't bear the thought either, Helen."

"You are so good with Marsha. She likes you so much and has learned so much from you. I think you make her feel good about herself. She has confidence because of you!"

"Well, thank you for the compliment. I am really just doing what I do best: inspiring little minds. I really do miss teaching little ones."

"Grace, you have no idea what you mean to us! I mean, look at Marsha now compared to when you started with her only a few months ago."

"Remember, Helen, teaching a child is a partnership between teacher and parent. One without the other doesn't work well. We have worked hard together, in fun ways."

"Oh, Grace, you are a gem! Are you sure I can't convince you to move to Europe with us?" Helen asked one more time.

"I wish I could, both for Marsha and the sheer adventure of it. But as I explained before, I simply can't!" she said with a slightly sad look on her face.

"I know, but you can't blame me for trying. Well then, can I pour you another cup of coffee?" Helen asked, trying to lighten the conversation again.

"Yes, please, and these cookies are simply scrumptious."

"Our relatives sent them from Germany. They are good, aren't they?"

The ladies sat a while drinking coffee and eating cookies while watching Marsha's inventive play.

"Helen, I feel like I could be your mother and Marsha's grandmother. Sometimes I feel like I am. You know my child is far away and I have no grandchildren of my own yet."

"Yes."

"I've seen you and Sam struggling for months now. I think you are still in pain because of what happened. Honey, please don't feel sorry for yourselves. It will only hold you back, and Marsha realizes more than you know. Be positive around her and always encourage her, promise me!" Grace lectured.

"Like I've been doing? You mean, telling her?" Helen asked to be sure that she understood the lady's request.

"Telling by showing, Helen, and repetition until she feels comfortable. And yes, encouraging words always help too. I know it's a lot, but see the rewards?" Grace said, motioning toward Marsha.

"You're right. We just have to take the time. It's everyday stuff that does it the best. Like folding laundry or anything to keep her involved, engaging her mind. I showed her over and over how to fold towels, and now she's pretty good at it. We just take so many mundane little things for granted, and Marsha is so thrilled to learn, Grace."

"Oh, I agree, and no matter what, Marsha will take longer. She'll need more time for everything. But in the end, she'll persevere if guided and reminded that it's OK."

"I'm sure she gets angry and frustrated, Grace. More than I know."

"That's OK, though. I've seen it too. Help her channel that anger in a positive way. Marsha forgets about her anger and directs her energy to learning something else."

"Grace, how do you know all these things?"

"Oh, from years of working with handicapped children.

It just stayed with me, I guess."

"Well, you have been a godsend to us, and we will all miss you beyond words!"

"Just promise me that you will not give up on Marsha. She is such a special child. I would love it if you could let me know how she is coming along from time to time. Maybe send me a little note or a picture. I have really become so attached!"

"Oh Grace, that is the least we can do. Of course I will let you know how Marsha grows up. When she learns to write, we can write you a note together. I'm sure she will remember you for years, Grace."

"That would make me so happy, Marsha, if you and Mama would write to me when you're in your new home," Grace said directly to Marsha as she got up from the table to leave.

Marsha looked at her mother and then at Grace, and gave her a big hug good-bye.

"Why can't you come with us?" and tears started rolling down her innocent little face as she started crying.

"Well, honey, I have to stay here and take care of other little children that are sick like you were. You are so much better now and ready to learn without me. Your mama and papa will always be there to help you, so you'll never be alone," Grace embraced Marsha and she willingly snuggled into her arms for the last time. "Now I have to go, and you need to promise me you'll be a big girl, OK?"

Grace felt a tear escaping. Quickly she wiped it away and composed herself. I can't let Marsha see me cry, she thought. It would be entirely too hard on her.

The showing of Grace's emotion did not evade Helen though, and she stepped in when she witnessed Grace fighting with her composure. "Marsha, sweetheart, Grace can be your pen pal. Won't that be fun? We can write to her and you'll get your very own mail. Oh, I wonder if the mailman will bring another letter from Papa today," and she and Grace embraced before Mrs. Baker hurried out the front door.

"Mama, why do we have to say bye-bye to everyone?" Marsha asked, looking like she might cry. She still didn't understand the concept completely.

"Honey, we are moving far away, to a new home, and we'll make new friends."

"Oh look, here is the mailman now, and look, he has a letter for us. I bet it's for you, from Papa."

Helen knew all this change had to be difficult for their daughter. But what could she do? Helping Marsha feel as secure as possible was Helen's best solution. *I'm giving her as much stability with me as I possibly can,* she thought to herself. *She gets attention from me all day long. There's nothing else I can do in our position!* Helen was thankful for Sam's letter to Marsha. It helped verify, to Marsha, he was thinking about her, which Helen kept reassuring her.

All day long Helen continued having Marsha by her side. She continued providing the most opportunities for learning.

"I need to keep Marsha's mind off Grace," she said out loud as she did the brunch dishes.

When it was time for Marsha's nap, Helen found herself taking one herself. She was so exhausted.

I really need to pack more, but a little nap won't hurt, she thought as she drifted off.

She woke up an hour later feeling much more energetic.

"Having your little one help really takes a lot of energy out of you," Helen said to no one in particular as she filled and closed the last suitcase.

The next morning came very quickly. The girls were up and ready when the buzzer for the front door sounded. The limo driver was here on time. Helen buzzed him up and walked one last time through the small apartment to make sure she didn't forget anything. As she returned to the family room the driver was coming up the stairs to get them. She left the key on the kitchen counter and turned off the light. She locked the doorknob from the inside and shut the door. As she approached the limo, she heard the driver talking to Marsha in a soft tone.

"Up you go, little lady, into the seat," said the airport limo driver. "We'll just put your wheelchair in the back with your mom's luggage and we'll be off to the airport. What airline, ma'am?" he asked as he folded the wheelchair and carried it to the back of the car.

"United, please," Helen said, climbing in the back next to Marsha.

"Mama? Help me. I can't close the seat belt," Marsha cried, almost panicky. Helen had noticed Marsha was quiet all morning and only now came to the realization that the anticipation of this trip must be making her scared.

"Mama, can we move back one row of seats? I'm scared!" These seats were so high and bouncy. Before the ride even started, Marsha felt extremely uneasy.

"What are you scared of, sweetheart?" Helen asked, concerned.

"The car, Mama, and the road moves so fast."

"Yes, honey, OK, here we go," Helen helped Marsha to the next row of seats. "Is this better?"

"Yes, Mama. Thank you."

Obviously Marsha's equilibrium couldn't handle the bumpy ride or the apparent side motion from the seats on the side of the back of the limo. This was a different motion of the world going by through the windows than she was used to.

"I'm right here, honey. Hold on to me for stability," Helen learned equilibrium is a very intricate and important part of brain function. Now she only hoped Marsha could travel on the airplane without discomfort. It would be a long nine hours in the air.

It was no time before they were at the airport. The limo driver quickly hailed a skycap and got the baggage handed off. He then helped Helen and Marsha to the United ticket counter before receiving his tip and wishing them a safe journey.

Helen handed the paperwork and passports to the woman behind the counter. The woman looked over the paperwork, then made a call. Helen was beginning to wonder if there was a problem, but before she had a chance to ask, a special United representative was there to assist them through customs and get them to the gate.

"Morning, ma'am. I'm James. I will help you and this lovely lady all the way onto the airplane!" The woman behind the counter handed the paperwork to James who took everything and began to push Marsha down the hall, and Helen followed closely behind.

After only a few minutes of waiting at the gate, Helen heard the announcement: "People traveling with young children or those requiring special assistance may board at this time."

James got up and pushed Marsha to the gate, and Helen sensed fellow passengers looking at her and Marsha and hoped her daughter didn't feel self-conscious. She tried to shield little Marsha from the continuous stares. These people were obviously not accustomed to handicapped children, nor were they aware of the pain their ogling inflicted on a parent or the psyche of the youngster.

"OK, Marsha, here we go," said Helen as she followed her daughter.

"Have a nice trip, little lady," said the attendant taking the tickets. She then looked at Helen as James pushed the wheelchair through the door. "Is this her first flight?"

"Y-Yes ma'am, her first international flight," said Helen.

Helen quickly followed Marsha in her wheelchair, down the tarmac and to the airplane's door.

"Now we need your chariot, little lady," said James at the entrance to the plane. "Can you walk from here? Do you need help with her, ma'am?"

"I think we can manage. Thank you. We are just a little slow."

"Don't worry, ma'am. Take your time," he said as he waved good-bye to the little girl before taking the wheelchair to the baggage storage hold.

The flight attendants quickly came to help. "Here, I'll take your bags to your seat, so you can assist your little one if she needs help."

"Thank you," Helen said as she followed the flight attendant and Marsha to seats 32A and B.

Marsha waited at their seats for instructions from her mother.

"Slide through to the window, honey. You'll be more comfortable when you go to sleep."

Marsha did as she was told and curiously looked out the window.

"When we start moving, pull down the shade so you don't get scared."

"OK, Mama."

When they were both settled, Helen made sure Marsha's seat belt was fastened snugly.

The helpful flight attendant reappeared and handed Marsha a 'United Wings' pin.

"You can have your mom put that on you and you will look just like me," and she showed Marsha her wings on her lapel. "There are blankets and pillows in the overhead compartments, if you need more than these two," she said as she handed Helen two white airline pillows. "If there's anything I can help you with, your call button is up here, ma'am," she motioned with a warm smile. "Depending on how full the flight is, I will ask the person next to you to move to another location so you and your daughter have extra room. I think there will be a few extra seats."

"Oh, thank you," Helen was impressed at the extent of helpfulness extended to her and Marsha. She felt almost embarrassed, although it sure made the trip more comfortable for her. Marsha pretended to be a fairy princess on her journey home to see her papa. She watched the hustle and bustle as people proceeded to stream by. She looked away, into her lap occasionally, as if the motion of people passing by was even too much for her.

Before she drifted off to sleep she thought, "Are these the people who will help me get home to my papa, Brisa?"

"Marsha, you've had a busy day. All these people are going to Brussels with you. The ones in the uniforms are the ones helping you get to your dad. It will take many

hours to get there. Remember that your papa will be waiting for you. Then you and your parents will go to your new home. Everyone else will go to wherever it is they have to go. Your mom will always be by your side, guiding you and making sure you're safe."

"How does Mama always know what I need?"

"A mother is wise, Marsha. A mother knows just by looking at you if you are scared or tired. She can tell these things because she has spent so much time with you. You are her little girl. You are her world. Your mother would give her life for yours, Marsha."

"Really?"

"Yes, Marsha, that's how much she loves you."

Marsha slept peacefully and dreamed of castles, princesses, and fairies. It seemed that she had just fallen asleep when she heard her mother's voice.

"Marsha, honey, wake up," her mother said as she bent and kissed her daughter on her forehead. "It's time for breakfast. Then we'll freshen up to see Papa in a little while."

"Are we home, Mama? Is Papa here?" Marsha asked yawning, stretching, and rubbing her eyes.

"No, sweetie, not yet. But it won't be too much longer," and she watched as Marsha slowly came out of her slumber. She marveled at the beauty of her powerful yet innocent little girl, and she proceeded to gently wipe the warm washcloth through her still sleepy little face and over her clenched fists. "Sweetheart, can you open your hands for Mama so I can clean them?"

"Uh huh. I need to go potty, Mama."

Again Helen felt the stares of passengers as they made their way to and from the lavatory. *Why are people so inconsiderate?* she thought. *I certainly didn't wish this for my child and Marsha is certainly not to blame. Why can't people have a heart, and why can't they see that staring hurts?*

Again Helen shielded her daughter's forlorn gaze as much as possible.

"Brisa, why do I feel people watching me, staring at me?"

"They're not used to seeing a little girl struggling to walk, that's all."

"But why do I hear giggling and whispers, Brisa? Am I doing something wrong? I'm really trying my best!"

"I know you're doing your best, Marsha, and keep doing that, OK? It's in your best interest, and don't worry about people who mock you. Ignore them! Someone who makes fun of you has no idea of the difficulties of being handicapped."

Marsha sat quietly and observed her mother buttering their toast. "Here you go, honey. I'll help you with your eggs and fruit if you like."

"No, let me do it."

"OK, you try first. That's good, honey."

Marsha slowly, precisely, and a bit shakily, picked up her white plastic fork her mother had extracted from its plastic covering. She placed it into her scrambled eggs and using both hands, the left to steady the right, separated a piece and slowly brought it to her mouth. She was getting much better with her motor skills, but the motion of the plane made it very difficult for a 'normal person', let alone a handicapped child. Nevertheless, Helen marveled at the progress her daughter had made so far, and silently counted her blessings once again.

"I did it, Brisa! I did it! Boy, this plane sure is bumpy."

"Of course you did it! You just have to concentrate on what you're doing and it'll get easier with time and practice. Remember, just don't give up on anything!"

"Baby, good job. Oh, that's great, honey! Look," Helen said, pointing to her lap, "Mama was messier than you were. May I help with your last bites, though? The trays are being collected. Then we will see Papa!"

"OK, Mama."

"Ma'am, we need to collect the breakfast tray now. We'll be starting our descent. The captain has turned on the seat belt sign. Can you make sure your daughter's seat belt is secure?" the stewardess said as she took their trays.

"Yes ma'am."

Marsha started whining. Her ears hurt and were making her dizzy. She clung to her mother to make the hurt go away, to make it stop, "hu-rt, Mama, oo, oww, oow!!!"

"Marsha, swallow, honey, swallow," and Helen turned to her daughter and demonstrated as the plane kept descending. "That's a girl. Keep doing that and your ears will feel better. It will all be over in a couple of minutes."

"Ma'am, a bottle of water for her to drink may help," said the flight attendant passing through. "Here's two, and is there anything else I can do before we land?"

"I think we're fine, thank you," answered Helen as she checked their seat belts again.

Marsha opened the shade on the window and peered out, as she drank the water. It was making her feel better. "It looks so soft, Mama, like pillows."

"Yes, it does, doesn't it? Those are the clouds we see up in the sky, honey, but from the top side. They are the same ones that sometimes rain on us."

"Is Heaven up here, Mama?"

"Now where did she get that?" thought Helen briefly before answering. What a bright child. What imagination. Helen wanted to nurture her daughter in every way, and felt all her questions deserved explanation. "Heaven is way above these clouds, honey. But maybe these are gates to heaven, I don't know."

"Does Brisa live here?" Marsha asked.

"Brisa, your friend?" asked Mama a bit off-center.

"My guardian angel, Mama."

"Oh, I suppose, maybe. But I think she would feel more comfortable living closer to heaven, further up there, closer to God, wouldn't you agree?"

Marsha looked at her mother with a dreamy, far away look, "Yes, Mama, I think her home would be closer to God."

Marsha sat quietly, and kept swallowing like Mama told her to. The pressure was getting stronger. She swallowed more frequently and it took all her concentration. Suddenly Marsha drew away from the window, put her head between her hands and gasped, “Oh, Mama!”

“Sweetheart, what’s wrong!” and Helen grasped her daughter in her arms. She pulled down the window shade.

“I di-zzy, Mama,” and Helen repositioned herself, putting one arm around Marsha and her left hand on her chest to steady her.

“Better now? We’ll be on the ground in a couple minutes. Just keep swallowing, baby.”

Marsha clung to her mother with one hand and her head with the other until the plane taxied and stopped at gate twenty-three.

“Better?”

“Yes, Mama. A little. Where’s Papa?” Marsha questioned, still holding on to her mother for comfort.

“Papa’s waiting inside. Let’s wait until these people get off and then we’ll go see him, in your royal chariot, OK?”

“Yes, Mama!” Marsha said with a wide smile, her headache miraculously gone.

Helen sensed Marsha’s excitement growing. She and Marsha waited patiently, then slowly made their way to the front of the plane without incident. Helen saw evidence of extra concentration and determination in her daughter. It’s either her equilibrium being off kilter or the anticipation of seeing her father, she thought.

Sam was waiting for the arrival half an hour already. He wanted to make absolutely sure that neither traffic nor an accident on the highway kept him from seeing his wife and daughter as soon as they disembarked from their plane. It was three full months since he saw them. Papa waited anxiously, pacing, and finally the plane had come into sight and taxied to the tarmac at gate number 23C. Helen and Marsha were the last ones off the airplane, and Marsha’s feeble appearance brightened instantly as she recognized her father at the end of the jetway.

“Hello, my angel, look at you,” Papa said as he swooped up his little girl into his arms. “And look, are you using crutches now? I’m so proud of you!” continued Papa as he snuggled his daughter. He looked at his wife and embraced her with his free arm. "Let's get you into your wheelchair and Papa will drive this time. If that's OK with you? I am so glad to see both of you! I have missed my family," he said as he tenderly embraced his wife and kissed her lusciously.

"Oh yes, Papa. Mama says my wheelchair is my chariot. Where're we going?"

"Oh, your chariot?" and Sam winked at Helen in amusement. "First we need to go get your luggage at baggage claim and then we're off to our new home."

"Do I have my own room, Papa?"

"Oh yes, and it's bigger than your old one and there's a yard, for you to play, pretty flowers for you and Mama to pick, I mean attend to," he said as he tickled his little girl playfully. He turned to Helen again and smiled. "You'll like the little house I found for us. I think we'll be happy there and it's not far from the American school Marsha will be attending."

"Oh, Sam, I'm sure it's wonderful. Anywhere would be wonderful, as long as we're with you. It's been hard. I've been so overwhelmed and out of sorts without you!" She hugged him again, nuzzling up to his neck and planting another kiss. I did get some much-needed rest on the flight, because Marsha slept peacefully almost the whole time. Oh, we did have to get up once and people were staring at our little girl the whole time. Sam, it was so uncomfortable, and so rude."

"Honey, it's OK now. You're at your new home now and we'll work it out together. I'm sure lots of people haven't experienced a handicapped child before and don't know how to act. They're just ignorant. You have to admit we've learned so much this past year, and still, every day can hold new challenges. Baby, it's going to be all right," he soothed again as he saw his wife shedding pent-up tears of despair.

"I'm so-r-ry! I'm just so tired! I-I find myself going, going, going, Sam, and then I just s-start crying," she sobbed as

Sam had his right arm around her waist. "I'm sorry," she sobbed again, attempting to gain control of herself.

Sam noticed Marsha, not used to seeing her mother cry, look on with concern. Helen tried her best to conceal her tears from her daughter as much as possible because she didn't want Marsha to feel uncomfortable or sad more than she already was with her limitations.

"Honey, it's OK. I know it's been hard and I understand. Life will be better now, I promise," and he embraced Helen once more and nodded to Marsha for her benefit. "Mama's just very excited to be here."

Marsha nodded, but didn't quite understand.

Sam retrieved the bags from the carousel and carried them to the nearest door, where Helen and Marsha joined him.

"Honey, stay here with Marsha and the bags and I'll bring the car right out front. Will you be OK now?"

"Y-yes, Sam. Thank you," and Helen's composure was almost back to normal.

"Papa will be back, angel. I just need to go get the car. Can you watch over Mama for me for a few minutes," he said to Marsha, smiling at her and giving a wink.

"Unconsciously he's already giving Marsha responsibilities to boost her confidence and self-esteem. What a wonderful man!" thought Helen.

Marsha nodded and smiled at her new duty.

Sam gave Helen a wink before disappearing through the electric double doors to the maze of parking lot across from the terminal. "Boy, am I glad to finally have my family home," he said out loud to himself, and let out a sigh.

"Excuse me, ma'am I was on the flight with you and noticed your little girl. She sure is cute!" said an older man. "It is apparent that you are doing an excellent job with her, because she's so confident."

"Thank you, yes, I do spend a lot of time with our daughter and am doing my best to teach her not to let her handicaps hinder her will to progress."

"You're apparently doing wonderfully," repeated the

man. "Oh, excuse me, I am a psychologist and my specialty is working with handicapped children and their families, ma'am."

"Maybe you can shed some light for me then. Why does everyone stare, and don't they know how uncomfortable it is, especially for the child? I felt most passengers on our flight staring whenever the opportunity presented itself."

"Ma'am, I'm sorry it upsets you so, but that's human nature, unfortunately. Maybe if society was a little more educated toward handicapped individuals it would help."

"Isn't it rather basic for others to know that staring at someone makes them feel uncomfortable and to a handicapped child it would be more so?"

"You're right, of course. However, the general public doesn't think in sympathetic terms. If you and your husband would like to discuss this and other issues concerning your daughter, I would be happy to help. Here's my card."

Helen looked at the card. "Thank you, Mr.—Mr. Taylor, but I think we're fine right now," and Helen turned her full attention back to Marsha. Helen felt a little annoyed at this man trying to cash in on their misfortune.

"Mama? —Who was that man?" Marsha asked. She had to keep her mama safe, Papa said so, and it was her job.

"Oh, darling, that was someone trying to help, and make money too!" continued Helen under her breath. She could hardly wait to be seated in their car, next to her husband. It had been a long day, a long journey, and she was so tired of being alone, tired of handling everything on her own. Now she looked forward to their new life, in their new home, with their daughter out of danger, and recovering beyond expectation.

"For the first time in a year I feel happy and there's light at the end of the tunnel," she whispered, and a smile of satisfaction appeared on her exuberant yet tired face.

"When is Papa coming back?" Marsha said, shifting in her wheelchair. She was tired of sitting.

"He should be here any minute, sweetheart. This is a

busy airport. Remember how busy the airport is from your airplane book?" Helen reminded, unconsciously taking the opportunity to teach memory.

"Uh huh. I just want to go home, Mama," Marsha yawned.

"I know. So do I, baby. It's been a long day," Helen said as she spotted Sam getting out of a green van at the curb.

Sam came in through the electric door and started pushing Marsha toward the car. "OK, angel, Papa's back. I wasn't gone for too long, was I? Did you take care of Mama for me?"

"Go home now?" Marsha asked with another yawn.

"Yes, just let me help Mama get this luggage in the car and we're off," and he started heaving bags into the back of the van. The little family felt as one again after months of separation, and Sam proudly opened the van doors for his wife and daughter.

Sam turned to lift Marsha from the wheelchair, but found her already struggling to stand and reaching for her crutches. Here, let me give you a little hand. "Your crutches, princess! You can stand—and walk all by yourself? Good job, baby!" Sam couldn't believe his eyes. Hearing Helen describe it was one thing, and actually seeing it was quite another. Three months ago, when he left, Marsha was barely on her feet, and with much assistance. Dr. Hanks had been correct. The operation made it possible for Marsha to walk again.

"Y-yes, Papa!" Marsha said proudly.

"We have to be very careful though, right, Marsha?" reminded Helen.

"Yes, Mama, no silly stuff!" Marsha repeated for the hundredth time.

"I'm so proud of you, angel!"

Papa glanced at his wife, and they both assisted Marsha comfortably in the back seat. The pillows that Helen had reminded Sam to bring were for Marsha's stability on the drive home. Mr. Walsch closed all of the doors on the van he borrowed from a colleague at work, and soon they were headed for their new home.

"It feels nice to have my wife beside me again," Sam said as he removed his right hand from the steering wheel to hold Helen's hand.

They sat in silence only a moment before Helen began telling Sam about Marsha's progress, physically, and mentally.

"Marsha follows me around on her crutches all day and is interested in everything I do. She asks questions all day long too, and I let her help when possible. Grace told me the best way for Marsha to learn is by example, and with lots of patience and love. I've noticed she doesn't get tired as quickly. She's pretty unbelievable, Sam."

"So are you, darling. You've worked so hard with Marsha and brought about a miracle for her. From what you've told me, Grace helped lots too, and I'm sure you're going to miss her."

"Oh, yes, Grace taught us so many things, hasn't she, honey?" and Helen looked at Marsha only to see her eyes closed. Helen began speaking in a softer voice so as not to wake up the tired little girl. "I enjoyed watching Grace and Marsha so much! The last few weeks she became more than Marsha's tutor, and we really got to know one another. Grace was with us most mornings and afternoons too. She made Marsha want to learn all day and..."

"Yes, you've told me many times how much Marsha enjoyed learning from her."

"It was more than that. It was like she saw into Marsha's soul and knew what she was thinking and how to bring the most and the best out of her."

"It sounds to me like we owe her a big thank you for sticking by Marsha and teaching her like she did. She sounds like a real Saint," Sam said with a smile.

"Marsha and I promised we would send a note every now and then. Maybe a picture or two to see how Marsha grows and develops."

"I'm sure she would like that."

"Yes, and I even suggested to Marsha she write something. Grace can be Marsha's pen pal," Helen said shrugging.

"That's a great idea, honey."

"Oh, Papa, look—big houses," exclaimed Marsha all of a sudden. Sam and Helen jumped at the sound of her outburst.

Sam grinned, "Brussels is an old city. The buildings in the city are brick row houses. There are many houses in one building that is why they look so big. Honey, look at the big, ornate church over there. Over there is another one."

Helen had been so preoccupied with the conversation and with her husband that she had failed to notice the gradual change in scenery. The last she remembered was the freeway. Helen gazed in awe at the beauty of the old, yet well-kept architecture of buildings lining the city streets.

"This is beautiful," she whispered. "Look, Marsha, the horse-drawn carriage over there. Do you suppose that's a real princess?"

"Where, Mama, where?" Marsha said, eagerly looking out the window.

"To your right, honey. Oh, look at the cobblestone street over there. Oh Sam, this is wonderful!" Helen gasped.

"I'm glad you like it. We'll come here sometime after we're settled. I heard of a little place for dinner. It isn't fancy, but the food is good and the building is quite old."

"That sounds wonderful, Sam. Is our house very far from the city?" Helen asked.

"No, about ten minutes. It's really very convenient to everything and very green."

"Green, Papa?" Marsha asked, unsure of her papa's statement.

"Yes, dear, with big, old trees and green grass yards to play in. We even live on a cobblestone road. As they proceeded, trees, indeed, started lining the roads and Papa's face took on a warm glow. He was proud of bringing his family home. Their street was lined, on either side, with big old homes, for their standards anyway. The car went bumpety-bump-bump before Papa stopped the car.

"Here we are. This is home," he said proudly and with a smile as he nodded towards the little bungalow-type house to their right. "It's the smallest house on this road, big enough for us, though, and the rent isn't bad."

"Oh Sam," gasped Helen. Their large living room window looked over a small font yard with a small flower bed with red roses and a multitude of colorful flowers to either side. Helen's first thought was, "This is so comfortable here. It's so quaint and quiet."

She listened through her now open car window, and heard the birds chirping in the trees, and let out a little sigh of contentment before turning to look at Marsha, who had fallen silent since they left the city limits.

She sat motionless, occasionally mumbling to herself. She seemed to be absorbed in the scenes of her new surroundings. All of a sudden a rabbit hopped into their front yard from neighboring bushes and sat there, in the sun.

"Bunny!" Marsha screeched and the startled rabbit darted back into the bushes again.

"Marsha, sweetheart, bunnies are scared of noise. Next time if you're quiet, we can watch it for a while. Sam, do you suppose there's other wildlife around here?"

"I suppose. There are woods behind our house and I'm still not sure where they end. I've seen lots of rabbits, squirrels, and birds and I'm sure something else has to be around. So, do you like it so far?" Papa questioned as he turned off the van's engine.

To their right was an inviting decoratively-paved patio, leading to the front door. Sam had even purchased a table with two wicker chairs for his ladies, and Helen immediately noticed the chairs had curved sides for Marsha's safety and comfort.

"You and Mama can sit and have tea parties," announced Papa as he saw Marsha's gaze fall onto the table and chairs. He knew she was dreaming of what might be, what could be in her future here. He carried his little girl over to the table and sat her in one of the chairs. "OK, angel," he interrupted, "why don't you sit here in your chair for a few minutes while Mama and I unpack and then I'll show you your room."

Shaken from the suddenness of being brought back to reality and all the new surroundings she was experiencing, Marsha felt overwhelmed. Her head hurt from all of the different motions she had experienced that day. "I tired, Papa, I tired. My head hur-rts."

"Sit right here and I'll get Mama to get your things first so you can lay down and rest. Just one minute, baby," and he was gone, leaving Marsha unattended.

Marsha sat quietly, only her eyes surveying her new surroundings and she considered her circumstance. "Brisa, Brisa, I need to talk to you. I don't think I like it here. Everything's so different and I'm so tired."

"Your mind can't handle all this new information very quickly, Marsha. You are on overload. That's why you have a headache. You're also in Europe now, that's on the opposite side of the world from where you were. There's a six-hour time difference. For you it's four o'clock in the morning. Of course you're tired. Give everything some time and you'll love your new home."

"You're always so positive and never want me to give up, Brisa."

"That was the deal, wasn't it? You made that choice, remember? You need to be positive and always determined to overcome any obstacle that comes along."

"But Brisa, I can't always do what I want, I mean, I can't."

"You try the best you can and try and try again, over and over again. That's the only way you can learn, both physically and mentally."

"Uh huh. It's so hard though."

"I know it's hard, Marsha, and I know you'll do your best!"

"Helen, you're doing too much. Marsha's outside. Why don't you go sit for a few minutes? Go relax with your daughter. She's tired, and told me she has a headache. Take her some milk and crackers maybe. I'll get her bags so you can get her ready for bed. I'll get the rest of the bags too. I've got to tell you again and again, you've done an excellent job. Marsha's skills, her ability to grasp the meaning of things, to reason, and communicate has improved tremendously. She has come so far in the short time I've been away; I can hardly believe it. We need to look into registering her at the American school for the fall. I started reading up on them and they offer special speech classes. I really think it'll be good for her."

"I'll look into it, Sam," said Helen over her shoulder on her way to join Marsha on their front porch. Sam is as concerned for Marsha and with all the work he's had, he's managed to look into Marsha's school already. "I bet you haven't been far from Papa's mind the last few months, young lady," Mama said cheerfully, only to end in a whisper as her gaze fell on the sleeping child. Helen stood a few moments, idealizing the picture of contentment before her. Marsha had managed to curl into somewhat of a ball on the wicker basket type chair Sam had left her in. Her head was resting on the chair's red pillow and the sun was just beginning to engulf her.

"These are happy tears, my dear," she whispered. "You and I are home with Papa now and everything's going to be all right."

She placed her arms around Marsha and gave her a hug, and kissed her little neck affectionately as she wiped her tears. "I've brought some juice and cookies for us. We'll have a picnic another time maybe."

"What's a picnic, Mama?" Marsha asked, apparently not fully asleep.

"Well, it's when we eat outside, honey. This way we can hear the birds sing and feel the warm sun."

"Oh, OK. Where's my papa, Mama?"

"Papa is finishing with our bags and then I'm sure he'll join us for our picnic, if you're not too tired. Would you like that?"

"Oh yes, Mama," Marsha said as she sat upright in the chair.

Helen observed how Marsha's face flushed a bit in anticipation. Obviously she had missed her father and the games he played with her, the attention he showered on her. Marsha really needs Sam, just like I do, thought Helen. Happiness and warmth filled her heart as she had visions of them together again as a family.

"How about some hamburgers on the grill tonight," announced Papa as he stepped out to join them. "Ah, I see the queen and the princess are having tea."

Sam smiled at his wife.

"Yes, would the king like to join us?" Mama said as she played along.

"Oh yes, my lovely ladies. But let's not spoil our appetites for the royal hamburgers. I just bought a fine grill to welcome our princess home!" Sam excused himself and returned with a crown and placed it on Marsha's little blonde, mussed hair. "Oh, you look beautiful," he continued as Marsha beamed the most Helen had seen in a long time, and enjoyed the show.

"Papa, this is fun. I like being princess. I no horse, though. I like tea party," and she continued beaming at her father as he played a part in his daughter's fantasy world.

Helen wondered if Marsha had actually just had a memory flash of her accident. Why had she uttered, "No horse, though?" Helen wondered if Sam caught the phrase too. Was it another step in Marsha's recovery process? Was her brain retrieving memories?

"Sam, Sam, did you hear that? Did you hear Marsha's comment about the horse just now?" Helen whispered in Sam's direction.

"Yes, honey, I did, and if the royal princess doesn't want a horse, that's just fine. Her royal servants will just carry her!" Sam just kept right on playing the game, to Marsha's delight and Helen sat watching how her husband brought out the playfulness in their usually quiet and reserved little girl. He could make her laugh when no one else could. Marsha seemed to forget about her handicaps and the pain and difficulties they caused when Papa was with her. There's nothing like a little girl playing with her papa, she thought and smiled broadly.

They played quietly for quite a while, and Sam went to scout the front yard with her. They sat side by side in the grass at the corner of the front yard and Sam pointed out their surroundings: the green grass, the buttercups, and the big trees over there with the wall of the neighbor's house behind it. All of a sudden the rabbit returned to nibble on some clover opposite them. This time Marsha stayed quiet and curiously watched the furry little creature. She sat, fascinated, and the bunny occasionally looked straight at her before resuming his munching.

Helen checked her watch and although it would only be breakfast time at home, it was afternoon here. She had to balance the times and slowly nudge Marsha into the new time zone. Although she was surprised at how Sam had been able to rejuvenate the seemingly exhausted child from the wicker chair moments earlier. She did have a couple catnaps and the excitement probably gave her extra energy, Helen rationalized.

"How about those royal hamburgers, King Sam? Should I bring them out for your grilling pleasure?" Helen's voice inquired, startling the rabbit, and he was gone.

"Princess? What do you think? Is your majesty hungry?"

"Hee hee," Marsha squealed with glee. "Yes, Papa, yes."

"All right then. Royal hamburgers are on the way."

Throughout dinner and the evening, Sam and Helen kept the game going. Marsha was having such fun and both parents agreed that through play, Marsha would grow and develop naturally.

"May the king take you to your royal bed?" Sam finally uttered, early in the evening, while watching Marsha stifle another yawn. Helen was still busy clearing dinner dishes.

"Yes, Papa, and weed me a bedtime story?"

"But of course, your majesty. Would *Sleeping Beauty* suit you tonight?"

"Oh yes."

"Once upon a time, in a land far, far away lived a king and queen. They only wanted one thing. They wanted a little girl. One day a frog at the water's edge, where they were sitting, told them he would grant them their wish."

"Can I have one wish, Papa?" Marsha interrupted.

"Of course you may, honey."

"Will it come true?"

"We'll see," Sam said smiling, before he continued to read the story. "The king and queen were so happy they had a big party to welcome their little girl. They invited everyone in the kingdom, but forgot to invite one of the fairies. The day of the party the little girl received special gifts from all the other fairies. Suddenly, the powerful fairy that hadn't been invited magically appeared and announced that on the little girl's sixteenth birthday a spell would be cast and she would fall into a deep sleep."

Papa looked up from the book and expected more questions. Instead, Marsha lay fast asleep. Sam bent forward, covered and kissed his little girl. She looked so content and snuggled amongst the yellow sheets covered with tiny white flowers, with her blanket and Mr. Teddy clasped close to her chest. "You've had a busy day, Princess," he whispered, and lingered, watching Marsha as she slept peacefully.

"Is Marsha asleep already, Sam?"

"Out like a light. She fell asleep only five paragraphs into Sleeping Beauty. I imagine she must have been exhausted after all the fun we had this afternoon. You know, she asked me if she could make one wish and I'm sure it was that she could be sleeping beauty, Helen."

"That is her favorite story. I agree she wants to be just like sleeping beauty. She wants to wake up from sleep and be able to play and live unencumbered, I'm sure. That's her ultimate wish," Helen sighed and sat on the living room couch.

"How do you know, honey? Has she told you?" Sam asked as he joined her, close by her side.

"I see Marsha watching other children play. I saw her watching people at the airport, and there are little things she'll say to me that just lets me know she wishes she could be like the other kids."

"OK, I understand now." With Helen's revelation, Sam felt his heart tightening and his mind racing. He wanted to have his little girl happy and didn't know what else to do. "Will you go to the private American school tomorrow, Helen, and see if we can sign her up for the fall? I think that getting her involved will be good for her and remember, they do offer special programs, which she'll need."

"Oh, Sam, do you really think we can afford it?"

"Things will be very tight around here. The private school is expensive, but worth it, especially with Marsha's circumstances. Exposing Marsha to another language besides English would be overwhelming right now. It would be too much for her. Remember to ask about different therapy classes that are included in the monthly tuition. I really think it's our best option, honey."

"I agree. It's just that I'm sure it'll be so hard for her to mingle with a whole class of children who will obviously have it much easier."

"Helen, I know this transition will be difficult for Marsha, but it's really the best for her, the best we can do for her."

"Marsha can only benefit from the exposure, don't you agree?"

"Grace seemed to be confident Marsha was ready."

"It's really the best option we have, Helen," and Sam and his wife's eyes met and Sam reached for and squeezed Helen's hand, reassuringly.

"While I'm registering Marsha tomorrow, I'll inquire about signing her up for speech therapy, and maybe I can talk to someone about Marsha's special situation and get some more information about individual teachers, the way they teach. Maybe one is better than the other for her. Maybe they even have a summer program she can attend to get used to her new school."

"Maybe they'll be able to give you some more ideas too, Helen."

"It sounds like a nice school and hopefully it has good teachers like Grace."

"It should, being a private school, and the money they

charge, Helen! Our baby deserves the best we can offer!" Sam and his wife sat in their modest little living room for a while longer.

Helen brought in a cup of hot tea to help her relax and Sam had a beer, enjoying being in their new home together.

"Honey, I know it's all so scary now. But Marsha will adapt quickly and she'll do just fine at her new school and if not, we'll do what we can to help her."

"It's a big step for her, for us too. I'll try to get some idea of what the second graders are covering the first few weeks so I can start working with Marsha now, Sam."

"That's a great idea. Get her familiarized with what they'll be doing in her classes. Even though she's covered the equivalent of first grade, It'll help her. Remember that she takes longer at everything. So we have to help her all we can," Sam gently reminded.

"It won't be easy, but I believe I can help her, Sam."

"Like I said, the biggest problem I see is the speed at which she does everything. Understandably, she needs at least twice as long to do everything. That's the biggest hurdle I see for her."

"I agree, and I don't see how we can help her there other than help her catch up with work at home. She needs to practice everything, physically and mentally," Helen sighed.

"I wonder how long it will be until Marsha writes her name?"

"Oh honey, she already does. I'm sure it won't be long before it is between the lines properly. It's just that she still has problems writing smoothly because of her fine motor tuning. That'll get better too. She has been doing a lot of coloring which helps immensely! Remember, a few months ago she couldn't hold a spoon, and look at her now! She's come so far, and I keep thinking how far she still has to go. It scares me sometimes, Sam," Helen began to sound distraught again.

"We're doing what's best for her future. All we can do is look forward, do our part and take things day by day.

Marsha will progress little by little with lots of hard work and God's blessings," Sam reassured.

"Yes, I've been trying to instill positive attitude in Marsha as best I can and it does seem like she's responding and just maybe God's angels are helping her. From time to time I see her sitting there, content, and it looks like she's in her very own world," Helen commented.

"I've noticed that too, and sometimes I get these thoughts in my head, like Marsha's telling me something, sending telepathic messages, communicating her thoughts to me. That sounds really crazy, doesn't it?" Sam said.

"It does sound a little off the wall, but you and Marsha have always had this very close relationship. She's Papa's girl, you know?"

"So you think she's trying to communicate with me, honey?"

"She could be, Sam. Why not?" Helen shrugged.

"Well, I feel she's really trying hard to get better and she's so determined, but I also think she's scared to death."

"Oh?" Helen gasped, worried at the thought.

"Just imagine how you would feel if you couldn't physically or mentally perform like other children around you. That you didn't understand but a portion of everything that was happening around you. You would be scared too. Just imagine."

"I would be frustrated, but scared?"

"Imagine yourself beginning to believe you're never going to amount to anything because you don't have the capabilities like everybody else."

"How do you know this, Sam? Has Marsha opened up to you? Has she told you how she feels?" Helen asked anxiously.

"Not exactly. But when we went on our little picnic this afternoon she told me about all these things she wishes she could do. I get the feeling that Marsha thinks her dreams can't come true because she's handicapped."

"Oh Sam, what did you tell her?"

"You can do and be anything you set your mind to. I

told Marsha never to give up. Only those that focus and persevere reach their potential, goals or dreams, whether handicapped or not. Some people succeed because they are destined to, most people succeed because they are determined to."

"You have such a way with words, Sam. Marsha looks up to you, so maybe she took what you said to heart."

"I hope so!" Sam said flatly.

"We have to help Marsha move forward and the more I think about it the more I agree, sending her to school will be the best, even if it results in hardships in the beginning. We'll just have to help her in every possible way," Helen continued.

"With us behind her, and you devoting precious time with her, Marsha will be fine, honey!" Sam exclaimed, reaching for his tired wife.

She felt his arms around her and felt more secure than she had in a very long time. "Thank you, sweetheart. Our being together helps our little girl so much, Sam," Helen whispered before drifting off to sleep in Sam's arms.

"Marsha is going to need you more than ever the next few months. School will become a love/hate relationship for her. You already know that more than anything she wants to learn. However, the new environment, including the many distractions, will be very difficult for her. Marsha will have problems concentrating, and her inabilities will cause extreme frustrations."

"Will anything else be disturbing to her?"

"Oh yes, the general daily procedures. She's not used to that at all."

"Will her inabilities cause her even more frustration?"

"She'll see other children move about freely and have fun all day long, while she can't. She's likely to become depressed and angry at herself at the same time."

"Should we even send her to school then?"

"Oh yes, you and Sam have come to the right decision. Marsha is ready and she needs the exposure. It's part of the rehabilitation process for her and she will succeed, in

time. Marsha will fight her way through, with many tears, but she'll make it, Helen. You're a great mother for standing by her and helping her through these difficult times. Besides, the longer you wait to expose Marsha to the real world, the harder it will be for her."

Helen woke with a start, looked at the clock; two fifteen. She looked to see if Sam was still beside her. He was fast asleep. Wow, now I know what he meant about communication about Marsha, from her spirit maybe or from an angel watching over her. Maybe it's an angel from God, protecting her and helping us help her, Helen thought. I wonder if it's that Brisa Marsha has told me about. She says that Brisa is a guardian angel. Maybe she really is. She lay awake for a few minutes before falling back to sleep, touching her husband for added comfort.

"Sam, Marsha is going to need you more than ever. She's going to be scared and intimidated. It's your job to make her understand that her handicaps are not forever. She can overcome them with practice and persistence. You need to keep reminding her and encouraging her. Marsha's also going to suffer psychologically and it's very important you do whatever it takes to let her know she is as good as the other children. Her disabilities don't make her less of a person. Marsha needs to be told and reminded that she's as special as anyone else is. Marsha needs encouragement. She idealizes you and your words of wisdom, Sam. You should be the one to talk to her about this first, and talk to Helen about this, because it is so important for Marsha's self-esteem.

"Thanks for your advice. I'm really not sure of the right path for her. I want what's absolutely the best we can offer Marsha. But Helen has so many responsibilities and is under so much pressure. I don't know how much more she can handle."

"Don't underestimate the power of a mother and what she is capable of doing for her child. What she needs from you is understanding, support, and your shoulder to cry on, Sam."

Ding, ding, ding, the alarm clock went off and Sam reached over and hit the snooze button. "Is it morning already?" he grumbled and reached over to hold Helen tightly. "Good morning, sweetheart. How did you sleep?"

"Good, I guess. I had a vivid dream about an angel, I think, giving me advice about Marsha. It was so real, Sam. It was so real and I remember it entirely."

"I had a dream, a message similar to yours and can also remember it vividly. This is really bazaar, Helen."

"Did you also feel like an angel was talking to you, Sam? What did she tell you?"

"How did you know it was female?"

"Well, In my dream I couldn't see her, but the voice was a woman's.

"OK, I guess, come to think of it, so was mine."

"Well, what did she say, Sam?" repeated Helen impatiently, who started praying after Marsha's accident and felt sure there were angels from the time of Marsha's miraculous recovery. Almost instantaneously Helen recollected the time she had the dream about Marsha's stages of recovery and how it all came to pass.

"Let's say it was Marsha's guardian angel that talked to me," said Sam. "She let me know we have a long, hard road ahead of us. She said that we could help Marsha's recovery immensely by always being positive with her; stand by her with understanding and encouragement. She told me everything Marsha does will be at least twice as hard for her to accomplish than it is for the rest of us."

"Sam, our little girl will be so defenseless and the world will seem like it's closing in around her and us. I guess we're getting instructions on how to handle everything we'll inevitably be faced with."

"Yes, dear, it seems that way, and we have to celebrate accomplishments and count our blessings," and Sam hugged his wife.

"Sam, Marsha's told me about Brisa, her guardian angel. Do you think it could be true? Could that be who spoke to us last night?"

"Could be. I don't know. Let's snuggle a few minutes longer before we have to get up," whispered Sam in Helen's ear.

"You won't get any argument from me, honey."

They laid there in silence for a while thinking about the possibility of an angel helping Marsha, and remembered all they had been through so far. Sam gave his wife a squeeze one last time before getting up. "I am so grateful our love is strong enough to handle this together."

Later that morning Helen felt empowered by the dreams of the preceding night. She felt herself accepting that Brisa had indeed been the force visiting the night before and that she in fact was Marsha's guardian angel. Helen now felt she had some direction and an unexplainable understanding that, though recovery for Marsha would be extremely difficult, it was definitely possible. "I see a light at the end of the tunnel," she whispered to herself, in front of Marsha, as they finished breakfast at the kitchen table.

"What, Mama?"

"Oh, honey, we are going to work real hard to get you well again, I promise."

"OK," and Marsha looked questioningly at her mother. "What are we going to do?"

"Well, right now we're going to visit your new school and then we'll sign you up for the fall semester. You're a big girl now, and you'll be going to the big girl school. Maybe we can explore a bit when we get there and talk to some of the teachers. We'll find out as much as we can so we can tell Papa this evening. Does that sound like fun?"

"Can I have ice cream after school?"

"Yes, Marsha, we'll get ice cream after school. Now let's go and have an adventure today."

"OK, Mama. Where is my new school? Will Grace be there?" Marsha asked as she climbed in the back of the family car.

"No, honey. But I'm sure there'll be a teacher you'll like just as much as Grace," Helen reassured.

"Will she play with me?"

"You will have more than one teacher, Marsha. Teachers are there to teach you new things, remember? You will be in a room with some other children, learning along with them. We're going to find out about special classes for you to be alone with one teacher who will play games with you to help you learn better, like Grace did. You always have to remember that Mama and Papa are here, and if you get scared or mad, you need to tell us, OK?" and Helen put her arm securely but lovingly around her daughter's waist to help her out of the back seat of their car.

"Uh huh, Mama," responded Marsha a little out of breath.

Walking didn't come easy yet and Helen hoped that wouldn't be an issue come fall. She planned on taking Marsha on lots of walking expeditions: around the new neighborhood, shopping, and to the park, if there was one. She remembered the words of Marsha's therapist in the United States, "Practice walking with Marsha as much as possible. The more she is on her feet, the stronger her legs will become, and the quicker."

"Brisa, I can't do this anymore, Brisa. This is so hard and I'm so tired."

"I know you're tired, Marsha. I told you the road to recovery is hard, and you agreed to go forth with it. You promised me, remember? Now pick yourself up and pull yourself together. Take it step by step, OK?"

"But..."

"Marsha! You've overcome great odds, and look at you, your motor skills are improving and you have the basic ability to walk. Now you need to focus and keep practicing. You need to get stronger, a lot stronger, and your mother is trying her best to help you."

"I have been trying so hard, Brisa, and I just can't do it. I c-c-can't."

"Keep practicing and you will. I know it seems impossible, but I know you will succeed! I can see it, Marsha!"

"You can?"

"Yes, I can see that you'll be walking better soon, and you'll be able to help your mama with big chores, too."

"Really?"

"Yes ma'am, so keep going and do what you're supposed to and never give up. You can do this, you hear me?"

"All right."

Over a year after their daughter's accident, little by little, Mr. and Mrs. Walsch realized, through their own education, that their fear and anger was best directed towards positive energy and useful deeds towards Marsha's rehabilitation.

"It takes a while to come to terms," Sam told his wife. "But I realize the best way to help is to accept the situation and move on. I've learned the power of love and positive energy from the book, *The Road Less Traveled,* by M. Scott Peck, MD. We need to instill this concept in Marsha too. It's really very important."

"I agree, Sam. You mean, teach Marsha to redirect her psychological pain towards outlets that benefit her?"

"Exactly."

"That way Marsha will hopefully forget her hardships a bit, for a little while anyway, while she's involved in crafts, for example."

"She'll notice her handicaps don't prevent her from doing everything. It builds self-esteem."

"Correct, Helen, and if we continue reinforcing her help is important to us, her self-esteem will be boosted even more."

"You and I also have to move on and stop feeling sorry for ourselves, leave the past behind and focus on the future."

Helen and Sam did their very best to help themselves and to think of anything and everything to help their little girl overcome her difficulties, her hardships, and her handicaps. They also realized they needed to leave the past behind. "Rereading *dis-ABILITY*, by Linda Lee Ratto[2], has helped me contend with our situation, Sam. Ratto describes the stages both Marsha and we go through and how to deal with them, how to handle them in a positive way. She tells how we can talk about our feelings, and that it is good therapy to talk about our issues."

"Sweetheart, somehow I can't imagine a book having that much of an impact, for our situation, I mean," countered Sam.

"Now I know it's OK for us to feel hurt and also frustrated. I feel better about what we are doing and what's ahead. Sam, we're not the only ones suffering like this, and it's natural. These books are giving me new strength to go forward. They've helped me tremendously!"

"That's wonderful, Helen. I'll have to read them again too, then."

"I think it's a good idea, honey."

Helen and Sam embraced and fell asleep almost immediately. Their days were long and hard, full of taking care of their little girl. Little did they know Brisa, Marsha's guardian angel, was also hard at work, encouraging her.

Days, weeks, then two months passed, and Helen diligently worked with Marsha, playing games with colors, shapes, and stories. Soon fall was upon them, and with it, the first day of school.

"Honey, you will have a wonderful day today," Helen told Marsha as she gave her one last hug and kiss before Marsha walked slowly, unsure, down the hallway of her new big-girl school.

Everything looked enormous, foreign, and even ominous to little Marsha. Helen stood watching until she disappeared in the sea of other students, noisily making their way to their classrooms.

Can Marsha handle all this? It's such a busy environment compared to what she's used to, Helen thought to herself. She slowly turned and made her way back to her car, doing the best to convince herself everything would be fine or would she get a phone call. Is Marsha ready for this monumental change? Helen and Sam discussed the many obstacles Marsha would face, over and over again, and no matter how much they prepared her, they realized she would be overwhelmed, probably for a long time. Only Marsha, her psyche, and her inner strength would decide how to handle her new world.

The first few days of school were the hardest, and long for Helen. She spent every moment from the time she left Marsha at school until she picked her up in the afternoon, thinking about her little girl. This was the first time in many months the two were separated, and Helen wondered if Marsha had as hard a time with their sudden separation as she did.

"It's strange when I turn around, look where Marsha would be, but she isn't there," she exclaimed to Sam over the telephone. "And I know she's struggling at school. Marsha is so tired when I pick her up in the afternoon, Sam. Most of the time she falls asleep on our way home from school or I'll find her curled up somewhere in the house fast asleep."

"That's OK though, isn't it, honey? I mean, we knew it would be anything but easy for her, and at least she isn't crying."

"Yes, that's an improvement over that other school in Pennsylvania."

"Has she said anything about school, Helen?"

"No, just that it's hard and it's noisy. I do let Marsha know I'm interested in what she's doing, and ask her what they've done in school every day. She gives me one word answers: fine, yes, we, noisy. But I'm not pushing for information, Sam. She'll tell me, or you, when she's ready."

"Honey, Marsha is probably overwhelmed by it all and needs time to register everything. I'm just glad she's accepted her new environment."

"You and me both. I'm staying in close touch with school, and they know where to reach either of us in case of emergency," Helen explained.

"You told them about Marsha, her background, the strides she's made, and how far she's come, right?"

"Oh yes, and they and her teachers are keeping an

eye on her. I've talked to them extensively too. They both seem very receptive and willing to work with us to do what is best for Marsha."

Days, weeks and then months went by and every day, five days a week, Helen took Marsha to school in the morning and then went to pick her up at the bus stop in the afternoon. School remained a challenge, but Marsha persevered. She did her best, improving little by little, and for the next couple years Marsha's teachers marveled at her dogged determination. What they didn't see were the tears Marsha shed from humiliation she endured from the other children most of the time. Marsha couldn't understand why her peers were so mean to her. She kept to herself as much as possible and didn't attract unwanted attention willingly. Marsha's face and shorter right leg made Marsha feel self-conscious. Marsha's face still had scars and her right leg was still about an inch shorter. At the beginning of school, Marsha needed to wear a two-inch lift under her corrective shoe, attracting unwanted attention and ridicule among the youngsters. The stares, comments, and laughter made school more difficult for the child.

Marsha's abilities for walking and activities were hampered, due to physical strains. With physical therapy, manipulation and massages, three times per week, doctors predicted Marsha's shorter limb would, over time, grow quicker and catch up with the length of the left leg. Experts felt sure that focus, determination and time would pay off. It was music to Helen's ears. Our baby will be free to run and jump with the other kids, she mused with a twinkle in her eyes.

Oh my God, this will be a dream come true for all of us, and her eyes involuntarily filled with tears. She let them trickle down her cheeks as she sat thinking a few moments longer of the possibilities, and she relayed her thoughts to her husband at work.

"Sounds very plausible, Helen. We'll just have to keep doing our part and keep our fingers crossed. Our strong little angel is bound to surprise us."

"Oh, Marsha, dar-ling, will you please help me? The napkins need to be arranged. The cook has me so overworked. Can you help me...please?" and Helen winked at her daughter who was laughing, enjoying every moment.

"Oh yes, I will. I will," and Marsha did her best to arrange the clean white paper napkins for the three of them. "Can I do the silverware too?"

"By all means, my dear," chimed Helen from across the small kitchen, and got Sam's attention so he could watch Marsha's efforts in setting the table the very first time. The two stood side by side for some time in awe of what effort Marsha exhibited and how meticulous she was.

"OK, little lady that looks perfect. Now, may Mama and I join you for breakfast?" Papa questioned.

"Yes, Papa, I'm hungry."

"OK, princess, let's eat."

The little family ate and enjoyed being together.

"Mama, school is so hard!" Marsha said suddenly, near the end of breakfast.

"Oh, honey, I'm so sorry. Do you want to talk about it? Can you tell Papa and me what's bothering you?"

"Ma-ama, it's so noisy. The other children all talk at once. It hurts my head, Mama," Marsha said, trying to explain as best that she could with the words she knew.

"I know, baby, I know. All the confusion is totally new to you," Mama soothed, reaching out to pull Marsha into her loving arms for a soothing hug and comfort. "Sam, that's exactly what I thought yesterday morning when I stopped by to pick her up for the doctor's appointment. The noise level bothered even me. There seemed to be so much confusion."

"Marsha, you've been sheltered for so long, honey," comforted Papa. "No wonder this is just too much for my little princess."

Both parents were trying to make their little girl feel better, although they had no clue of answers to the problem. "Maybe if you talk to her teacher again, Helen. Maybe she can shield Marsha from commotion a bit."

"I'll talk to her, Sam. But I don't know how much she can do with twenty-five students in her class," Helen was at a loss.

"Helen, maybe it will help, though!" suggested Sam.

"Oh Sam, I wish I could shield Marsha from what's hurting her," and she coddled her still-sniffling daughter. "What else, honey? What else is bothering you?"

"Everybody gets into their seats so fast, Mama, all at once."

"Like a mad rush, honey?"

"Yes."

"Fast movements have bothered her since the accident, if you remember, Helen."

"Yes, Sam. What else, honey?"

"Everybody is all over the pl-ace, Mama. I get dizzy," Marsha cried, and more tears rolled down her face.

"Well, I guess all this disorganization is a lot for you," soothed Papa and took his daughter's hand in his. He looked deep into her blue, forlorn eyes. "You need to learn to focus on what you're doing and tune everything else out, sweetie. It's part of your learning process. You need to learn how to handle your new environment. I really don't know what else Mama and I can do to help you when you're away from us."

"Everyone talks at once, Papa. I get all confused!"

"I'm sure it seems like that, Marsha. Isn't it quiet when Mrs. Sure teaches the class, honey?" Papa asked.

"Someone always talks, Papa."

Sam looked at Marsha, then his wife, with a tiny frown. He was trying to think of what else could be done.

"It'll get easier every day, honey," Mama continued. "Everything is a learning process, for all of us, really. Just do the best you can, honey, and try not to let the disruptions bother you. I'll go to school Monday and talk to Mrs. Sure about your worries, though. Maybe she'll have a solution or a suggestion."

"We'll work on it, honey. We'll do the best we can," said Papa, picking Marsha up gently, but firmly, kissing her neck, and Marsha squealed in delight as her anxieties quickly dissipated into giggles.

"Ooooooo, Papa, more, more, Papa, more!" the little girl begged to be tickled.

"Her equilibrium seems to be improving, Sam. Maybe everything will be OK down the road, and it's just a matter of facing her fears, doubts, and anxieties," suggested Helen.

"It's really up to Marsha and her body's ability to heal. Next time I'll try putting her on my shoulders, maybe. We need to help her practice her abilities to increase her confidence."

Helen stood up and joined her husband and daughter in the middle of their living room for a family hug. They stood there for what seemed a long time, swaying to the sounds of Carol King's, *You've Got A Friend.*

"When nothing's going right, Close your eyes and think of me," Helen sang quietly, with her arms around both Sam and their precious little girl. She hoped Marsha heard the words of the song.

...You just call out my name,
And you know wherever I am,
I'll come running to see you again...

Helen had her eyes closed and her head on Sam's shoulder. Sam whispered, "Honey, I think Marsha fell asleep."

...Winter, Spring, Summer or Fall
All you have to do is call,
And I'll be there.
You've got a friend...

Sure enough, Marsha's little head, covered with golden locks, lay on Sam's other shoulder. "School must really be rough on her, honey. I really can't begin to imagine!"

Sam took Marsha to her room and laid her on the bed. He returned to find Helen at the kitchen table, tears in her eyes and a sad, distant look on her face.

"Years ago," stated Helen, "as a teacher, I had a little

girl with a learning disability in my class, and I remember it was very hard for her to deal with the classroom environment, let alone learning quickly."

"How did you handle it?" Sam asked, sitting in the chair beside his distraught wife, reaching out and taking her hands in his for comfort.

"I shielded her as much as I could and gave her a little more attention to help her learn. Jodi couldn't focus properly. It took her a while to learn and understand things. Children can be so mean to each other, Sam, and I tried to intercede and intervene between her and the students bothering her. Oh, Sam, it broke my heart! The next year I heard Jodi went to a different school and repeated second grade."

"You have some knowledge of Marsha's situation then."

"I just don't know what else we can do besides the speech therapy program and talk to her teachers, Sam. I never imagined our daughter in a similar situation," Helen whimpered, collapsing into her husband's arms.

"I know, honey. It's hard, so h-ard!" Both parents leaned on each other for comfort and support.

"What are we going to do? What else can we do to help her, Sam?" Helen pleaded for an answer.

"We'll just see how she progresses, keep working with her. In the future, who knows what medical or technological advances could help her."

"Yes, we'll provide her with the best resources we can afford, and the rest is up to her," Helen stated, trying to convince herself that Marsha would persevere through her own abilities as well and everything would turn out for the best, or was she dreaming a fairy tale?

"Yes, Helen, that's really the gist of it, what it all boils down to. Marsha ultimately has to help herself. I know you would do anything for Marsha, and so would I, but there's only so much we can do, honey. At some point it's just out of our hands."

What I Know For Sure

"What do you give when you've given your all, and it seems like you can't make it through?"

The answer lies in the simple refrain: "You just stand."

That's where strength comes from—our ability to stand up, face resistance, and walk through it.

It's not that people with the courage to persevere don't ever feel doubt, fear, and exhaustion.

They do.

But in the toughest moments, we can have faith that if we take just one step more than we feel we're capable of, if we draw on the incredible resolve every human being possesses, we'll learn some of the most profound lessons that life has to offer.

What I know for sure is that there is no strength without challenge, adversity, resistance, and often pain. The problems that make you want to throw your hands up and holler "Mercy!" will build your tenacity, courage, discipline, and determination.

I just take what comes.

I've learned to rely on the strength I inherited from all those who came before me—the grandmothers, sisters, aunts, and brothers whose spirits were tested with unimaginable hardships, yet survived.

"I go forth alone, and stand as ten thousand," Maya Angelou proclaims in her poem "Our Grandmothers," I bring all my history with me—all the people who paved the way for me are part of who I am. I take my greatest strength from their strength. I try to view the challenges in my life not as annoyances, but as confirmations of fortitude.

The words of Eleanor Roosevelt, in her 1960 book, "You Learn By Living," are some of the wisest I know: "You are able to say to yourself, I lived through this horror. I can take the next thing that comes along... You must do the thing you think you cannot do."

As you walk into what you fear, know that you already have the enduring power you're asking for—then say thank you because you understand your deepest struggles will produce your greatest strength. And what do you do in that moment when you feel like you can't make it through?

You just stand.

~Author Unknown

Monday morning Helen got up bright and early to fix a quick breakfast, before awakening Marsha. She had taken a few extra moments dressing and fixing her hair and makeup.

"Mama is going to speak with Mrs. Sure this morning."

"Why, Mama?"

"I'm going to ask her if she'll help make school a happier place for you," stated Helen.

"How, Mama?" Marsha asked as she pulled on her shirt and directed her full attention towards her mother.

"I'm sure she can make it less scary for you, honey."

Helen noticed increased cognitive ability. Marsha still faced problems focusing and it continued being one of Marsha's bigger challenges, as was balance, and fine motor tuning. The motion and communication in a class of twenty-five had to, at times, be unbearable for a child with learning disabilities of this magnitude. Thank goodness Marsha's condition was steadily improving. A year ago Marsha's intellectual recovery was very questionable. Now Marsha had the capability to learn as well as read, and Helen saw her vigor. Her learning process was slow, but it was there! Marsha was steadfast.

Helen noticed Marsha's writing ability improved with her improvement of motor skills. Her first attempts with Grace were very shaky, without any structure or framework. Her shaky little hand did not cooperate at all then. In time, with practice at home, and physical therapy, Marsha's motor skills improved, as did her coordination, just like doctors predicted. With practice and patience her reading speed and comprehension also dramatically improved. She did not give up on their daughter then and she was going to do all she could to help her now.

Reflecting, Helen and Sam could see how time, and their continued perseverance, caused miracles. Soon Marsha would have more plastic surgery on her face. With that and her growth, her scars would also increasingly disappear over time. The added pressures of ridicule due to a flawed appearance would also dissipate, and Helen and Sam hoped memories would too. But no one realized the extent or years of trauma Marsha endured. They would linger only in Marsha's memory. She would never be free of her past. Each and every little jostling of Marsha's being upset her terribly. It brought back feelings of being not normal and worthy.

In fourth grade Marsha was excelling, but never spoke of friends. She was getting good grades and her teachers praised her, but she never praised herself. She praised everything *but* herself. Marsha didn't talk about school very much, and rarely gave detailed answers about what was going on in school. She didn't fit in. She felt like an outcast.

"The kids look at me like some kind of freak."

The fall picnic was the Friday before Halloween and Marsha didn't want to go. "Mama, I don't want to go to the school picnic!" Marsha stated at breakfast.

"Why, honey?" Helen asked, looking up from her newspaper.

"I can't play ball or tag and nobody likes me anyway. They all call me names and stuff."

"OK, Marsha. We don't have to go to the picnic. We'll do something else together, if you like," Helen suggested.

"No, Mama, I'll just stay home and play by myself," Marsha stated flatly, ending the conversation with her tone.

I feel more comfortable just being by myself than being judged by everybody and made fun of on top of it, she thought. I hate my life!

Helen and Sam realized their daughter was withdrawing socially. What could they do? They tried to compensate with outings and excursions with Marsha and included her in their grown-up gatherings with their friends. Marsha was the little girl growing up in an adult environment, and she was flourishing in her parents' eyes.

Helen saw and held on to the possibility Marsha would someday lead a normal life, a life free of noticeable handicaps and she wondered if Marsha somehow read her mind.

"Mama, why can't I do things like other children? No one in school likes me, Mama. Why does my teacher do everything for me?" Marsha asked.

"Oh, honey, I know your life is a challenge, and it will likely for a long time. Your teachers are trying to help you the best way they know how and your classmates, unfortunately, don't understand your difficulties. Teasing and ridicule is how kids react to what they're not familiar with, and that's unfortunate. People, who love you, will always try to do things for you because they want to help you. They might not even realize it's not fair to you not to challenge you. When you do things on your own, you're learning and sometimes it's the only way to learn. Yes, other children will be frustrated with you because you cannot perform as fast or as good as they do. But be strong and keep going, keep practicing. Repetition will cause you to learn. Look what you've learned by doing things over and over again so far. Don't give up, honey. Every day you're learning and every day you are getting closer to being like the other kids. One day you'll have lots of friends, I promise, honey."

"OK, Mama. That's what my friend Brisa tells me, not to give up."

"Who's Brisa, honey?" Helen asked.

"She's my friend. She talks to me and tells me stuff. I told you about her a long time ago," Marsha said quietly. "Remember?"

"What kind of—?" Helen was trying to think of a Brisa at school.

"Brisa is nice to me. She likes me. Brisa explains everything and doesn't judge me. She also always tells me never to give up my fight. She's been telling me that for a long time, Mama."

"I'm glad you have a friend like that, sweetie. She's smart and I think you should listen to her."

Helen couldn't remember a friend named Brisa, but she sounded smart and supportive, the kind of friend Marsha needed.

"OK, Mama, I will."

"Good," Helen replied with a feeling she had just won a major battle.

She couldn't imagine the frustration of not being accepted by classmates, having no friends to play or clown around with. How lonely Marsha must feel without a friend to share her childhood with, Helen thought as she watched her daughter playing with her baby doll, for the hundredth time, in the corner of their living room she had designated as her baby's spot. Marsha tucked her baby in her bed and sat by her side, stroking her gently. She sat there, almost mesmerized, and Helen wondered what was going through her mind. What was she thinking about? Helen couldn't begin to imagine. She only hoped that they were happy thoughts.

"Brisa, I told my mama about you and she understood. She knows I have you for a friend, at least. I think you are my only friend sometimes."

"Your mama thinks I'm your imaginary friend, not your guardian angel. She's just glad to know that you understand you must help yourself too, to get onto your own two feet again. She is very smart to understand that doing everything for you is not beneficial for you."

"She is the only one who understands and doesn't judge me. Most of the time, when I'm away from home, I feel I'm no good, Brisa. I'm useless—"

"Nonsense! Nothing hurts worse than feeling unappreciated, unrecognized, even trapped—"

"That's exactly how I feel most of the time, and trapped inside of myself, too. I want so much to do things and I just can't, especially when I see others having fun. When I do try, I get taunted or laughed at. It hurts, Brisa. It really hurts me, and I just want to die."

"I know, Marsha. It's hard to be different and I'm trying to think of ways to let your parents know what you're going through, the pain you're enduring. Listen, as hard as it is, stand up for yourself and focus on being your very best."

"You won't let me get down on myself, will you, Brisa? You always have positive answers for me."

"Yes, I do. It's my job as your guardian angel. Your positive attitude will help your recovery and shape your life, Marsha."

"Does Mama know all this?"

"Oh, deep down, I think she does."

Helen was brought back to reality by the familiar sound of the garage door opening. She blinked her eyes a few times and brushed her face dry from her happy tears.

"Mama, Papa's home!" Marsha announced, getting up from her 'Doll Spot'.

"Yes, dear, I hear. Do you want to meet him at the door?" and Marsha was already halfway to the steps leading to the lower level and to the garage entrance. "Come, and we'll both be there when he walks in, like a surprise."

"Yes, Mama, OK!"

The door opened and there stood Papa. "Oh my gosh. What's this? I get to be greeted by my two favorite girls at the door? Oh, I'm so lucky!" and he swept Marsha into his arms, giving Helen a wink. "How is my special angel today? Did you learn lots at school today? Papa has some news that will affect all of us," he said, and saw Helen's concerned, questioning look out of the corner of his eye as he continued playing and cuddling with Marsha.

Aware of her instant worry, he gave his wife a reassuring nod. Sam was aware that their financial situation concerned Helen greatly. There was the private school and numerous medical bills and expenses every month. Marsha's welfare and happiness came first and foremost at this stage. But they were concerned for their future!

Would they be able to provide what Marsha needed for rehabilitation? To what extent would Marsha recover? How would Marsha be received as an adult?

Released of immediate worry by the smile and nod from her husband, Helen enjoyed sitting back and observing Marsha interact with her father. The two saw so little of one another, with Sam working late most evenings. Their time was precious, quality time.

"You love your papa, don't you? And Papa loves you so much! You have no idea!" she whispered and continued fondly observing Sam as he listened to Marsha's stories of the day.

"Papa, I saw a big frog today at school. He was a green frog and we decided to name him Froggy."

"Where did you find him, honey?"

"Tommy found him in his backyard."

"Oh, did you talk about frogs then?"

"Uh-huh, they live in wet mud. There are brown ones too and they're called toads."

"That's correct, and we could probably find some around here if we tried, Marsha."

"Can we, Papa, can we please—?"

"It's getting late now, and the frogs and toads are probably sleeping now anyway. Maybe we can find some this weekend though, during the day. We'll go to the lake, OK?"

"Can I pick some flowers too?"

"Of course, my little angel," and he reached for Marsha and hugged her. It was the first time Sam had heard Marsha requested something she used to love to do. Sam remembered Helen telling him how Marsha always came home with flowers for her. He remembered lots of little vases all over the house with little yellow, blue, and pink flowers, mostly weeds. Sam didn't remember their names, but when all of a sudden, the flowers were gone, and so was life with his little girl, as he remembered it. Since then, whenever he smelled flowers, it reminded him of Marsha, and now the flowers were returning. "You can pick a whole bunch of pretty flowers, honey. We'll pick a bunch for Mama this weekend, if you like."

Marsha gazed at her father and flashed him a smile in response. Sam held her close and nuzzled her blond head. "Oooo, Papa," and Marsha cuddled into his chest. She closed her eyes and hugged her papa back.

I wonder if the beat of Sam's heart is soothing her, thought Helen, while she smiled and nodded to Sam to take their little sleepy girl to bed.

"I'll be right up, honey," and she quickly picked up the pillows and blanket on the floor, the ones they'd been playing and cuddling with.

It's been another long day, Helen thought, and let out a yawn. I wonder what Sam has up his sleeve. Whatever it is must be good, because he's been in good spirits all evening.

"We're going back to the United States, Helen. We've been here almost three years and the company is moving us back to Pittsburgh," Sam whispered to his tired but inquisitive wife. He could sense her anxiousness.

"Oh, Sam, you got the promotion?"

"Yes, honey."

"Oh Sam, just think of the possibilities for Marsha, for us!" Helen squealed. Helen's eyes were now moist as she came alive from her exhaustion. "When do you need to be there? Do we have to pack right away? Will Marsha be able to finish school this year? Will you have to go to the US and leave us alone like you did before?"

"Slow down! Slow down, honey! Please," and he took his wife into his arms. "They want me there by the end of next month and have agreed to let us live in a corporate hotel until we find our new home."

"Oh Sam, that's wonderful!"

"We'll have almost two months to pack, and Marsha won't miss any school..."

"We'll have all summer to look for a house," continued Helen excitedly, "and Marsha can help. She'll like that, I think. When should we tell her Sam?"

"Tomorrow. You think she'll be excited?" asked a relieved Sam.

"I'm not sure, really. She's still so unsure of herself and uncertain about new things. She certainly won't remember when we lived there before. Do you think?"

"I don't know, Helen. She probably will, at least bits and pieces, given how smart she is. But the language will be easier for her, for one thing."

"Lots of things will be, Sam!" Helen stated in a happy tone.

"Yes, I guess so. Life is likely going to improve. But we still have work to do. Nothing good comes without a fight or struggle. It'll just be a little easier."

"We've been struggling for a long time, wouldn't you say? We've paid our dues, I think, Sam."

"Honey, you've taken most of the burden and it's going to be better from now on, I promise," and he laid his finger on her mouth to quiet her response. "Tomorrow's the start of our new adventure and we have to get some rest, OK?"

Helen yawned and had no objections.

Helen slept well that night and woke up alone in bed. She looked at the clock, seven forty-five. She had slept in. That hadn't happened in many years. She stretched and went to look for Sam and Marsha. Marsha wasn't in her room. Helen walked out into the hallway and heard her family downstairs in the kitchen. She went to see what was going on. When she entered the kitchen, Marsha looked up from the big atlas sitting on the table. The atlas Helen had used to show her where Brussels was three years ago.

"Mama, Mama, this is where we're going, look," pointed Marsha on the map. She and Papa had already talked about their journey to America and how they were going to find a new home, one more time. "Papa said Pittsburgh, right?"

"Yes, dear, Pittsburgh."

"What's it like there? Is it pretty?"

"Pittsburgh is an industrial city. But we won't be living in Pittsburgh. We'll live somewhere outside the city, and yes, it's pretty there. It's hilly, with lots of trees."

"We lived there before we moved here. Do you remember that?" asked Helen, measuring the extent of Marsha's current memory.

"I know we lived in a big house. But I don't remember where and what everything looked like, Mama."

"That's OK, honey. When we get the boxes unpacked, in our new home, I'll show you some pictures and maybe you'll remember. If not, that's OK too."

"When are we going to go to Pittsburgh, Mama, so I can unpack my doll's furniture?"

"We're leaving in a few weeks, sweetie."

"Is Papa coming with us this time?" Marsha asked, looking at her father with pleading eyes.

"Yes, you'll sit between Papa and me on the airplane."

"Yaa," Marsha cheered, clapping and bouncing slightly in her seat.

Time flew by. It was amazing how far Marsha had come in two months, since Sam got word of his transfer.

"How fortunate Marsha always had a thirst for knowledge. Remember at first how I had to help her with the workload of reading and writing, so she was able to keep up. Even though they had issues with the rate of learning, Marsha had learned and stayed with the class. How could Marsha keep up with her slower comprehension and writing ability? She was, and is, as intelligent or better than some students. I persisted every year and finally, after lots of discussion, it was decided with extra tutoring at home, Marsha would be able to keep up with the rest of the class," Helen reminded Sam as they discussed the schooling options when they return to the US. "As before, no matter where she goes, we'll just have to work at home with her a little more."

"Marsha will continue progressing, with expected frustrations, and we'll just have to live with that. We'll have to help her with that!" Sam reminded Helen.

As Marsha finished grade school she was academically pretty much in line with other students, teachers told Helen. She still had some difficulty with her reading and writing speed. But compared to previously, she was doing well.

"She even excels in some subjects. Her favorite is English, Marsha tells me," Helen said proudly. "Just the other day she came home all excited saying, 'Mama, I got a B for my description of the beach! Look, Mama, look!' She was so proud of herself."

"She has every right to be. And we are proud of her, too!" stated Sam. "How did you handle it?"

"I was washing dishes and quickly dried my hands of dish soap to read her work. We sat down at the kitchen table together and Marsha was still fidgeting with excitement. I said, 'Good job, sweetie, let me see. Look at this! Mama is so proud of you!' and I gave her a big hug. I know how important recognition and praise is for her development," she told Sam.

"That's great, honey! Marsha is going to be ready for fifth grade, no matter where she goes!" Sam said proudly, ending the conversation with a final nod and a smile.

Unknown to her parents, Marsha was having a conversation of her own in the other room.

"Brisa, I can't believe I got a B on my report, and Mama was so happy, and Papa said he was proud of me."

"Of course. They're happy you're seeing how intelligent you are. Writing about the beach wasn't hard, was it, Marsha?"

"No, not really."

"It came natural to you, right? You just did it, right?"

"Well, yes."

"How do you see yourself, Marsha, compared to the other kids, I mean."

"Sometimes I feel like a failure because I can't do things, no matter how hard I try. Sometimes I think I'm a burden because everything takes me so long. Everybody always has to wait for me. Everyone thinks they have to help me or do things for me. The adults want to help me, anyway, and I don't want help. I don't want any pity because that makes kids laugh at me even more. I think I'm as smart as everyone, maybe even smarter sometimes. But I feel like I just don't belong. The only problem, Brisa, is everyone looks at me as some kind of freak, because I read and write slower and I still have some equilibrium problems. I really hate gym class because I can't participate like the others. Like when we play volleyball, I get hit with the ball all the time and get laughed at." <Sniff, sniff>

"Marsha, don't feel bad. You're doing super! You're participating and not giving up and you're learning by trying as hard as you can. Equilibrium problems and slower reaction time is something you're going to have to learn to live with. It will get better though, in time; and that's just something kids don't understand. But you do, and that's important. Just keep doing your best and don't stop!"

Marsha was aware of the prejudice against her for a long time. But this year was worse. She faced daily psychological pain from the sneers, jokes, and laughter she faced.

"Mama, I don't want to go to school anymore. They all make fun of me. It hu-u-rts, Mama. It hurts so bad!" Marsha cried in her mother's chest.

"Marsha, honey, I'm sorry," consoled Helen. "They have no idea what a special little girl you are. Maybe try talking about something that you can do to those kids that bother you. Do you think that might help?"

"I don't know, Mama."

"Sweetheart, you just focus on your strengths and don't worry about what anyone says. They don't understand you, and you know what?" Mama said, lifting Marsha's chin so that their eyes met.

"What?" <Sniff, sniff>

"Everyone has something they're not good at, sometimes more than one. I have trouble chewing gum and walking at the same time. And I'll tell you a secret. Papa can't ride a bike!" Mama said, as Marsha looked a little less stressed and even giggled a little at that revelation. "I'm sure you're not the only one that gets picked on."

"Mike got laughed at today," Marsha said, thinking back.

"There you go, and what did he do when they laughed at him?"

"Stuck out his tongue and walked away. Maybe I'll laugh back at them too. OK, I'll just laugh back at them," Marsha said, making the internal decision out-loud.

"There you go. That's my girl," and Helen knew she had won another battle, making her daughter feel better, for now at least.

"OK, Brisa, I've made up my mind. I won't let the other kids bother me any more. Mama helped me see that tonight. I don't want to feel like a failure and be unhappy all the time. Mama says I should remember my strengths and focus on them. She said I shouldn't worry about what others say or do. That's what smart kids do."

"Your mother is very wise, Marsha. I know she loves you and wants only the best for you. She only knows your situation from a bystander's view. Nevertheless, she knows you're troubled and in pain and in turn, it brings her pain too."

"You mean she hurts like I do?"

"Yes, in a sense. You might try telling her when something is bothering you, like you did tonight. I know she and your father would do anything to help you if they can."

"Sometimes I don't know how to explain what's bothering me and sometimes I don't think anyone would understand, Brisa."

"There is no better person to talk to about anything than your mother or father, Marsha. No matter what it is, silly or not, and they will always love you."

"I know, sometimes I just need to hear that, just like I need to remember the only way to overcome my shortcomings is to persevere."

"Yes, Marsha, and I don't let you forget that. I'm very proud of your vigor to go forward, learn, and succeed. You can bet your parents are amazed and proud of your will. They recognized your urge and fed it from the very beginning."

"You mean in helping me learn?"

"Yes, ma'am. You wouldn't be this far along without them. They've been by your side every step of the way."

Helen walked into Marsha's room a short time later. Marsha was sitting on her bed facing the window with her eyes wide open, not really looking at anything. Helen couldn't decide if she was daydreaming or asleep. Needless to say, life was tough on Marsha, and she needed all of the time to regroup that she could get.

"Honey, sweetheart, wake up. It's time for dinner."

"Oh, Ma-ma, I was daydreaming," Marsha said with a start.

"I know. You must have had another hard day at school today."

"I talked to Brisa and she told me to be strong and stand up to those kids who've been bothering me. I really think I can do it, Mama."

"That's wonderful. Good for you, honey, and I'm glad your friend agrees with me you have to be strong to fend off bullies, Marsha."

School quickly ended and the trip to the United States went smoothly. Marsha quickly fell into a normal routine and enjoyed spending the entire summer with her parents. They found a house and made it their home and Marsha made friends with the neighborhood children. Though she always felt a little strange playing actively, she learned to cope and to say no.

Helen and Sam still spent weekends focusing on their daughter, taking her to parks, museums, and activities. Marsha enjoyed the outdoors immensely and Sam found himself buying a tent and going camping with his family. Whatever the little family did, Marsha was always hungry to learn, and her parents made every effort to satisfy their daughter's curiosity. Fall approached and Marsha was enrolled in the local public school. It was challenging, but with a little extra work at home every day, Marsha kept up and excelled, far beyond what anyone had anticipated.

Life went on through puberty with many of the same issues and problems of being different in an ocean of similar fish. Each year got better as Marsha progressed and matured and learned to deal with people, and situations of growing up.

Junior high laid the groundwork for change, in Marsha's mind, and high school started the turning point.

"I am going to take control of my life," she said to herself in the mirror as she proudly went to school each morning. "In my mind I know I'm special. I know I'm smart and I'm going to focus on what I do best, learn all I can."

"I want to go to college," she announced to her parents, without knowing exactly why at first. All she knew was she wanted to help others in some way because she was given a second chance, a second chance at life.

"You have really grown up fast, Marsha. You're doing well in school and stand up for yourself. I'm so proud of you," Mama said with a tear in her eye.

"I love you, Mama."

"I love you too, Marsha," and mother and daughter held hands, looked into each other's eyes and both shed a tear.

XVII. Goals And Dreams Come To Fruition: Isn't Life Amazing?

Marsha awoke from the daydream of her life. She found herself still sitting among the family pictures scattered around her on the living room floor. She had no idea how long she had been there. She quickly went to check on Justin and found him sleeping peacefully in his crib. She admired her newborn for a few minutes. Just watching him sleep was intoxicating. He was so small, so perfect! Now, he was hers. She thought about all that she and Brad had gone through to get him, and she marveled at how lucky she truly was.

Her stomach growled and woke her from her thoughts. She checked Justin just one more time and headed to the kitchen. As she approached, she heard her parents talking. She couldn't hear what they were saying, but did catch her name in the conversation.

"What are you two talking about?" Marsha asked as she entered the comfy kitchen.

"You," her father answered.

"Really?" she asked, getting a cup of coffee.

"Actually, we were talking about your accident and how at times, we thought you wouldn't make it. But you did, and you persevered," Sam said in a proud fatherly tone, "and now we have a beautiful grandson."

"Now tell me, how did you take charge of your life, honey and become the wonderful lady and mother you are today? How did my challenged, scared, little girl become such a vibrant and successful woman? You surprised Papa and me when you announced your decision to go to college. There again, you had great ambitions. That was only one of the great advances you made," Mama said as Marsha joined them at the kitchen table.

"Somehow I came to the revelation that the only way I was going to change anything was to do it myself. I had to work on myself, my self-esteem, and learn as much as possible in order to get ahead. No one was going to do it for me! I read somewhere a quote that has always stuck with me: 'It's important to have a goal in mind. Accept the fact that there will be setbacks and obstacles. But if you continue to visualize the goal and work toward it, one day you will achieve it. Do what has to be done without complaint and think only positively. Don't allow yourself to think negatively'. I think of it as my motto."

"You sure went through a lot growing up. Mama and I wished we could have helped you more, but we knew you had to do most of it on your own," Sam stated with a smile.

"Through the four years of high school I slowly emerged from my shell. I still experienced ridicule, directly or indirectly, on a daily basis because I was different. The scars and the lift under my right shoe, making the length of the right and left leg equal, were no more, but the way I acted was different. After all, I was mature for my age. A life changing experience gives you a different perspective from those around you, whether you know it or not, forever. Others seemed less determined, more carefree and loud. I was quiet, determined, and very focused, probably strange to them, and that never changed. I finally ignored such behavior as bullying, since there was nothing I could do, and I realized getting upset took up lots of time and energy. Brisa told me to direct my fears and anger to useful activities, ones to benefit me," she recounted. "I guess I dedicated myself to writing. My English teacher gave an assignment, a written report with a ten-minute oral report. I remember I chose to do my project about shells and included my shell collection as an exhibit. I really dedicated myself, did a great job and got a really good grade. Mama, Papa, I think that report turned things around for me. It gave me more confidence, confidence in myself. My focus was to learn as much as possible and excel, and remember, my dream became to go to college to be a physician's assistant, Mama?"

"I remember. I asked you why not just become a doctor," said Papa. "And your response was, 'To be a doctor takes too long and it is too much responsibility'."

"Why did you want to be a physician's assistant, honey?" asked Mama.

"Since I spent so much time in hospitals, I guess I felt a subconscious need to help the sick. I was a candy striper for a couple years too, remember? Adults understand handicaps, and there was no peer pressure. No one made fun of me at the hospital. I needed to somehow feel good about myself in the midst of all the criticism I was getting, and as a candy striper at the hospital I helped people who were worse off than I was. I felt alone and scared of my future and needed to find some worth. I needed to feel good about myself again and I realized the nurses and doctors would be nice to me. They had taken care of me before and would understand now. Besides, I liked being with adults because they didn't judge me on my shortcomings. Everyone appreciated me, and what I did. Actually, I think I felt more comfortable in the adult environment, since that's how I grew up. Maybe volunteering was a way to use my anger and my pity in a positive way."

"Remember how patients used to ask for you, when you weren't working?" Mama asked.

"Yes, I remember, and that's exactly why I enjoyed it so much. I was a positive influence on the patients. They respected me for who I was. I really enjoyed bringing a smile to their faces. Volunteering at the hospital gave me a sense of self-worth I lacked. I felt like I was both needed and making a difference. It gave me a confidence boost and furthered my desire to pursue college."

"We were so concerned about you going to college, honey," interjected Papa.

"Why, Papa?"

"Mama and I had a grave concern that if you didn't succeed, you'd give up. We didn't want you to be disillusioned or disappointment. We wondered how we could pick you up from major disappointed."

"Did you know my dream of becoming a physician's assistant was in fact a dream? That I would never actually get there?"

"Yes, Marsha. Your mathematical and science skills weren't the best. But you gave us so many surprises we couldn't deny you your intentions. You were so determined, and we decided it was best to let you learn your own strengths and weaknesses. If you wanted to study, Mama and I were not going to stop you. The Physician Assistant Program wasn't the only program at Queen's College, after all. We figured once you were there, you would work things out for yourself."

"Oh, Papa, it was so hard my freshman year, before I changed my major to communications and marketing. I suppose you really only excel at your passion. I really should have known from my love of writing all those years, and I know now that some lessons have to be learned through experience."

"You are so right, my dear," answered Papa proudly. "We tried to shield you from as much hardship and failure as possible because we loved you so much and maybe deep down inside still felt guilty for the past. We just never knew what little thing might cause you to give up and we couldn't deal with that!"

"Oh, Papa, I decided, a long time ago, to take charge of my life, and nothing was going to stop me! I knew I had to go on. I knew I had a purpose for living, with no idea what that purpose was yet. Yes, there were quirks along the way; times I struggled with issues inherent to my condition, and obnoxious situations. Marsha Walsch still went home and cried on many occasions, but she was not going to give up! I had collected quotes that were a positive influence on me. I memorized most of them. Another of my favorites was, 'A combination of discipline and learning leads to confidence. Remember that everyone is a beginner at some point in his life, even your teacher was once a pupil'."

"That is very true," Papa said, nodding his head.

"Yet another of my favorites was, 'Face your fears and conquer them. If you do something you have previously been afraid to do, you will begin to crack the egg of your insecurity. Accomplishing something difficult gives you the strength to go on to further successes.' These quotes really helped me over the years. I would say them to myself over and over, almost like a prayer of sorts."

"I always fretted when you would disappear in your room and I would hear you crying," interjected Mama, with a pained expression on her face. "I had no idea about the troubles you faced with your peers. I didn't know kids were so mean to you, honey. I wish I had known!"

"Marsha, I'm sorry you had to handle all that alone back then, and I must commend you for handling it yourself. You sure were a strong little girl!" added her father.

"I really liked my teachers the best," continued Marsha, with a far off look in her eyes as she remembered her past. "They were always nice to me, probably because they knew I was really trying to learn what they were teaching. Outside of class, teachers gave me extra help if I had questions, especially our math teacher, Mr. Pluto."

"Oh yes, I remember Mr. Pluto. He was a nice guy. I met him once at a parent/teacher conference night, when I was in town and not on business somewhere. I'm really sorry I couldn't be around more when you were going through school and all that silent misery, sweetie," said Papa sincerely. "I had no idea about any of this except for your inability at mathematics."

"Oh yes," teased Marsha. "You couldn't understand why I didn't understand math because you are so proficient in mathematics, and lots of times I felt like I was a failure or a burden because I just couldn't understand."

"Yes," answered her father. "I was too wrapped up in my affairs to really understand how my daughter could possibly not have mathematical ability. I was hard on you..."

"I remember helping Marsha when you were not home and we spent lots of time researching for her papers and reports. Looking back, I probably helped a little bit much, but I was compensating for your father not being there and..."

"Mama, Papa, it's OK," interrupted Marsha. "I got through it. How, I don't know, but I did. I even managed to get average grades in math. I did work more than anyone, probably, but enjoyed it, and that's probably another reason why I couldn't identify with any of the other kids. Oh, and remember, secondary and high school were so sports oriented, remember? If you weren't good in sports, forget it."

"I remember that very well, honey," responded Mama.

"I tried to stay away from things I knew I couldn't play, which was about everything. But sometimes I just wanted to play and I'd get so humiliated when I failed again. Playing Ball I'd get hit, every time, because my reaction time was impaired and my equilibrium impairment made everything else questionable to impossible. But I overcame that misery too, the questioning, the taunting, the humiliation from the other students."

"Honey, I do remember you telling me about how important sports were and how you wished you could be like the other kids," said Helen. "I told you that sports weren't everything, that you have a mind that gave you lots of opportunities. But I had no idea about the extent of psychological abuse."

"I couldn't identify with anyone and felt so alone, and when the other kids teased me I didn't fight back because I couldn't react quickly and besides, I didn't like conflict."

"Your responses were just fine at home, sweetheart. I had no idea," Mama declared, shaking her head at the thought of what her daughter really went through.

"Yes, Mama, school was a different world. I felt like an outsider; trapped, worthless, unrecognized, and unappreciated. I was in lots of pain!"

"Marsha, why are you telling us all this now?" demanded Papa. "We feel guilty enough for what you had to go through, what we did to you..."

"Oh, no, Papa! Please don't feel guilty. What happened to me wasn't your fault. I'm telling you and Mama this, what I've been through and how I feel, so others can see what their children, in similar situations, are going through as they recover from tragedies, as they grow up. I want to be a role model for those who think there is no hope to go on. I want to be an inspiration for those who perceive their pain to be too much to handle. If I can help one person, one family, with their problems or choices, I will have fulfilled my desire and purpose. That's why I put my heart and soul into this adoption. I was giving a child a second chance and helping someone who really needed it, in more than one way, I hope. I'll never forget your faces when you first laid eyes on your grandchild."

"Oh, honey," Marsha's parents gasped, almost simultaneously, sitting side by side at the kitchen table, as the true meaning of Marsha's quest became evident to them. A tear rolled down Helen's cheek and Sam had a look of revelation in his eyes.

Sam put his arm around his somewhat distraught wife

and looking at his strong and independent daughter, said, "Marsha, you are really and truly amazing!"

Helen nodded her head in agreement, wiping away tears of respect for her daughter. Sam looked at his daughter and said, "Go ahead, go on, tell us the rest when you're ready, dear."

Marsha got up from the table and refilled her coffee. She motioned to her parents to join her on the couch in the sitting room where they could be more comfortable and hear the baby if he woke up.

"I have to do this. It is part of my healing process, Mama, Papa," she continued, looking at her somewhat transfixed parents.

"It's also your destiny, helping others through your experiences, Marsha. You are using your talents to make a difference, and that's commendable!" stated a proud Papa. He finally comprehended and understood his daughter's adult quest.

"Oh, honey. I'm just flabbergasted at what you've done. Please go on. Your father is right, even though it hurts to hear about your painful past, your gift is priceless!"

"I had made up my mind to go on, to go forward, no matter what, remember? And I fully realized I had a long and difficult road ahead, more difficult than anyone I knew. I also knew everything would take me twice as long to learn and accomplish, probably for the rest of my life. There were times when I really questioned what I was doing, Mama, because life was so hard for me outside of our home. Yet there was always a tiny voice telling me someday I would make an important difference, and that little voice really made the ultimate difference for me."

"You always acted so strong and willing to go to school, to learn, though," said Sam.

"It was mostly an act. I had to challenge myself. I realized it was the only way to get ahead. Remember, you two always told me so."

"Yes, we did, didn't we?"

"All those papers, reading assignments, reports. I

wanted to excel. It was tough, but fun. No one bothered me when I was working by myself. Writing papers and reports was what I enjoyed the most in school."

"You certainly exercised your mind, honey," her mother sighed in recollection. "I sat with you and helped you any way I could or was allowed to."

"I'd see other kids playing, running, and having fun outside and I knew I couldn't do that. So I did what I could do, something that wouldn't make me feel bad or self-conscious. I focused on myself and making myself better, smarter. I also figured if I stayed at home, no one would pick on me. I really tried to stay away from the other kids as much as possible."

"You had friends though, honey, and you did go out and have fun."

"Sure I did, on occasion. When there was someone who didn't care about my shortcomings, like our neighbors. Or if we were away from peer pressure."

"Oh, honey," interrupted Papa. "You were always special in our eyes. And there were so many friends, relatives, and others that thought you were amazing."

"But Papa, that didn't matter! My peers, the kids around me, the ones that were supposed to be my friends, the kids I should have been chumming around with, were *all* mean to me. They teased me, made fun of me, and put me down – constantly! High school was supposed to be the best time in my life, and for me it was the worst! I've done my best to block out the details. It's a time I'd really rather forget."

"I'm sure it wasn't that bad, Marsha. I mean, you had been through a lot worse."

"Yah, but this was totally out of my hands. There was nothing I could do. Verbal and sometimes even physical ugliness and rejection just kept coming nonstop. I was living it, continuously, every day and there was nothing I could do about it. Nothing is worse than feeling trapped, unrecognized, and unappreciated! Nothing!"

"OK, princess, you've made your point," finished Papa.

"Mama and I didn't realize your world was so cruel, did we?"

Helen was bowing and shaking her head in answer.

"I tried to shield you as much as possible," she whispered. "I'm sorry for the psychological scars it must have left."

"Well, Mama, I think I've learned a lot about people and life itself every day of my life, because of what I went through. It's made me a stronger person. Everything I've accomplished has taken more energy for me, and therefore, I think I'm more appreciative of everything. I dedicated myself to learning. Remember how I'd spend hours reading, writing, and studying?"

"I remember, Marsha, you spent lots of time with pencils, paper, and books. It was not uncommon to see you playing with your dog, Jessica, either, or sitting with the adults talking. You were absorbing, learning all you could. No wonder you grew up so quickly."

"We were your role models," muttered Sam.

"Yah, Mama, and you know why? I needed to feel good about myself, because I needed that positive energy to do my best in school. I looked at school as my job. Did you know that?"

"No!" Helen said flatly.

"You always had an iron will when it came to going to school, and I was so proud of you, Marsha," offered Papa.

"I wish you would have told me! Really, Papa, it would have made such a difference to me! Expressing your approval or your pride for me would have helped my self-esteem. I always felt I didn't measure up. Or, that anything I did wasn't good enough. So I went through my teenage years depressed and annoyed at myself. I did the best I could for you and for myself because I wanted to go to college. Remember you and Mama questioned my decision? But I wasn't going to be discouraged!"

"Yes, I remember," replied Papa. "Your doggedness made us think you could do it. I agreed you should have the opportunity to..."

"And college made me blossom," interjected Marsha quickly, interrupting her father mid-sentence. "No one knew me, or my shortcomings. I had a clean slate and I started over."

Marsha shifted in her seat, sat up straight, and appeared to take on a new identity, merely telling about her newfound freedom.

"I decided I wanted a healthy start and a new me. The first day at college I started exercising in the weight room and continued throughout my next four years. Not only was it a physically healthy choice, but a mental one as well. I knew I was the only person who could change Marsha Walsch."

"I remember that the first semester was so hard for you, Marsha," Sam interjected. "Mama told me how you called home three or four times a week because you were homesick. The one weekend I picked up the phone you were crying, remember?"

"Yes, I do. I had a really hard week and needed to have a big assignment ready and typed by Monday, and I had no idea how to get that done."

"I suggested finding someone to type it for you. Didn't one of the girls in your dormitory end up doing it?"

"Yes, I forget her name, but she did it for me as a favor. Papa, I was so relieved."

"I know, honey, typing was not one of your strengths. We were so proud of you though, because you worked around the obstacles those four years, and stuck it out—once again, doing your very best."

"Oh Papa, I wish you had told me how proud you were more often. I mean, I knew you were, but it would have been so nice to actually hear it!" Marsha said with her voice breaking, as she held back a flood of tears.

Sam and Helen sat there a little dazed by the story their daughter was weaving, the story of her amazing past. The hidden secrets they never knew.

Finally Sam exclaimed, "I hope by you unraveling your experiences and pain, someone else's parents will have a better understanding of what their son or daughter is experiencing, and learn from the mistakes we've made."

They looked at Marsha and nodded for her to continue when she had her composure again.

"At college, psychologically I felt like a new person, free of intimidation and anxiety. I was able to focus on my strengths and develop them without emotional hindrance. It was an incredible feeling of freedom."

"The first time you came home from college, I remember, you did seem a little more confidant," suggested Papa. "That was Thanksgiving, right? You were away at school almost three months by then."

"Yah, Papa, and I was so glad to be home, although besides seeing you and Mama, I couldn't have cared less about coming back to that town. Afterwards though, being away from home became easier, although we did still talk once a week during the four years I was there. I always felt an extraordinary tie between us, more than most other college students, it seemed. They mostly thought of their parents as a gravy train or a money tree. I thought of you as an extension of me, somehow, and I always looked forward to calling home."

"Uh-Huh, I remember the escalation in our phone bill after you left for college," teased Papa.

"Oh, Sam, I really did enjoy talking to Marsha, away in her new college world. I enjoyed hearing about the new life she was experiencing and her difficulties too."

"Yah, me too. Hey, remember when I was trying to help you with a math problem over the telephone? I think it was your junior year," interjected Papa. "We must have been on the phone almost an hour."

They all halfheartedly chuckled.

"Mathematics never was a strength," commented Marsha.

"But even in college you still managed to get an average grade," praised Mama.

"Oh, please! I asked for help from everyone, and I guess some of it sunk in. I really don't know how I managed it," and she looked at her father with a smile and a shrug of her shoulders.

"You are really incredibly smart, Marsha, and you've grown into one amazing woman," exclaimed Papa again, his eyes a little watery.

"At that point in my life I felt like I needed to prove myself to me and nobody else. I was focused and studied as hard as I possibly could. I wanted it all and hung on to the dream that I would have it all some day. Funny thing though, I had no idea what I was going to do, how I was going to do it, or where I wanted to go. I had no clue. But that little voice kept telling me I would make a difference someday. I stayed confident and bullheaded," Marsha exclaimed and looked towards her father again. "Yah, Papa, I guess I got that from you."

"Lucky for you. They're not such bad traits to have. Are they?" questioned Papa in a teasing manner, as Helen shifted in her seat.

Marsha continued, "I suppose you know that I wrote poetry a lot. I did it for fun and sort of like therapy for myself. Writing poetry was a way for me to both create and release my inner feelings: some of which were very sad and others quite beautiful. College was tough in many ways, and I wasn't totally free of the disabilities or anxieties I faced in high school. So, naturally, I learned to handle my shortcomings and face my fears, focusing on my strengths."

"Whenever you came home, during holiday breaks, I always noticed you were busy writing something," volunteered Helen. "You were always writing letters or something. I'm sorry I never paid much attention."

"Oh, no, Mama, you did ask me several times. But I never answered much. To tell you the truth, I never knew what or why I was writing. I had no direction in mind for what I was doing. I just lived in my own little world, writing about my feelings, pains, and dreams and actually never thought it would take me anywhere."

Marsha moved next to her mother on the sofa because she could see the distraught look on her mother's face.

Helen let Marsha take her hand, comfortingly squeezing it, "Mama, you did the best you could. I know that now. You know I finally did get one of my poems published, right?"

"You did? I never knew that, honey. Which one? What was it about?" Helen asked, her face brightening a bit.

"*Summer Love*. It was about a boy I fell in love with during one of our vacations at the beach. I wrote that one in the sand at sunrise one morning. It was so beautiful, just me, the sand, and the ocean breeze greeting the new day," Marsha recounted with a faraway look in her blue eyes. "It was published in *American Collegiate Poets,* spring 1983 edition."

Marsha felt like she was baring her sole, and it felt good. These were the memories she held dear. She never figured her parents cared about her feelings and it touched her to find out that they really did.

"Do you still have a copy so we can read it?"

"Of course I do, on one of my bookshelves. I'll find it for you later. It just shows you how continuous positive thinking leads to personal victories and that's just the beginning. I learned to learn from the past and build on that knowledge. Life's not a dress rehearsal. Even back then, when, I guess I was in my early teens, I thought how phenomenal it would be to write my own book, one about my experiences, someday. I knew I could make a difference for many suffering parents and provide understanding to others touched by tragedy, like mine so many years ago now. Maybe that's what Brisa was referring to when she told me I had purpose."

"You also got involved with the media department at college didn't you?" asked Papa.

"Yes, I did. I put my talent for writing to work, writing the early morning news report for our college radio station. I started spreading my wings and interacting with people my own age. Being a member of the college radio station and gave me a sense of belonging and realization I could interact with others. I actually found myself having fun and looked for opportunities utilizing my love for writing. I found myself thinking about a career with writing. I needed those four years of college to gain the confidence for what lay ahead, and looking back, the time went so fast."

"Oh, honey, I would have never thought college would have agreed with you like it did," said Helen.

"You did really excel, Marsha," interjected Papa. "I know it was hard for you. We were so proud, honey."

"But you never said that. You never told me you were proud! I didn't know!" repeated Marsha.

"I thought you knew. We showed you we cared. We gave you whatever we could," Sam said helplessly.

"Dad, I'm just saying, everything would have been more positive for me if you would have told me. Using phrases like, 'I am so proud of you', or even 'Good job'. It would have made all the difference in the world."

"Does verbal praise really matter that much to you?"

"Yes, and to a challenged child it's even more vital; that's what research has taught me," Marsha said as her voice trailed and she reached out for her father's hand, to let him know all was forgiven.

"Once you decided to focus on English and marketing courses, there was no stopping you," he recalled. "There was one professor who really noticed you, Dr. Whiting, wasn't it?"

"Yes, he was the Director of the Communications Department," Marsha remembered how she applied herself and caught Dr. Whiting's attention. "I studied hard for all my classes, especially Dr. Whiting's communications courses. Not only were they interesting, but also, they involved research and writing, both of which I enjoyed. Dr. Whiting was different. He cared about his students and expected his students to learn through research and using the written word in the form of reports. What set Dr. Whiting apart was, he made us think and create on our own. Dr. Whiting prepared us for real life. He had a very basic teaching philosophy, really. Expectations were placed on each individual student. The principle of Dr. Whiting's philosophy was that the student was in charge of him- or herself. It is up to the student's thirst for knowledge, the efforts he or she exhibits that make him or her become a successful college graduate. With guidelines set by Dr. Whiting through dictation and discussion, I completed papers and reports through extra research. Independent study promotes ingenuity and causes students to excel and achieve. I discovered the need to change from adolescent ways of having things done for me to the appreciation of doing for myself. I learned that tedious work must be done to get ahead, and learned the essence of dotting the i's and crossing the t's to get things done. There is a definite awakening and joy of discovery when a youngster learns the power of research and the ability to create a project from start to finish. Dr. Whiting's successful students learned through hard work. He didn't give me a break either, even after he learned of my lingering difficulty of slow writing. He suggested that I get complete notes from fellow students and offered to answer questions after class. I suppose I excelled because I was used to hard work and challenges and I really liked researching and writing. It was what I did best."

"You met his high expectations, honey, even with your problems. Dr. Whiting realized your tenacity and problem-solving ability too, I'm sure," Helen said.

"Oh, yes, Mama, he realized my intense interest to learn, and he knew I would get assignments done, no matter what it took, with enthusiasm and pride. When I decided on communications for my major, Dr. Whiting became my college advisor and mentor without my knowledge, moving mountains for me. He took me under his wing, but made me work for everything, just like any other student."

"I remember you calling home on several occasions, complaining about his nonstop dictation, endless information, and specifically that report you had to research, write, and type in three days."

"Oh yes, the one where I first had to get the basic notes from a classmate before I could even begin research. That was the assignment where some kids arrived at class on Monday and looked like they hadn't slept or showered in three days," Marsha laughed.

Marsha had spent all weekend working nonstop and arranged to have her five-page report typed for her. "That weekend was hellish for me. But I got the assignment done and Dr. Whiting realized, no doubt, how hard I worked."

"That just goes to show, if you apply yourself to something, no matter what it is, you are likely to get help and succeed. Dr. Whiting helped you because you were doing everything you could to help yourself..."

"You probably worked harder and longer than any of his other students," interjected Marsha's mother.

"I can safely say I probably did, Mama," responded Marsha quietly, remembering. "And remember Senior Seminar? I spent the entire semester researching and writing a fifty-page report *Women In Advertising, America Compared To Germany,* with an oral report and visuals to go with it. It was a lot of work compiling information from different media, researching, writing and comparing the two cultures. Since marketing was my minor, all the knowledge I acquired was interesting to me and furthered my education, a step closer to my goal, still unknown to me at the time. I worked on my senior seminar project every day with enthusiasm."

Subconsciously, Marsha learned a very important lesson that she would recollect years later: *Do what you're interested in and you will succeed and excel!*

"I remember. Your cousin and I collected magazines and newspapers for you when Papa and I visited Germany that autumn. We were so proud of you and wanted to help any way we could."

"Mama, I was so grateful you went to Germany that year, and I remember your and Papa's concern about taking on such a monumental research project. In fact, I did two projects in one, and when I finished at the end of the semester I felt so proud and accomplished!"

"You had every reason to feel exuberant! What you did was monumental, once again! Your mother and I were beginning to see that whatever you set your mind to, you did. You were amazing then, as you are now!" beamed Sam.

"Oh Dad, doing the research and creating the fifty page research project was one thing. Then came the hard part, I had to present in front of a class of thirty-five students and Dr. Whiting. I was so nervous! I couldn't help stuttering, and felt myself shaking. I remember focusing on one particular student, shutting out the world around me until I came to grips with myself. I had all kinds of information and visuals to share and a twenty-minute presentation turned into forty-five. Towards the end I answered questions with confidence and was even arguing with Dr. Whiting. The entire class was at the edge of their seats. No one dared argue with Dr. Whiting, ever! Oh, Mama, I felt so good. I knew my subject and backed it up with confidence. I had confidence, Mama! Confidence! It was amazing! I felt amazing!"

"That's probably why Whiting argued with you. He wanted to get that confidence out in you," Papa stated.

"I never thought of it that way. But yah, you're probably right. Dr. Whiting was so amazing. I wonder what he's doing now?" and Marsha had that far away look in her blue eyes again as she imagined Dr. Whiting in New York, filming another documentary or maybe even something bigger. She knew years ago when she was at college, and he was both a professor and the Director of the Communications Department, Dr. Whiting was heavily involved in the media and she had dreamed about working with him some day.

"Marsha, are you OK? What are you thinking about?" inquired her mother, now newly fascinated by her daughter's dreams and accomplishments, the ones she and Sam never knew about.

"I was just wondering where Dr. Whiting is now. Do you know, as tough as he was, I always thought working with him someday would be an honor. How much I could learn from him. I don't really remember if I actually had a vision doing that: working with him."

"Honey, you obviously respected and admired him very much, and look at yourself now. You are using communications skills too. You're writing about your experiences. You're creating, Marsha. You are writing books to help others, to help future generations through similar tough situations."

"And I still hear Dr. Whiting's words, 'Work hard and you'll make it, Marsha, I'm sure of it'."

"Dr. Whiting truly was your mentor, Marsha. He guided and encouraged you without you knowing, at the time. You ultimately took the ball and ran with it. That's how a mentor/ student relationship works. Because he pushed you to your limits and you persevered. He believed in you, and he stayed with you all these years. You never forget mentors."

"Yah, Papa, he stayed on my mind all these years, and you're right, he's helped me without me knowing it, not just in college, but throughout my adult years. I never forgot him, just like Brisa. Their words and encouragement stayed with me and guided me. But you have to have the determination and perseverance to go foreword yourself, to excel!"

"And you did!" proudly stated Sam.

"One thing he told me always stuck with me and I'll never forget, 'You can't sit back and wait for breaks to come your way. They don't happen by hoping: they happen because of positive actions. Maintain a positive attitude about anything you want to achieve, and do what has to be done.' It was another for my quote collection," Marsha said, fading off into thought again.

"When Marsha Walsch graduated with a Bachelors degree in communications, with a minor in marketing, in 1986, four years later, many accomplishments had been met. I was no longer the intimidated, scared little girl I was in high school. I had trained myself to think on my own, research, write, and take responsibility. I had continued to work hard and independently and through my talents and resourcefulness, I started shaping a vision of and for the future. The difference was I needed to work a little harder because of my shortcomings. Sitting here now, Mama, Papa, I understand what goal-setting is all about. Our final goal is at the very end of a line of little goals we set for ourselves. Each progressive goal leads us closer to our chosen destination. It's all about persistence and perseverance."

"You learned so many valuable lessons, possibly because you are different from others because you've had a difficult road," commented her father. "I'm sure Dr. Whiting saw your extreme desire to learn, get past your disabilities, and your doggedness towards everything. Well, I know he took great pride in being your mentor and seeing you succeed. We had dinner together with him and his wife after your graduation ceremony, remember? Dr. Whiting had nothing but praise for you and wanted nothing but the best for you. I remember him saying you realized your potential and that anything was possible if you worked for it."

"Didn't he also remind Marsha to focus on her strengths? Influential people are likely to notice your passion to succeed and extend themselves to assist you."

"Yes, I remember that, Helen, and he was so wise in sharing that with Marsha," recalled Sam. "Dr. Whiting really made a remarkable difference in our daughter's life."

"I was about to enter another stage of my life, another chapter. You knew it was coming. You knew it was an inevitable evolution of growing up. Your helpless little girl had overcome, succeeded, and blossomed. Now she was about to enter the real world, the workforce. With the protective atmosphere of the college campus gone now, I got the feeling that you prayed I wouldn't run into too many disappointments. I was already experiencing my chances at work were diminished, due to my minimal disabilities. I know you hoped and prayed to God I wouldn't give up. I always imagined that you asked yourselves questions like 'What will happen to Marsha if she can't find a job?', 'What if she gets depressed and gives up?', 'What are we going to do?', 'What can we do?' Both of you were always so worried about me. I guess that comes with being a parent and our circumstances. You needed to keep a positive attitude for me," Marsha said. "I had no room for negativity. I remember Papa saying, 'Marsha, don't be silly, be realistic'. And I was, Papa. I couldn't think of what might happen or could go wrong if I wasn't willing to work through my disabilities. There are others with handicaps worse than mine were and many of those people are employed. Mama, you said 'Don't give up sweetheart. There are opportunities out there. We just need to find them.' It really helped me."

"We did what we could. You didn't let us help you much," said Papa.

"I remember you telling me, 'Start in the mail room and before you know it you could be working with the president of the company.' And, best of all, it was true."

"Of course it was," Sam said with confidence.

"I personally went to business and hotels in the town and talked to managers for employment. I wasn't afraid to stand up for myself and ask questions because I knew I had to make things happen. My pursuit paid off at the local hotel where a position for the general manager's secretary hadn't been advertised yet. Mama, Papa, I need to move away from home. I need to break away."

"We understood," said her father. "We were too overbearing for your grown up personality. You needed to spread your wings. I remember telling you that when you finished your probationary period at the hotel, we would get a little apartment for you. That way you would have your independence."

Marsha's parents had understood their daughter was growing up and despite her challenges, had unbelievable determination and ambition to succeed. Sam and Helen vowed to keep that intention and spirit alive. They believed in their daughter, and somehow, deep down, they knew she would triumph. Marsha's parents wanted to provide their daughter with as normal a life as possible.

"Mama and I wanted you to develop independently and socially," finished Papa. "Why not? We raised you to understand that anything is possible with intense dedication."

"And we were close by if you needed us," interjected Helen.

"I had been thinking about how to ask you if you would let me live on my own. I had been working at the hotel, in their customer service position for two months. I enjoyed my work; screening phone calls for the front office and the general manager, collecting and distributing mail, writing guest memos, and other light office duties. I enjoyed the responsibilities and the recognition of being productive. The work was nonstop, all day long, but the duties fit my abilities. My self-esteem grew again, after weeks and months of rejection. I think I sent out at least three dozen resumes and visited at least thirty businesses before I got that position."

"Yes, there were many, and you persevered again!" Helen smiled.

"I felt worthwhile again and..."

"Oh honey, was it that bad?" Helen interrupted.

"Yes Mama. Just imagine coming home from college and nobody wants you solely because you can't write a hundred miles an hour or type fifty words per minute! I don't think you knew the extreme mental blows I suffered. Well, realistically, how could you or anyone for that matter, unless they actually experienced similar shortfalls? For a handicapped person, psychologically it's harder because the pain is cumulative and ongoing and it never goes away. Anyway, the customer service position taught me the importance of public relations and working as a team. I learned there are things you can change about yourself and others you can't and it's OK to have weaknesses. Once I realized and accepted that, I became a much happier person. You are really the only one with the power to change your life, little by little."

"How did you get so smart, my daughter," asked Sam, beaming admirably at Marsha, now sitting proudly beside him.

"Oh Papa!" Marsha blushed; a little embarrassed by his praise.

"What really made you decide to keep going, honey? What was it that gave you the will and inner strength to, combat the seemingly impossible? Can you describe it?" asked Helen.

"Remember Brisa?"

"She was your imaginary friend. The one who helped you cope with yourself and your problems when you had no other friends to turn to, right?"

"Well, Mama, she was more than an imaginary friend. Brisa was and is my guardian angel. I still hear her voice, encouraging me, when I get frustrated or defeated."

"Oh?" her parents gasped.

"She's the one who told me, early on after the accident, that I would move mountains and make a difference for others, someday. Brisa always instilled in me I had the power to succeed. Brisa's voice was imbedded in my unconscious. I heard it every time I encountered hardships, every time I thought about giving up. Brisa's words were loud and clear, *'Don't give up. There is a purpose to your life.'* Every time I ran into what seemed like a brick wall, I heard her, *'You are going to make a big difference for others. Those people will need you. They're counting on you and you can't let them down.'* She never let me get down on myself."

"She was right, you did have unbelievable strength to go on and succeed over and over again, honey. We wondered where that amazing energy and vigor came from," Mama said, looking at her husband.

"Brisa helped me understand lots of things about survival. She helped me see the mind and body really do work together. She told me if I wasn't willing to make a true effort to survive, my physical body couldn't do it alone. That's when I was first introduced to teamwork, not that you could tell I used that much growing up. I was a loner, which isn't a bad thing. I learned how to handle things by myself, which prepared me for adulthood. Of course as a child, I was lonely and didn't think it was beneficial. I felt so alone, unsubstantial, and worthless. Brisa pushed me to think positively, and I battled with reality for a long time. Sometimes I felt so miserable, I thought about suicide. Did you have any idea?"

"No!" Marsha's parents said almost in unison. "We had no idea..." Both parents sat erect at the mention of suicide. To think the daughter they had come so close to losing wanted to take her own life, take her own life after her miraculous recovery and promise for the future.

"I remember the preteen years being the most traumatic. No doubt puberty added to my hardships and frustration, making certain times and experiences almost unbearable. It did get better every year, dealing with everything, I mean."

"What made you decide to continue, Marsha," Helen said as her anguish unleashed itself as she burst into tears.

"Brisa's encouragement, optimism, and promises, and your unconditional love. I couldn't leave you, and remember, I had a purpose and Brisa also told me it wasn't my time yet. So I persevered and struggled one day at a time towards my destination, unknown to me at the time."

"Oh Marsha," sobbed Helen as she let Marsha's father comfort her.

"We really had no idea," Sam said, shaking his head.

"It's OK. I got stronger as I matured and was able to deal with life much better."

"You were lucky to have Brisa, your guardian angel, to guide you," added Helen in a daze, recollecting the many years of what must have been torturous recovery for her daughter, her child, her little girl, with no end in sight.

"It was a hard road to travel, primary, secondary, high school, college, and a time afterwards when I finally learned to totally redirect my energy of sadness and self pity to things I enjoyed, making my inner misery more bearable. Always, I heard Brisa's message not to give up, and I didn't!" Marsha said proudly. "I learned you can't depend on others to make you happy. You must be able to accept yourself the way you are. You have to be able to look at yourself in the mirror and appreciate the person looking back at you."

"And you didn't?" Helen sobbed.

"No, Mama, not for a long time...until I found my passion. Before then I felt somehow unworthy, alone, unfulfilled."

"It's like that for everyone though, Marsha!" commented Papa.

"Yes, I know that now. But for someone with disabilities, no matter how small, finding that passion, a passion to build upon, by yourself, like being an artist, gives a sense of new worth, self worth. For me it came as a joy from within. Here is something I can do, improve, enrich, strengthen, and elaborate on. I have something that I'm good at. You have no idea how that changed my life. It changes the world for a challenged individual."

"Your life, as you've described it, has been a real challenge, Marsha. And I see now why telling us your challenges and feelings is so important," Sam said sadly.

"Yes, Papa, and growing up is especially hard for all who are challenged. Every step forward is cause for celebration. Every movement in the right direction makes a handicapped child feel better about him- or herself and helps them persevere. What makes the difference is how he or she wishes to live life. What you do to overcome your hardships is your choice. You'll likely face many hardships, like I did. However, when you make the commitment to hold your ground, growth and change is inevitable, and growth is change. This growth, in turn, gave me the positive attitude and outlook I needed to go on. Positive energy creates more of the same and rejections and negativity fall by the wayside," said Marsha with another one of those far away looks in her blue eyes. "I pushed onward and did what I believed in, working toward my goal of being all I could be. I wanted to be happy, and I was determined to make that happen!"

"You certainly were never a quitter or one to take no for an answer," muttered Papa quietly, almost inaudibly, so not to spoil Marsha's thoughts.

"Learning to live well means trying to see the positive things, even if they're really horrible at the time. Life is a bigger challenge for people like me. But in time, I came to terms with my situation, and turned it into something positive. Turning your bad situation into good means you're changing for the better, and growing to love yourself. Your joy radiates from within and soon your life will take new direction, take on new meaning, and the world will look at you differently too. You'll become a happier person with each positive step you take."

"Honey, you are talking from experience!" interjected Mama.

"Yes, she is!" commented Papa with an approving smile.

"You really made big changes during your young life, and many by yourself. It took lots of courage to do what you did! I have a quote of my own, 'Man can be defeated but not destroyed. A defeat is simply that, and not the end of the world. Treat defeat as a temporary setback. Learn from it and try again with renewed vigor and determination.' See, you're not the only one in the family with a motto," said Sam with pride

"I made changes because I realized I needed to, to make myself a better person, to go forward, and to make a difference for myself and ultimately for others. But I didn't really do it alone."

"Oh?" Mama asked.

"No, once you learn to accept and love yourself, you become a positive person, you attract others like you. These people are determined and dedicated and hard working, just like you. They are likely to want to make a difference and know about mentoring and teamwork to make that happen."

"Friends are based on similar interests. I'll agree with that, Marsha," Papa said.

"No, Papa, it's much more than that. I drew courage, power, and knowledge from not only experiences but also the wonderful, helpful people I encountered throughout my journey, similar to Dr. Whiting. People like Mrs. Baker when I was very young, your friends, whom I spent countless hours with also, and the people who saw me for who I was and gave me a chance. Even the bad experiences taught me. Everything that happened to me over the years, due to my hardships helped me develop into the strong, compassionate person I am today."

"You have learned so much, honey," exclaimed Helen with a sigh.

"You have certainly beaten incredible odds and turned your life around," commented Sam, shifting to put his arm around his wife.

"Much like President Theodore Roosevelt did in the movie, *Pearl Harbor*, when he got up out of his wheelchair to prove anything is possible," Marsha said.

"You certainly have done what everyone thought impossible!" Mama exclaimed with a smile.

"You are what they define as a hero, honey," Sam exclaimed proudly. "Webster's defines a hero as 'someone with great courage whom others would like to emulate'. You will be a role model for little boys and girls and their parents who have experienced tragedy."

"And you haven't stopped there. Now you and your husband are looking at giving another child a second chance. Justin is a lucky little boy!" Mama said as she beamed at her remarkable daughter.

"With your love and perseverance you will continue to make us proud!" finished Marsha's father as he heard a small cry coming from the nursery.

(Endnotes)

[2] Ratto, Linda Lee, *dis-ABILITY*, Penman Publishing, 2004.

Direct quotes from: Norris, Chuck, with Joe Hyams, *The Secret of Inner Strength*, Little, Brown And Company, 1988.

Life is what you make it.

It is up to you.

Triumph over Tragedy!

Postscript

Fifteen years after that horrific day, Marsha faced and met the challenges of society and the workforce. Though lingering challenges remain to this day, quitting was never an option. Positive attitude and persistence prevailed and opportunities were seized. Marsha felt like the world was against her most of the time. But from time to time, as a result of persistence, came the realization that society does give those who make special efforts a chance. Dr. Whiting's teaching philosophy prevailed. Marsha unconsciously exercised hard work into her lifestyle, and still does to this day. Some people do look past limitations and see those possessing mental, psychological, and physical strength. Society itself is also evolving. It is realizing, at an agonizingly slow pace, that those with limitations or handicaps are worthwhile and can make a definite contribution too.

At age thirty-one, Marsha married. Until that year, Marsha thought she would be alone the rest of her life. She felt no one understood her; a young strong woman, heavily bruised from years of harassment, yet still sweet, enduring, unfailing, and with an unwavering positive attitude.

Marsha's misfortune prompted her and her husband to consider adoption. Although there were no diagnosed medical issues, both felt there were questions such as: Could there be problems with a pregnancy? Hadn't Marsha endured enough complications? Though Marsha and her husband understood adoption was not easy or without issues, the choice was made to become adoptive parents. They wanted to provide a child with a second chance, similar to but different from Marsha's experience.

With the adoption of their first and then second child, the author decided to continue making a difference for the world community by writing about the psychological and emotional aspects of adoption in *The Adoption Eclipse*, her first book. No one should enter the adoption experience blindly.

Appendix 1

Trauma Centers

Essential to the development of a successful trauma system is the designation of trauma care facilities.

The American College of Surgeons (ACS) is a national organization dedicated to improving the care of the surgical patients and education of surgeons. The ACS Committee on Trauma focuses on improving the care of the injured patient, always believing that trauma is a surgical disease demanding surgical leadership. The Committee on Trauma has developed a resource document with established guidelines for the care of the injured patient called: "Resources For The Optimal Care of The Injured Patient." The published edition is known as, ***The Golden Book***.

Ray Georgen, MD, FACS, Medical Director of the Trauma Blue Program at Theda Clark and a member of the Board of Trustees of TheraCare: "No one should have to worry about the quality of care they or a family member receive following a life-threatening event."

Level I

A Level I trauma center is the highest-level trauma center. Because of the large personnel and facility resources required, most Level I trauma centers are university-based teaching hospitals. A Level I trauma center has acute patient care responsibilities and leadership in the roles of education, research, and system planning. A Level I center should have greater than 1,200 trauma admissions per year. The surgical staff and surgical units are usually in-house, and operating 24 hours a day. A general surgical residency program and ATLS are two more requirements. There is a research component to being a Level I center.

Level II

A Level II trauma center is also expected to provide definitive trauma care utilizing a full range of services. The care given to trauma patients at a Level II center is the same as that provided at a Level I center. Surgeons, however, are not in-house but are promptly available 24 hours a day. A Level II must also provide appropriate transfer to specialized care facilities and serve as regional resources for education and injury prevention activities.

Level III

A Level III center can provide prompt assessment, resuscitation, and stabilization of trauma victims, arranging for possible transfer to a facility that can provide definitive trauma care. The availability of general surgeons is a requirement. Transfer arrangements or agreements are made with nearby Level I and II trauma centers for patients requiring definitive or more specialized care. Standardized treatment protocols must be in place.

Level IV

A Level IV facility provides advanced trauma life support prior to patient transfer. This is usually in a more remote or rural area where no higher level of care is available. Many times this facility may be a clinic or a hospital that may not have a physician available. The Level IV institution is committed to providing optimal care within its resources. Transfer agreements with a higher level trauma center is required. Treatment protocols are necessary.

Appendix 2

Disability Resources

1) **Kids Together**
   A site about including people with disabilities in society.
   http://www.kidstogether.com

2) **Access Services**
   A non-profit Christian therapy agency serving children and adults with special mental health needs. Including creative living options, home support, foster care, employment, and counseling.
   http://www.accessservices.org

3) **Accessible PA**
   Provides nformation on programs and services for people of all ages with disabilities, as well as their families, and support providers.
   http://www.accessiblepa.state.pa.us

4) **AgrAbility for Pennsylvanians**
   Provides information and service to farmers and farm family members affected by disability in rural areas of the Commonwealth.
   http://agexted.cas.psu.edu/agrab

5) **National Federation of the Blind of Pennsylvania**
   This site links to other sites for resources for blind persons.
   http://www.nfbp.org

6) **Parent Education Network**
   Information resource for parents of children with special needs.
   http://www.parentednet.org

7) Parent-to-Parent Internet of PA

An e-mail support group for parents of children with special needs that allows parents to give and receive support, advice, information, resources, as well as share some of the challenges and successes of parenting children with disabilities.
http://www.voicenet.com/famserv

8) Pennsylvania Developmental Disabilities Council

Includes members, news, plans and activities, online publications, and updated legislative information.
http://www.paddc.org

9) Self-Determination Housing Project of Pennsylvania, Inc. (SDHP)

A nonprofit organization that expands access to public and private housing programs and self-determination in housing for persons with developmental disabilities. History, description of services, and contact details are available online.
http://www.sdhp.org

10) Speaking for Ourselves

Self-advocacy organization in Pennsylvania for people with disabilities.
http://www.speaking.org

Contact local and state organizations/agencies, i.e.: power companies for possible assistance with expenses, hospital and rehabilitation centers, religious centers, etc.

For additional information contact your Human Services Council.

Appendix 3

Hints For Success

Primary Advice:

1) Search for the best physicians and appropriate hospitals.
2) Make arrangements with the insurance companies to ensure the fullest and highest quality care.
3) Provide constant encouragement for the child to endure the many surgical and therapeutic procedures he or she will face.

General Good Ideas:

1) Persevere.
2) Don't give up. Help yourself.
3) Accept your situation and move forward.
4) Face your fears.
5) Positive thinking is power and leads to victories.
6) Take action.
7) Learn to love yourself.
8) Each step, no matter how small, is a step ahead.
9) Have direction, a plan or goal.
10) Focus.
11) Have a dream.
12) Think ahead.
13) Learn from your experiences.
14) Educate yourself.
15) Build on accomplishments.
16) Learn by listening and doing.
17) Helping others will help you help yourself.
18) Learn from ones who have been there.
19) Apply yourself, others will notice and will help.
20) Find a passion and devote yourself to it.

21) Never stop reaching for your dream.
22) The more you strive/work towards a passion, the more opportunities will come your way.
23) Find a passion, a hobby, or a cause to connect with others with similar interests.

You are a very special person.

Be courageous.

Be a hero!

Sources & Recommended Reading

1) Kubler-Ross, Elisabeth, DR, 1969, *On Death and Dying*, Touchstone 1997. ISBN: 0-684-83938-5
2) Manning, Greg, *Love, Greg & Lauren*, Bantom Books, 2002. ISBN: 0553-38189-X
3) Norris, Chuck, with Hyams, Joe, *The Secret of Inner Strength*, Little, Brown And Company, 1988. ISBN: 0-316-66119-13
4) Peck, M. Scott, MD. 1978. *The Road Less Traveled*, Touchstone Books, 2003. ISBN: 0-7432-3825-7
5) Ratto, Linda Lee, *dis- ABILITY*, Penman Publishing, 2004. ISBN: 0-974508-2-9
6) Reeve, Christopher, *Christopher Reeve Still Me*, Random House, 1998. ISBN: 0-679-45235-4
7) International Publications, Spring Concours, American Collegiate Poets, 1983.

To be published:

AWAKENING the GREATNESS
in EVERY LEARNER:
The Challenge, The Possibilities,
and The Invitation
by: William G. Spady, Ph.D.,
Linda Lee Ratto, Ed.M.,
Barbara McCombs, Ph.D.,
Al Row, Bette Moore,
Eileen Kostolini, Lisa Rudd,
Rita Perea, and The HeartLight Team
Inquiries, contact Linda Lee Ratto: lratto@HeartLight.US

ORDER FORM

Marsha's Song
A Celebration Of Life

by
Ines Arnsberger Hatch

ISBN 1-932496-19-X
Price: $18.00 plus $2.00 Shipping & Handling

Stellar A Productions
P.O. Box 13
Tyrone, GA 30290

www.StellarAProductions.com

Please send______copies of *Marsha's Song* to:

Name: ________________________________

Address: ______________________________

City/State:____________________Zip______

Enclosed please find check or money order for:

$___________ (No cash or C.O.D. please)